Human Security and the New Diplomacy

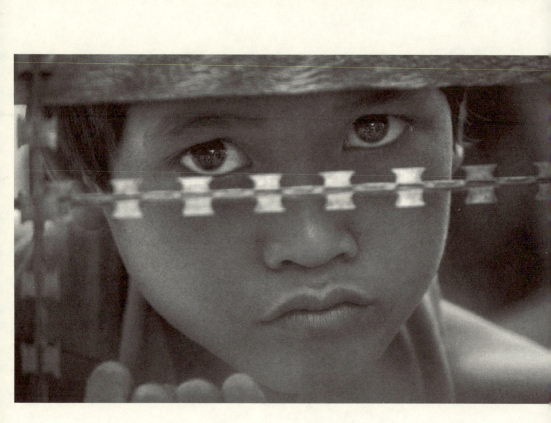

Human Security and the New Diplomacy

Protecting People, Promoting Peace

EDITED BY

ROB MCRAE & DON HUBERT

McGill-Queen's University Press
Montreal & Kingston · London · Ithaca

© McGill-Queen's University Press 2001
ISBN 0-7735-2218-2
ISBN 0-7735-2200-X

Legal deposit first quarter 2001
Bibliothèque nationale du Québec

Printed in Canada on acid-free paper

McGill-Queen's University Press acknowledges the financial support of the Government of Canada through the Book Publishing Industry Development Program (BPIDP) for its activities. It also acknowledges the support of the Canada Council for the Arts for its publishing program.

Canadian Cataloguing in Publication Data

Main entry under title:
  Human security and the new diplomacy: protecting people, promoting peace
  Includes bibliographical references
  ISBN 0-7735-2200-X (bound)
  ISBN 0-7735-2218-2 (pbk)
  1. Security, International. 2. Peace. 3. Intervention (International law)
  I. McRae, Robert Grant II. Hubert, Don
  JZ5584.C3H85 2001   327.1'72   C00-901665-1

This book was typeset by Typo Litho Composition Inc.
in 10/12 Baskerville.

Frontispiece photograph by David Longstreath, CP Picture Archives.

To all those Canadians who have kept the peace, delivered the aid, and provided support for countless people at risk and suffering around the world. This book is dedicated to them, their families, and in certain tragic instances, their memory.

Contents

Textboxes and Figures

Abbreviations

ACRI   African Crisis Response Initiative (US State Department)

AFRC   Armed Forces Ruling Council (Sierra Leone)

APEC   Asia-Pacific Economic Cooperation

APM   antipersonnel mine

ASEAN   Association of Southeast Asian Nations

AWACS   Airbone Warning and Control System

BiH   Bosnia and Herzegovina

BONUCA   UN Peacebuilding Support Office (MINURCA)

C3   command, control, and communications

CANADEM   The Canadian Resource Bank for Democracy and Human Rights

CCSA   Canadian Centre on Substance Abuse

CCW   1980 Certain Conventional Weapons Convention

CIDA   Canadian International Development Agency

CNN   Cable News Network

CPP   Cambodian People's Party

DDF   Democratic Development Fund (CIDA)

DDR   disarmament, demobilization, and reintegration

DFAIT Department of Foreign Affairs and International Trade

DND Canadian Department of National Defence

ECOMOG Military Observer Group of the Economic Community of West African States

ECOSOC UN Economic and Social Council

ECOWAS Economic Community of West African States

ESDI European Security and Defence Identity

EU European Union

EUTELSAT European Telecommunications Satellite Organization

FATF Financial Action Task Force (OECD)

FRELIMO Front for the Liberation of Mozambique

FRY Federal Republic of Yugoslavia

FYROM Former Yugoslavia Republic of Macedonia

G-7 Group of 7

G-8 Group of 8 (7 and Russia)

HIV/AIDS Human Immunodeficiency Virus/Acquired Immune Deficiency

HNP Haitian National Police

ICBL International Campaign to Ban Landmines

ICC International Criminal Court

ICRC International Committee of the Red Cross

ICTR International Criminal Tribunal for Rwanda

ICTY International Criminal Tribunal for the former Yugoslavia

IFOR Implementation Force (NATO-led, Bosnia)

IHL international humanitarian law

IMF International Monetary Fund

INTERFET International Force in East Timor

JMC Joint Military Commission

KFOR Kosovo Force (NATO-led)

KLA/UCK Kosovo Liberation Army

MAI Multilateral Agreement on Investment

MEM Multilateral Evaluation Mechanism (OAS)

MICAH International Civilian Support Mission in Haiti

MICIVIH International Civilian Mission in Haiti (UN/OAS)

MINUGUA United Nations Verification Mission in Guatemala

MINURCA UN Mission in the Central African Republic

MINURSO UN Mission for the Referendum in Western Sahara

MIPONUH UN Civilian Police Mission in Haiti

MIPONUH United Nations Civilian Police Mission in Haiti

MNF multinational force

MONUC UN Organization Mission in the Democratic Republic of the Congo

NAFTA North American Free Trade Agreement

NAM Nonaligned Movement

NATO North Atlantic Treaty Organization

NGO nongovernmental organization

NPRC National Provisional Ruling Council (Sierra Leone)

OAS Organization of American States

OAU Organization of African Unity

OCHA Office for the Coordination of Humanitarian Affairs

ODA official development assistance

OECD Organization for Economic Cooperation and Development

ONUC United Nations Operation in the Congo

ONUCA United Nations Observor Group in Central America

ONUSAL United Nations Observor Mission in El Salvador

OSCE Organization for Security and Cooperation in Europe

P-5 Permanent 5 Members of the Security Council

PIC   Peace Implementation Council (Bosnia and Herzegovina)

PSO   peace support operation

RCMP   Royal Canadian Mounted Police

RECAMP   Reinforcement of Capabilities of Africain Missions of
Peacekeeping (France)

RENAMO   Mozambican National Resistance

RSG   Representative of the Secretary-General

RUF   Revolutionary United Front (Sierra Leone)

SFOR   Stabilisation Force (NATO-led, Bosnia)

SHIRBRIG   Standby High Readiness Brigade

SRSG   Special Representative of the Secretary-General

UAVS   unmanned aerial vehicles

UN   United Nations

UNAMET   UN Assistance Mission in East Timor

UNAMIR   UN Assistance Mission in Rwanda

UNAMSIL   UN Mission in Sierra Leone

UNDP   United Nations Development Program

UNESCO   United Nations Educational, Scientific, and Cultural
Organization

UNFICYP   United Nations Peacekeeping Force in Cyprus

UNGA   United Nations General Assembly

UNHCR   United Nations High Commissioner for Refugees

UNICEF   United Nations Children's Fund

UNITA   National Union for the Total Independence of Angola

UNMIBH   United Nations Mission in Bosnia and Herzegovina

UNMIH   United Nations Mission in Haiti

UNMIK   United Nations Interim Administration Mission in Kosovo

UNMOT   United Nations Mission of Observers in Tajikistan

UNOA   United Nations Office in Angola

UNOGBIS   United Nations Peace Support Office in Guinea-Bisseau

UNOMSIL   UN Observer Mission in Sierra Leone

UNPROFOR   UN Protection Force (in the former Yugoslavia)

UNSC   United Nations Security Council

UNSMIH   United Nations Support Mission to Haiti

UNTAC   United Nations Transitional Authority in Cambodia

UNTAET   UN Transitional Administration in East Timor

UNTMIH   United Nations Transition Mission in Haiti

URNG   Guatemala National Revolutionary Unity

USAID   United States Agency for International Development

UXO   Unexploded Ordnance

VC-ATOD   Virtual Clearinghouse on Alcohol, Tobacco, and Other Drugs

VJ   Yugoslav Army

WTO   World Trade Organization

YIIP   Canada's Youth International Internship Program

Foreword

KOFI A. ANNAN

During the cold war, security tended to be defined almost entirely in terms of military might and the balance of terror. Today, we know that "security" means far more than the absence of conflict. We also have a greater appreciation for nonmilitary sources of conflict. We know that lasting peace requires a broader vision encompassing areas such as education and health, democracy and human rights, protection against environmental degradation, and the proliferation of deadly weapons. We know that we cannot be secure amidst starvation, that we cannot build peace without alleviating poverty, and that we cannot build freedom on foundations of injustice. These pillars of what we now understand as the people-centred concept of "human security" are interrelated and mutually reinforcing. And perhaps most crucially, no country, however powerful, can achieve human security on its own, and none is exempt from risks and costs if it chooses to do without the multilateral cooperation that can help us reach this goal.

In the following pages, the government of Canada paints a stark picture of life today for many of the world's people: civilian victims of internal armed conflicts; poor and marginalized people who have yet to experience the benefits of globalization; hundreds of millions of men, women, and children around the world who live in squalor, without even the most basic of life's necessities. But this book also offers hope. In it, Canada challenges the conventional wisdom of what it means to be secure, proposes ways to make the protection of people a priority, and points us in the direction of a new diplomacy that responds to a new set of circumstances in world affairs. In doing so, Canada displays yet again its long-standing commitment to the United Nations (UN) and the joint efforts to build an international community of collective action, responsibility, and conscience.

In an increasingly interdependent world, nations and peoples must think afresh about how we manage our joint activities, advance our shared interests, and confront our common threats. No shift in the way we think or act is more critical than that of putting people at the centre of everything we do. That is the essence of human security. That is something that all people – in rich and poor countries alike, in civil society or the precincts of officialdom – can agree on. And it is something that, with political will, can be placed at the heart of the work of the UN – our work to create security where it has been lost, where it is under threat, or where it has never existed.

Editors' Preface

This is a rather special book. It is an account of the early years of a Canadian initiative to develop and lead a radically new foreign policy agenda, built around the concept of human security. Our goal was to take stock of this first phase of work. Cumulatively, the chapters highlight just how much has been accomplished in such a relatively brief span of time. But they also point the way forward to the challenges of the future. The human security paradigm not only changes the way we look at the world, it leads to a new way of acting in the world – and to a new diplomacy.

This book is special for another reason. The authors of the chapters are all foreign policy practitioners, professionals from the Department of Foreign Affairs and International Trade. Finding time to write when they could, they contributed to the book under a very short deadline, while advancing their issues in the world of diplomacy during the day. Their papers are not academic studies, but "insider" accounts of how each issue developed and what obstacles were overcome. We did not seek out success stories as much as narratives with interesting lessons learned, for better or worse. Even the blind alleys taught us something along the way. Hence, it goes without saying that what follows is not "official government policy," but rather the more personal accounts of individuals who are ultimately responsible for the views reflected in these chapters. This book is unique in that respect too.

Of course many of the issues described in these chapters will continue to evolve in the months and years to come. Recent developments can be tracked at the following web site: http://www.dfait-maeci.gc.ca/protectingpeople/

As editors, we have benefited enormously from the advice and active assistance of the editorial board. Chaired by Paul Heinbecker, the board members included Mark Ross from Mr Axworthy's office, Lillian Thomsen, André Ouellette, David Sproule, Alexandra MacKenzie, and Jill Sinclair. Two other board members deserve special mention: Michael Small helped shape the vision of the book and provided wise advice each step of the way, and Christine Cadieux, as our project coordinator, skillfully ensured that all of the parts of the book came together, while working closely with the authors to that end. We wish to thank all of the members of the Department of Foreign Affairs and International Trade whose contribution to various aspects of the book cannot be detailed here. The editors remain deeply indebted to them.

Don Hubert
Rob McRae
July, 2000

Human Security and the New Diplomacy

Introduction

LLOYD AXWORTHY

In the time since I became foreign minister of Canada, a shift has occurred in what it means to be secure. Today, the language of foreign affairs includes protecting civilians, war-affected children, the threat posed by terrorism, drug trafficking, and forced migration, not just states' rights and national sovereignty. This represents an important progression in the global lexicon. It is also a much needed and welcome change in perspective.

Beyond the language of human security, this perspective has become an important element in Canadian foreign policy. What we have advanced as our human security policy is a direct reflection of the changing world reality.

What is different? Why is this happening? These are questions that this book attempts to answer. Each of the following chapters describes events or initiatives that have given shape to an emerging policy. This book is an effort to describe the evolution of what is an important new way of viewing the world.

Canada began using the language of human security when it became clear that, in the aftermath of the cold war, a new foreign policy paradigm was needed. By just reading the newspaper or watching the evening news, it has become clear that in today's conflicts civilians are most often the victims, if not the primary targets of violence. It was obvious to us then that protecting individuals should be a major focus of our foreign policy.

The term human security was not, of course, our invention; it was first popularized by the United Nations Development Program

(UNDP). Nor is the concept really all that new. A recognition that people's rights are at least as important as those of states has been gaining momentum since the end of the Second World War. The United Nations (UN) Charter, the Universal Declaration of Human Rights, and the Geneva Conventions all recognize the inherent right of people to personal security. Focusing the concept on protecting people from acts of violence and helping build a greater sense of security in the personal sphere, however, have been principally Canada's initiatives.

The UNDP Human Development Report was a useful point of departure. It was a comprehensive review of the seven dimensions that constitute security: economic, food, health, environment, personal, community, and political. But what made it so encompassing also made it awkward as a policy framework. In a postcold war world, where the most extreme threat to people is violence from intrastate conflict, such a broad focus tended to distract from the central realization that underdevelopment cannot be addressed in the presence of war and its attendant insecurity.

What is the utility of an infrastructure program when neighbours are killing neighbours because they are of different ethnic identities? What is the use of providing food to populations in need if rebel gangs are just going to hijack it to fortify their own ranks? How does one tackle the epidemic of HIV/AIDS when continuous war and conflict engender its spread? These are not easy questions to answer or even consider. There can be no doubt that development assistance plays a vital role in preventing conflict or rebuilding societies after fighting has ended. But when the lives of hundreds of thousands of people are dominated by the dynamics of violent conflict, they cannot be ignored.

In the past decade, more than 80 percent of casualties of conflict have been civilian. The figures are shocking. Worldwide, more than 30 million people have been displaced from their homes, countless others have been denied access to basic necessities, and millions of men, women, and children have been killed. Many of these defenceless individuals were targeted with intent: they rarely have adequate protection, and they certainly have little recourse to justice after their rights have been violated. Worse still, even after conflict has ended, many remain subject to indiscriminant violence. This has been amply demonstrated in the case of the impact of antipersonnel land mines, and the surplus of light weapons left over from the proxy battles of the cold war.

In the immediate aftermath of war, fewer weapons have been more indiscriminate or represent a more serious threat to human security than undetected, un-exploded mines. Antipersonnel landmines have a tremendous negative impact on people's attempts to rebuild their lives. These weapons represent a violation of every humane sensibility.

They are not a strategic ordinance; they cannot be specifically targeted against belligerents. In short, there are no smart mines. They only need a trigger, anything will do – a child walking to school, a mother the sole bread winner of a family, working in a field. One misstep and a life, an entire family, can be devastated.

I recall the morning when we opened the landmines treaty for signature. With Prime Minister Chrétien, UN Secretary-General Annan, and soon to be Nobel Peace Prize winner Jody Williams of the International Campaign to Ban Landmines (ICBL) in attendance, the human security agenda had its first major accomplishment. This campaign succeeded despite the fact that some said that a ban was not practical or politically possible, and that undertaking it in the manner that we did – outside the usual, at times ponderous disarmament system – would weaken the overall regime. But those who saw the necessity of a convention and the means to achieve a ban pressed on, confident that they would strengthen the overall impetus for disarmament. The result is greater safety for individuals put at risk by land mines around the world.

The Ottawa Convention represents a victory for a new kind of global politics. Never before had such a coalition come together and produced such sweeping change in such short order. That day in Ottawa was a confirmation that government, civil society, and nongovernmental organizations (NGOs) could work together to effect change for the benefit of the world's people. It demonstrated the utility and power of the new diplomacy, where nontraditional actors, citizen-diplomats, have an important role to play in the formulation, promotion, and enactment of foreign policy. The speed with which the treaty was ratified and entered into force, and the compliance with its letter by nations who initially opposed it, is clear evidence of the impact of nonstate actors and the increasing centrality of human security to the conduct of international affairs.

The landmines coalition took the Canadian tradition of building multilateral momentum for promoting international peace and security a step further. By seeking partnerships beyond traditional coalitions of states, Canada has helped legitimize the participation of civil society and NGOs in the policy process. These organizations usually have greater leeway than states to speak out and take action, and are, therefore, more able to push specific agendas. The *internationalization of conscience* by these new actors has been an instrumental tool in the development and promotion of the human security agenda.

Several years ago, few were talking about human security. Today, at every forum I attend or meeting I participate in, states of all station and tradition are using the term, and more important, are accepting the usefulness of the idea. When I gave my first United Nations

General Assembly speech outlining the human security concept as "protection for civilians," it was little understood or accepted. Four years later, as I presided over Canada's April 2000 presidency of the Security Council, the human security perspective was ever-present – nearly everyone was relating to it or using the language. On the agenda were issues like protecting civilians in armed conflict, reforming sanctions regimes to mitigate negative humanitarian outcomes, bolstering the rights of women in places like Afghanistan, and the necessity of humanitarian intervention to protect against a future Rwanda or Srebrenica.

Despite how quickly the concept has been validated, getting states to practice human security remains a difficult and uneven process. We have witnessed failures, back-filling, and hesitancy to act in defence of defenceless people. In recent times, Rwanda, Bosnia, Kosovo, East Timor, Sierra Leone, and the Congo have posed major challenges with very different results.

The campaign to end the repression of ethnic Albanians by the Milosevic regime was a serious test of both international will and readiness to turn the talk of protecting people into concrete action. For the most part we passed. The North Atlantic Treaty Organization (NATO) reversed the ethnic cleansing practice and saved the lives of untold numbers of people. But the Kosovo experience left some troubling questions about the willingness of the members of the UN Security Council to place international peace and security above individual national interests.

Intervention to end the suffering of hundreds of thousands of ethnic Albanians should have had Security Council authorization from the outset. It did not. And that denial, as a result of the obvious threat of a veto, seriously damaged the credibility of the UN. More immediately, by not acting in the face of clear violations of international standards, the Security Council abrogated its duty to enforce international peace and security.

The result was a transfer of responsibility for enforcement action to NATO. This was not an easy decision to make, not least because it posed a number of serious questions about the propriety of the action and strained relations among several key states. Countless efforts were made to negotiate an accommodation between demands for autonomy by the ethnic population versus centralized control and repression of their rights by the Milosevic regime. Ultimately, military action was necessary to enforce the Rambouillet Accord against the systematic violations of fundamental humanitarian standards perpetrated by the Milosevic government. The decision to use the power of the international community to protect these civilians was monumental. As a result, the Kosovo experience has substantially altered the debate on the conduct of international affairs.

I recall well the meeting of G-8 foreign ministers at Cologne which had been convened to seek a way to end the fighting in Kosovo. It proved a useful venue because it brought together NATO members with Russia, thus allowing the conditions for Kosovo to be conveyed to the Security Council for resolution. After roughly sixteen hours of marathon negotiations on every word of the text, it was a surreal experience as each minister spoke loudly into their respective cellphones, instructing ambassadors in New York to move within the hour to ratify the deal and adopt a resolution. It was a vivid demonstration of the new multilateralism at work. A body originally conceived as a sounding forum on global economic issues had evolved into an important political tool to solve a security crisis and was able to facilitate a linkup back into the council – all this demonstrating the need to retool and reform international institutions and practices to meet a changing global reality.

The Kosovo crisis has also engendered a major debate on the limits and uses of humanitarian intervention. Under whose auspices, by what criteria, recognizing what standards, using what tools – are all questions of looming importance. Secretary-General Kofi Annan courageously raised these issues at the General Assembly in the fall of 1999 when he called for a major examination of these questions. But since then the negative reaction of many countries and a certain degree of timidity by the secretariat has resulted in a diminishing of official interest in pursuing a dialogue on the question of intervention.

Canada has called for the establishment of an International Commission on Humanitarian Intervention as a way of forwarding debate and dialogue on the issues surrounding the fundamental questions of intervention. Without honest inquiry and reasoned recommendations, we will face an unending sequence of ad hoc, sporadic decision making, which will do little to increase people's security or their faith that the international community is willing and able to uphold the basic dignity of humankind.

This uncertainty has been reinforced by recent events in East Timor, Sierra Leone, and the Congo, which, while different in circumstances, have each put pressure on the international community and, in particular, the UN to intervene for humanitarian reasons. Each of these efforts has been troubled by uncertainty in timing, mandate, resources, and commitment – relying on individual efforts by particular countries or regional groupings to fill the vacuum. One could argue that each case adds to the experience, and each time further develops international/UN capacity for response. Unfortunately, the evidence does not support this evolutionary argument. The actual result is a system too frequently unprepared and unwilling to act.

This weakness is also evident in postconflict situations where the UN and others are often expected to rebuild ravaged, divided societies. Again in Kosovo, East Timor, and Sierra Leone recent experience demonstrates that the task of "peacebuilding" is approached in a rudimentary, ill-resourced way. It is not easy to reconstruct out of chaos, ethnic enmity, and the breakdown of local capacity, especially after the television cameras leave. Without constant reminding, the public in many key donor countries loses interest. What's more, the resources allocated to the task are invariably minuscule compared to military contributions.

In this case, Canada has tried to focus on how to support postconflict rebuilding with resources comparable to what was spent on the peacemaking actions. In Kosovo, over $220 million over two years has been dedicated thus far to peacebuilding activities, with special emphasis on education, corrections, and police services. In Sierra Leone, our priority has been the demobilization and rehabilitation of combatants, especially child soldiers. In Haiti, our efforts have focused on the justice system.

In situations where we have decided to become involved, our modus operandi has been to do what we can, where we can have a discernable and positive impact, and to do so to the best of our abilities. The best Canadian foreign policy remains an independent policy based on our competences and capacity to deliver. Acting with independence, but in partnership with our allies, has, over the past half century, made Canada a vital and respected member of the world community. And it has given us a voice and influence more substantial than our political and military might would suggest. This independence is a credit to Canadians and their desire to have a distinct international voice. This is especially significant given that we live next door to the world's political, military, and economic superpower.

Canadians want their country to be more than a junior partner to the United States. They expect their government to have a voice that reflects their priorities and concerns. Lester Pearson first took Canada onto the world stage as an independent actor in a sustained way in the 1950s and 1960s – a time of critical realignment in international relations. He crafted a distinct Canadian foreign policy identity and utilized the newly emerging postwar multilateral infrastructure to promote an agenda of international peace, security, and development. He saw the UN as the preeminent vehicle to drive this agenda, and he used it to successfully promote new ideas and practices, most famously peacekeeping. While the end of the cold war era, has not made the issues or the tools of Pearson's day obsolete, it has meant that new issues are emerging that necessitate the international community find alternative ways of thinking and acting multilaterally.

At the cold war's end, we are attempting, as Pearson did at its beginning, to place Canada in a strong leadership position. The human security agenda is a basis for a new way forward. It attempts to deal with new and newly transformed threats to the lives and safety of individuals, both at home and abroad. This agenda is crucial not only for the security of individuals, but also to maintain Canada's role as a leading voice on the world stage. These are the considerations that have been motivating our efforts.

We began this process by examining the utility of soft power. Some have taken soft power to mean weakness, or lacking hard power. That is a wrong, and perhaps politically motivated, rebranding of an essentially positive phrase. Soft power relies on diplomatic resources, persuasion, information capacity, and creative use of selective military tools rather than coercive force to promote a country's interests or project its influence on the world stage. It means maximizing our talent for coalition building, developing ideas, and making use of the multilateral system. Exercising the soft power option is not a retreat from any great hard power tradition and it does not reduce Canada's influence abroad. On the contrary, it enhances Canada's ability to promote its interests and pursue the human security agenda.

With a worldwide network of embassies, high commissions, and consulates, active parliamentarians, and a strong trust built with civil society during the landmines campaign and in the development of the International Criminal Court (ICC), Canada is well positioned to advance the concept of human security. To facilitate this process, we have also begun to build a new global network of like-minded countries associated with international organizations and NGOs to work together on human security subjects. Started by ourselves and Norway two years ago, the Human Security Network (the Lysøen Group) has grown to include thirteen countries which meet and communicate regularly on a variety of common interests and initiatives related to human security.

Starting from the central premise of "protection for civilians," we set out to examine, what at the time seemed many divergent, but what would be revealed to be intrinsically related, ideas and issues. The landmines treaty was the first concrete, public expression of the human security agenda, but it was not the only dimension. At the same time as the landmines campaign was underway, the idea for a permanent international criminal court was emerging. As these were both being developed, we were examining the plight of the world's young people and started to piece together a strategic policy framework on children's issues. Each of these have produced substantive results, including the Rome Statute of the International Criminal Court and the Optional Protocol to the Convention on the Rights of the Child on minimum ages for recruitment and deployment of soldiers. Along with these initiatives, we have identified the spread of small arms and light weapons as an increasing cause of insecurity and instability. Moreover, we have dedicated an increasing amount of time to forge new conventions prohibiting the transfer of these armaments, and have also sponsored significant efforts at facilitating microdisarmament projects in various parts of the world, especially West Africa.

Similarly, we have identified the rise of drug trafficking and organized crime networks as additional serious threats. This has been particularly true in our own hemisphere where we have sponsored a number of multilateral efforts at cooperation and coordination to combat the destabilizing influence they have on governments and the security of people. During the June 2000 Organization of American States (OAS) General Assembly held in Canada, the human security agenda was a centre point of discussion. It focused on, among other things, ways to offset the political, social, and economic corrosion of the drug trade on both producer and consumer societies. And in that respect, a more recent addition to our agenda has been to zero in on the increasingly destructive role played by some nonstate actors. These are the drug traders, arms merchants, and diamond traders who contribute to violence, destruction, and general instability. Our initiatives at the UN to expose the sanction's busters in Angola, both in government and the private sector, the broader review of the humanitarian impact of sanctions and our sponsorship of a study on the emerging "war economy" is serving to highlight the need for rules, legislation, and practices to limit the damage of these predators.

As each of these initiatives suggests, we have pursued human security where we have seen an urgent need and where we have thought we could make a difference. Issues have emerged and events transpired that have helped refine the concept and focus our policy initiatives. They have occurred both consecutively and concurrently. This book is, in part, a reflection on that process, and an acknowledgement of the breadth that this agenda has assumed. Contrary to the assertions of some critics, human security is not, just the landmines campaign; it is not, as some have suggested, "a one trick pony." Human security has become a central organizing principle of international relations and a major catalyst for finding a new approach to conducting diplomacy.

Pursuing this agenda has been as much an exercise in domestic coalition building and realignment as it has been an international one. We have found that human security not only transcends borders, but also traditional competencies within governments. The landmines treaty would not have been possible without consultations with, and the cooperation of, the Department of Defence. Defence was also instrumental in our ability to adopt the Optional Protocol to the Convention on the Rights of the Child, raising the age of participation in combat to eighteen and the minimum age of recruitment to sixteen. And, of course, there remains the crucial connection between our human security interests and our capacity as peacemakers – one reason why I have always supported the strategic modernization of our armed forces. On other fronts, the implementation of legislation to change Canada's Criminal Code and amendments to the laws governing the treatment of war criminals to enable ratification of the Rome Statute of the International Criminal Court required close cooperation with the Department of Justice. Similar cooperation is needed with the Royal Canadian Mounted Police (RCMP), Immigration, and the Solicitor General's Office on issues such as drug trafficking, illegal trafficking in people, and money laundering, all of which pose serious threats to the human security of Canadians and people around the world. And the Canadian International Development Agency (CIDA) has been a vital player in supplying needed resources for peacebuilding activities and engaging in its own direct initiatives related to the spread of HIV/AIDS, the necessity of education for women, and the advancement of good governance practices.

None of this would be possible, however, without the support and commitment of the prime minister, the government, and the Parliament of Canada. In the early days, this agenda did not have many converts at home. However, the success of the Ottawa Convention prompted a closer examination of the concept and its implications for Canadians. It has become clear that problems in one part of the world can have a serious impact in another, including here at home. What this means for Canadians is that violent and nonviolent threats pose a greater challenge to their security regardless of where they might originate – geography is less and less of a defence. Whether it is a terrorist bomb exploding and killing or injuring Canadians travelling or working abroad, or a sexual predator half way around the world talking to a child who is using the Internet in Charlottetown, increasingly we cannot protect our citizens with armies and bombs alone.

Given its recognition of this new global reality, the government has made human security a priority. It gave the agenda prominence in the

Speech From the Throne opening the latest session of Parliament. And the year 2000 budget for the first time provided funding dedicated specifically to issues of human security. This recognition is the result of a continuing process of bringing these issues to the cabinet table, the broader parliamentary caucus, and ultimately the Canadian people. There still remains, however, the task of convincing those in the bureaucracy, media, and NGO community that the promotion of human security is vital to Canada's domestic interests. For that reason a broadening of the dialogue is needed.

We have launched a Public Diplomacy Program that seeks to involve and include Canadians in this dialogue. Through our National Public Forum initiative, there are annual consultations on human security issues. There are also annual week-long consultations with NGOs on human rights and peacebuilding. A free publication called *Canada World View* now reaches 50,000 subscribers and is available on the internet. And an active program of developing UN clubs and landmines initiatives has been started in our high schools, colleges, and universities.

Ultimately, human security is the young people's agenda. I am constantly impressed when I meet with or talk to young people at their ability to understand the concept and see the way forward of the agenda. We are laying the foundations; they will build the edifice.

Canada's Youth International Internship Programme (YIIP) is an example of our commitment to promoting human security with young people. Each year we fund young Canadian graduates to travel overseas to work with NGOs and various UN programs to gain international experience and to share their expertise in societies which often do not have access to the sorts of advantages they have had. These internships are exposing them to the new global reality, granting them valuable experiences, preparing them for work in an interconnected world, giving them rich cultural exposure, and perhaps, most important, allowing them to make a difference in the lives of people.

The human security agenda is an attempt to respond to a new global reality. The road forward has many paths. What unites them is a very simple aspiration – security for all people, everywhere. It is, in essence, an effort to construct a global society where the safety of the individual is the central priority. It is a motivating force for international action, where universal humanitarian standards and the rule of law are woven into a coherent web protecting the individual; where those who violate these standards are held accountable; where our global, regional and bilateral institutions are built and equipped to enhance and enforce them.

Advancing human security is also the reason for developing innovative global partnerships linking like-minded countries, institutions, and NGOs. Such coalitions between governments and civil society are harbingers of the future, demonstrating the power of noble intent, good ideas, and pooled resources. Their energy, expertise, and ideas are indispensable in the pursuit of human security.

Vaclav Havel observed: "The sovereignty of the community, the region, the nation, the state ... makes sense only if it is derived from the one genuine sovereignty – that is, from the sovereignty of the individual." In a similar vein, I believe that the concept of peace and security – national, regional, and global – makes sense only if it is derived from people's security. This is the basis of Canada's foreign policy today. This is what we mean by human security. This is what this book seeks to explain.

In conclusion, I would like to thank my staff for all of their contributions to this agenda. In particular, Eric Hoskins for his commitment, and Mark Ross for his assistance in the preparation of this book.

1 Human Security in a Globalized World

ROB MCRAE

Globalization, that much overused word, is, nonetheless, the word most of us use to describe the profound changes affecting the international environment in the last few years. It means different things to different people, but for most globalization includes:

- the global reach of new communications technologies (the "death of distance");
- the emergence of global markets, and the "triumph" of capitalism (and consumerism) over its alternatives;
- the spread of democracy and western political values;
- and the nascent appearance of a global civil society.

By and large, these changes have been positive. The number of democracies in the international system has grown significantly, and most regions, with the notable exception of Africa, have experienced real economic growth and rising living standards. But what has become equally apparent is that globalization brings with it many new problems: these, if left unchecked, could reverse the gains of recent years and eventually threaten the international system itself. This is the dark side of globalization, and includes such things as international crime, mass migration, ethnically and religiously-based conflict, environmental degradation, pandemics and, last but not least, the widening gap between a rich and ageing North and a increasingly youthful and impoverished South.

All of these trends have been present for some time, but the end of the cold war has accelerated them in ways that we are just now coming to understand. The cold war stand-off effectively enhanced the role of alliances and state control, in what was an interlocking bipolar world, based on ideological allegiance. The wars of this era tended to be interstate wars, most often proxy wars fought with the support of one or the other alliance. The obligations (and benefits) of fealty tended to suppress those internal ethnic rivalries that had resulted from the often chaotic post-World War Two decolonisation. The end of the cold war, and the collapse of communism, removed these fault lines from the deep freeze. And it did so at a time when many former client states lost the political, military, and economic support of their superpower benefactor. While failed states were occasional during the cold war, they have come to plague the post cold war world, often with deadly consequences for their citizens.

Not that anyone should be nostalgic for Mutually Assured Destruction. But the fact remains that the post cold war world is more unstable and less predictable. The threats we face are more diffuse and multidimensional. In many ways, the world is less safe today, particularly for civilians. When states fail, civilians suffer foremost. Because the international system that grew up in the twentieth century was designed to protect states and state sovereignty, and to enhance security between states, the international system is struggling to protect civilians within states. The tools are not there, though some are now being developed in the face of some staggering challenges. These new foreign policy instruments, which are largely the focus of this book, reflect a broader change in foreign policy itself. This is the "Copernican Revolution" that makes human security, rather than state security, a new measure of success for international security, and for the international system.

THE HUMAN SECURITY PARADIGM

Of course, the concept of human security is, in principle, quite broad. It takes the individual as the nexus of its concern, the life *as lived*, as the true lens through which we should view the political, economic, and social environment. At its most basic level, human security means freedom from fear. These concerns have been traditionally the domain of nation-states, and where there was democracy those concerns were at least addressed, if not always successfully. Internationally, the security of our citizens was promoted through a set of interlocking agreements between governments, through international organizations, and through the voluntary sector. The concern about *human* security has been central to the work of the Red Cross going back to the nineteenth century, and the Geneva Conventions, which emerged following World War Two, and sought to codify the humane treatment of civilians in times of war.

There are other antecedents of human security too. The United Nations (UN) has taken a leading role on human rights issues generally, and contributed substantially to a developing body of international human rights law. Both the UN Charter and the Declaration on Human Rights are ample testimony to the this body's leading role, including the fact that the UN has woven human rights considerations into the work of virtually all of its agencies and commissions. So too has the UN been active in the investigation and condemnation of specific human rights abuses around the world, bringing to attention the plight of specific individuals and communities. Special *rapporteurs* have been established in some cases that have not only led to debate but occasionally the negotiation of international agreements or even the imposition of sanctions. Clearly, many of these human rights instruments are relevant to the promotion of human security and, like human development, human rights are a key constituent of human security. However, in conflict situations, human security is a concern not only with rights but with the safety of civilians from violence. It is a concern which underlies the use of a much broader set of instruments than the traditionally normative approach of human rights. In both cases, the counter-claims of national sovereignty have had a direct impact on international action. The promotion of human rights and human security naturally leads to a reconsideration of sovereignty in all its aspects, a reconsideration that is part of the broader process of globalization.

International aid and development assistance have made, and still make, an enduring contribution to human security. Emergency humanitarian relief has always taken the individual – this particular woman, this child, this man – as the focus of its effort. Humanitarian action of this kind has sought to respond to basic needs in a moment of crisis, to fend off starvation, or to build temporary accommodation for the dispossessed. Development assistance has complemented humanitarian aid by building sustainable economies and by strengthening the capacity of developing societies to manage both internal and external political fault-lines. But even here, human security provides a new insight: development projects that strengthen economies at the macro level, whether through market reforms or liberalization, can produce unintended effects locally. Smaller economies, especially in the developing world, are sometimes battered by the winds of globalization in ways no economist can truly measure.

What lies behind the unhappiness of some smaller states with the World Trade Organization (WTO), the International Monetary Fund (IMF), and the World Bank, is a plea to consider more carefully the micro impact of international policies and agreements on the human security of their citizens. So too environmental security proposes that we measure international economic and environmental agreements against the impact they have at the level of civil society, including the impact they have on the environmental security of individuals. Human security, viewed through an environmental lens, leads us to examine the welfare of individuals as a function of a total ecology, both physical and psychological. An environmental diplomacy that departs from this humanitarian standpoint would take quality of life and health, in addition to life-expectancy, as the real measure of successful environmental and health policies. Where environmental degradation or preventable diseases have a negative impact on health and create chronic disabilities, life-expectancy measures are rendered meaningless. It is the quality of the life lived, in addition to the abstract calculation of years, that is the focus of human security. But while all of these areas of international relations reveal evidence of a paradigm shift in the making, that shift is most apparent – and most needed – when we look at international security.

GLOBALIZATION AND THE NEW CONFLICTS

What has led to this reconsideration of international relations, and the diplomacy we use to pursue them? The first trend is, unquestionably, globalization. If the safety and security of civilians, and their welfare, has traditionally been the responsibility of nation-states, it has become increasingly clear that, in a globalized world, these states no longer possess all of the means to deliver. Whether developed or developing nations, all have come to recognize the need for international trade agreements to regulate commerce, arms agreements to promote international security and stability, global environmental accords to tackle truly global environmental problems, or international human rights accords to guarantee certain basic freedoms. Many more examples could be given, but the point is that we can no longer treat "domestic policy" in isolation from the international context: every domestic issue has an international dimension and vice versa.

Globalization, whether we mean markets, democratic systems of government, technology, or the spread of global values, is pushing down into the affairs of states and affecting the lives of individuals everywhere. This process is far from universal, and there are plenty of ghettos in globalization, but it is now a discernable broad-scale trend. The unanswered question is whether or not it can be managed, and by whom. The current phase might best be called "frontier globalization," because it reflects many of the attributes of the Wild West. Globalization often looks more like ungoverned territory than the promised land, marked by gold rushes and greed, robber-barons, and mass extinctions, – responsible, it would seem, to no one, at least not to most of the people who inhabit its precincts. The future challenge here is a challenge of international governance, and the development of new instruments that both enhances the opportunities of globalization, while tackling its "dark side."

Because the dark side of globalization *does* pose a threat to human security. This is the second trend that is leading to a reconsideration of our foreign policy instruments, to our paradigm shift. The other side of the coin to globalization is localization. We see it everywhere, almost always mixed up together. The opposites converge in the image of a coca-cola drinking, jean-clad, AK-47 equipped paramilitary youth defending ethnic or religious purity by attacking helpless civilians from another clan, tribe, or village. Localization is both a reaction against globalization (and often the West), and yet facilitated and made more deadly by it. The retreat into tribalism (in the broadest sense of this term) is a reaction against the uncertainties wrought by globalization and the disappearance of traditional economies and ways of life, even of cultures and languages. When identities are so threatened, extremism and violence become self-affirming. The current phase of globalization is inherently dislocating, with political, economic, even psychological dimensions. If ever there was an age of anxiety, this is it.

Moreover, globalization makes localization and local conflict more deadly, for a variety of reasons. Foremost, it empowers nonstate actors as never before. Stateless international arms dealers are ready to sell to any side, even both sides, of a nascent conflict. The sides in question are as often as not nonstate paramilitaries, who support themselves through the illegal control of a local resource (diamonds, drugs, people) or black markets, who trade that resource through international markets, and then launder the criminal gains via overseas banks in order to pay for the guns. These, the conflicts of localization, of ethnic and religious homelands, spread their tentacles far and wide. They have a global impact because they promote international crime, terrorism, and extortion, often through the witting or unwitting cooperation of an ethnic diaspora, which may itself be virtually global in geographic extent. The export of deadly local conflicts to other parts of the world is exacerbated by globalization. In the future, we may find that "homeland" conflicts are directly driven by such aspects of globalization as the ongoing assault on traditional economies, and by such global phenomena as the impact of global warming, environmental degradation, and water shortages. We have a plethora of intergovernmental agreements to tackle many of these problems, but the new threats to human security in both the developing and developed world seem to be particularly resistant to such an approach. Why is this so?

In seeking to prevent conflict, the international system has long relied on the negotiation of interstate treaties and agreements as the preferred option, based on the assumption that states exercise sovereign control within their borders. There have been two problems with this approach, just now becoming apparent. While we have a web of international agreements, the way in which they interact and together have an impact on specific countries, including vulnerable communities and individuals, is still not well understood. By focusing on human security, we focus on the actual impact of these intergovernmental agreements, where the individual is the nexus of competing and sometimes conflicting international and national laws and treaties, or even policies (e.g., the IMF or World Bank strictures). We are just now coming to terms with the unintended effects on people's lives of this plethora of national and international instruments. It would seem that sometimes the policy challenge is better understood at the micro level than through macro analysis.

But the second reason that traditional intergovernmental processes are not always successful in protecting human security is that governments are sometimes not willing or able to implement their international obligations. When such states are not willing to abide by international commitments, their refusal is often couched in terms of the supremacy of national sovereignty over all other considerations. The civilians of such countries are left in a legal limbo of competing rights and responsibilities, whether they be economic, environmental, or political. Other states are simply unable to implement international obligations due to a lack of control, or governance, within their borders. This can be due to a variety of factors, ranging from a dearth of institutional capacity and resources, to the breakdown of order, or even ongoing conflict. These are weak and failing states, where disorder is often accompanied not only by conflict but by economic and social collapse, including famine and mass migration. Here, human security evaporates altogether. Indeed, we are better to speak of traumatic insecurity as the daily fare of the citizens of these noncountries. In both circumstances, where states willfully threaten the security of their citizens, or where states are unable to ensure such security, the international community must ask itself how it can best extend assistance to such civilians. The answer is not always self-evident.

The reason for this is that intergovernmental agreements and organizations do not possess all of the instruments necessary to protect the security of civilians from fear or violence. On the economic side, development assistance, both official and private, has sought to strengthen human security by establishing a basic level of *economic* security. In responding to basic human needs, and in building the capacity of developing countries so that they can profit from international assistance in a sustainable way, economic development is key to long-term political stability. But without a minimal level of security, there can be no sustainable economic development, and even international humanitarian assistance of the most basic kind can be precluded by endemic violence and insecurity. Yet, it is precisely where international assistance is most needed to protect human security that the international system is the weakest. The intergovernmental framework that has grown up since World War Two has developed mechanisms to prevent, and contain, interstate conflicts. These are wars of territorial aggression between states, fought across, and over, borders.

But current conflicts often take place within states, between rival factions, where interstate mechanisms do not penetrate, and where the claims of sovereignty can be used to block international humanitarian action. The challenge has been to develop new instruments, both governmental and nongovernmental, to protect civilians in situations of armed conflict. It is this dimension of human security that is the main concern of this book. It is precisely here where the international instruments are most in need of development, based on a better understanding of the new conflicts, and a better appreciation of the constituents of human security. This is the paradigm shift for international security: from a concern with protecting and enhancing the security of states, to the protection and security of civilians. The shift results both from a failure of the previous paradigm to comprehend what is going on and to provide satisfactory solutions, and from the emergence of new norms among foreign policy practitioners and in civil society more broadly. Hence, this is also a shift in value systems, representing new concerns and feeding a new international advocacy. Perhaps what we are witnessing is the emergence of a global civil society because this is precisely what seems to be energizing the new multilateralism, a multilateralism that brings together states, international organizations, nongovernmental organizations (NGOs), and individuals in radically new combinations.

ADDRESSING THE COSTS OF WAR

In the field of international security, a focus on the individual as the nexus of concern enables us to understand both the broad spectrum of threats, and their interlocking nature, in any given context. The new conflicts are unique to their local milieu, and indelibly sui generis. But there are some important similarities too: frequently rooted in ethnic rivalries, they often "benefit" from the cheap availability of small arms; paramilitaries and mercenaries almost always play an important role, including the use of child soldiers; such conflicts are often funded through local and international crime and corruption; and vital resources, such as fuel and oil, are controlled through black markets run by local warlords. In fact, it is often economic advantage, whether the control of a resource or access to the spoils of a corrupt regime, that are the hidden motives behind what first appears as a bloody ethnic conflict.

In these new conflicts, the civilians are not only pawns, they are often the targets, and vehicles, for complicated power struggles involving opposing warlords or clans. Moreover, the civilians affected by these conflicts are not just those in the immediate vicinity of the conflict. The crime and clan structures that support these conflicts are truly international: drug deals in North America might pay for small arms shipments from Europe that are intended to equip insurgents in Africa. Crime, corruption, and black markets have been not merely ancillary to the conflicts in West Africa or the Balkans, they have been key to the prosecution of the wars of ethnic-cleansing there. Civilians have even been used as instruments of war, where death and mutilation in such countries as Algeria and Sierra Leone have been used to terrorize the population and weaken public authority; or when the ethnic Albanian population of Kosovo was pushed across the border in an effort to destabilize neighbouring countries and overwhelm the North Atlantic Treaty Organization (NATO) forces stationed there. Nor are these new conflicts strictly "intrastate." The truth is that, while internal ethnic-based conflicts have been on the rise, there is almost always a state dimension to these conflicts, and often an interstate dimension. Some countries have sometimes had an interest in promoting division and instability on their borders, by aiding and abetting insurgents in neighbouring countries. The objective can be as simple as putting in place a sympathetic neighbouring regime, or as complicated as the control of an important resource.

But ethnic conflict can also be the by-product of more unwitting circumstances. Religious decrees, the breakdown of state authority, blatant corruption, even rumours of food shortages, can lead to the outbreak of violence and its contagion throughout a country. Haphazard decolonisation, rather than reflecting the contours of ethnic communities, sometimes placed borders so as seemingly to maximize internal strife. In all cases, economic factors play an important role. When states fail, it is, in part, because their economies are failing. These countries live in globalization's ghettos, the places where global economic growth does not penetrate or benefit. It is precisely where globalization does not go that our development assistance programs are so crucial in building capacity. But more often than not, development assistance is ineffective or undermined if there is no human security, no security for a civilian population in pursuit of its economic well being. By developing mechanisms to protect and enhance human security, we build stability and protect the human capital upon which the prosperity of future generations depend.

By focusing on threats to human security, and specifically on preventative measures, peacebuilding, and the protection of civilians in conflict situations, it has become increasingly apparent that we need new instruments, often complemented by old, in order to take effective action. The salutary adaptation of existing instruments, including our militaries, is one of the lessons of the last decade. Indeed, the creative use of military deployments has become one of the more striking elements of recent humanitarian intervention. This successful adaptation of our militaries belies the arguments of some that human security is no substitute for the "real security" provided by more traditional means. Human security and traditional security are not alternatives: security is a single continuum, and is protected and enhanced by a series of interlocking instruments and policies. Similarly development assistance, without relinquishing its traditional focus on basic human needs, has come to tailor its assistance so as to promote both peacebuilding and the reconstruction of political, economic, judicial, and institutional capacities in war-ravaged societies. The old instruments are neither discarded nor superseded – they become integral to a new, more comprehensive approach centred on the protective welfare of civilians. The challenge is to adapt the mandates and institutional arrangements governing our armed forces, our development assistance agencies, even our police, to the new security environment, so as to make them more flexible and more responsive.

Though normally an act of last resort, political-military intervention can be the decisive factor in dealing with humanitarian crises. The ethnic conflicts in Sierra Leone, East Timor, and Kosovo demonstrated that the selective application of military force, in tandem with diplomatic initiatives, can be key to bringing internecine conflict to an end. But they also showed that military force can win the war, but it cannot win the peace, at least not alone. In Bosnia, military force was used to bring ethnic conflict to an end, to separate the combatants, and to secure the area of operation for the implementation of an international political settlement. But at least initially, all support for the civilian mission in Bosnia was sloughed off by the force commanders as "mission creep." It was only due to public pressure for such things as the arrest of war criminals, and the realization that even the holding of elections required the protection of ballot boxes and polling stations, that an effort was made to knit together the military and civilian operations. The lesson was simple: complex postconflict situations required complex and highly-integrated missions.

Indeed, in some cases, the peace support operation is expected not only to support the civilian peacebuilding operation, it is required to take on some civilian tasks where there is no other option. In the Balkans, Africa, and East Timor, our militaries have built and managed refugee camps, and provided the basic needs when the United Nations High Commission for Refugees (UNHCR) or other international organizations have been slow to respond. The military command structure, and standing forces (especially when already in theatre), are particularly adept at responding quickly to humanitarian crises. The need for this, especially on the margins of peace support operations, will likely persist if not grow in the future. It is all part of the adaptation of existing instruments to new missions, including missions with a human security focus. Peacebuilding in postconflict situations, whether or not a peace support operation is in place, also requires the rapid mobilization of financial and human resources if the entire effort is not to be undermined. Without reconstruction, without even minimal salaries for local police, doctors, judges, or civil servants, former combatants and civilians will have no stake in the future. Especially when the international community is asking war-traumatized people to relinquish the certainties of clan allegiance for an uncertain future based on democracy, the respect for human rights, and a free economy. Only economic and political development can lead war-torn societies from recrimination to reconstruction.

Another lesson of recent peace support operations, such as in Haiti, is the key role that international police play in peacebuilding. Soldiers simply cannot perform most police work, whether this is criminal investigation or the preparation of evidence that will hold up in a court. Moreover, without international police, nascent local police forces cannot be properly trained and organized. When an insufficient number of international civilian police are deployed, especially where the local police is heavily compromised or absent, the result is a condition of lawlessness. In situations of deepening insecurity, people's stake in the economic and political future is weak. The answer must lie in a more organized international effort to deploy international civilian police – perhaps a new instrument altogether, one that would include a "rapid response" mechanism.

FIRST STEPS AND FUTURE CHALLENGES

The obvious conclusion from these examples and others is that we are just at the beginning in the development of the right instruments to protect and strengthen human security. Whether this be preventative diplomacy, the deployment of peace support operations, or peace-building efforts, each human security crisis calls for a different set of instruments calibrated to local circumstances. Some of those instruments we now have, others have barely been created, and some are still but a gleam in the eye of forward-looking foreign ministers. The Copernican Revolution in foreign policy – that is, in human security – not only more accurately reflects the new international context, it also changes the way we look at the world. The thematic chapters below focus on trends in the international environment, which are then illustrated by a series of case studies. Both the thematic chapters and the case studies throw light on the development of new foreign policy instruments. Equally important, they offer some thoughts on what direction future work should take.

Key to the future of human security will be our ability to engage our own citizens in both the issues involved and in the development of crisis response mechanisms. Public understanding of human security crises and public support for sometimes complex solutions are the conditions for success. When the high-profile fighting stops, can we retain support for the long road to peace and reconciliation? How do we engage, and connect, our citizens, while increasing their sense of foreign policy ownership? The biggest challenge will be to develop a set of instruments that will enable us to prevent major human security crises, and their attendant loss of life, from occurring. This will be no easy task, since it poses some difficult questions. For example, on the basis of abstract principles of human rights, the scope of action is seemingly limitless. It is when we encode those rights in international agreements that we have a proper mandate and scope for action. But when those agreements do not exist, when there is a legal vacuum, can we still act on the basis of principle, even when such action transgresses the principles of national sovereignty? Like human rights, the protection of human security, especially the protection of civilians in armed conflict, transcends borders. Yet, the principle of sovereignty and respect for international borders was enshrined by the international community as a response to the horrific interstate wars of the twentieth century.

Some of the new instruments to protect human security both target intrastate conflicts while seeking to engage governments. Such things as the Ottawa Convention (banning antipersonnel landmines), the International Criminal Court (ICC), and the Optional Protocol to the Convention on the Rights of the Child, all require the cooperation of states while simultaneously limiting their sovereignty. This, in itself, is not a new phenomenon. International agreements regulating trading practices or environmental protection have pushed international standards of behaviour deep into the traditionally domestic concerns of states. The new intergovernmental accords in the area of human security, such as those mentioned above, internationalize security issues that were once the traditional concerns of domestic policy. The use of landmines, the commission of war crimes, or the conscription of child soldiers were previously veiled from international scrutiny by the claims of state sovereignty. This is increasingly no longer the case.

But what has caused an ever-larger number of states to relinquish their sovereignty in this way? Part of the answer lies with the process leading to these agreements, which is why the landmines campaign makes such an interesting case study. We find that a coalition of interests was built up, in both state and civil society, in support of the intergovernmental process – though most of the progress was achieved outside its confines. This coalition of interests coalesced around an initiative that proved capable of mobilizing broad-based support, which was instrumental in widening the circle of supporting states. Coalitions of the willing, that by-product of uncertain security environments, have this distinctive advantage in mobilizing people and governments because their mandates are clear and unambiguous, unlike the typical products of the intergovernmental negotiating process. Moreover, success for these coalitions often depends to a higher degree on the exercise of soft power, i.e., the ability to attract potential supporters to your cause (rather than by leveraging support through coercion or the trade-off of interests). Sometimes sovereignty can prove more porous to soft power than to hard.

Of course, putting an emphasis on preventative action does not mean that we will be immune from moral dilemmas. In seeking to avert the worst, we may find ourselves negotiating with dictators and suspected war criminals. Can this be justified on the basis of a projected future good? At what point do we stop seeing such figures as part of the solution, and start viewing them as part of the problem? At the end of the day, is it right to seek to undermine, or even over- throw, regimes that threaten the human security of its citizens and neighbours? And when peace settlements are agreed or imposed, es- pecially those which succeed ethnic conflict, is it practical to insist on western models of multiethnic societies, when ethnic cantonisation and border changes may provide the only near-term exit strategy for cash-strapped international agencies? When seeking to develop new human security instruments similar to the Ottawa Convention, are we willing to pay an acceptable price for the purity of their intentions by sacrificing the universality that comes from the traditional intergov- ernmental process? There are answers to these questions, but they are difficult and in need of more public debate.

Though military force is only one instrument out of a range of in- struments that can be used to protect human security, it is the most controversial. We need to ask ourselves what are the conditions that justify the use of such force, and whether they can be encoded. It may turn out that the development of a doctrine of humanitarian interven- tion is either too difficult, or too politically sensitive, to obtain broad international support. It would have to set out standards for the treat- ment of civilians in armed conflict, and agreed actions in response. And even for those countries that support humanitarian intervention, would the development of such a doctrine introduce obligations to- ward future crises that no government would be willing to accept? Clearly, we need a range of possible actions, short of military action, in order to both address threats to human security and to protect civilians before conflicts get out of hand. Some of these new approaches will likely be hybrid combinations of existing tools, such as the further de- velopment of "muscular" international monitors, perhaps backed up by military force just over the horizon. We need to look into the eco- nomic factors behind much conflict, including support from the diaspora, and find new ways to affect the economic bases of war and conflict. Finally, the new technologies now available, especially the Internet, present both new channels to promote instability and imagi- native technological means to deter potential aggressors and to connect potential peacebuilders.

These are only some of the questions touched on in this book, ques- tions that deepen our consideration of the challenges posed by human security. After all, our Copernican Revolution is still in its early days. The next generation will no doubt see our "new" foreign policy, and our "new diplomacy," as second nature, at a time when a range of in- struments is available to prevent, or halt, threats to a more broadly conceived human security.

REFERENCES

Charter of the United Nations. San Francisco, 26 June 1945.

Department of Foreign Affairs and International Trade. *Human Security: Safety for People in a Changing World.* Ottawa, Canada: DFAIT, 1999.

Geneva Convention Relative to the Protection of Civilian Persons in Time of War. Geneva, 12 August 1949; *Protocol I and II Additional to the Geneva Conventions of 12 August 1949.* Geneva, 8 June 1977.

Univerval Declaration of Human Rights. New York, 10 December 1948.

CASE STUDY

Landmines and Human Security

MARK GWOZDECKY AND
JILL SINCLAIR

The preamble from the Ottawa Convention on the prohibition of the use, stockpiling production, and transfer of antipersonnel mines and their destruction begins in the following way:

Determined to put an end to the suffering and casualties caused by anti-personnel mines, that kill or maim hundreds of people every week, mostly innocent and defenceless civilians and especially children, obstruct economic development and reconstruction, inhibit the repatriation of refugees and internally displaced persons, and have other severe consequences for years after emplacement.[1]

These words open what is arguably the most unlikely and innovative disarmament convention ever concluded. Right from the opening sentence of the convention, it is clear that this international instrument is more than a disarmament agreement – indeed, it seeks to bring life to the humanitarian norm which limits the right of combatants to choose the means of war.

When the Ottawa Convention was being negotiated, the concept of human security was in its infancy. In fact, the ban was possible because its proponents were able to superimpose a human security framework over what had traditionally been treated as an arms control and disarmament issue. The purpose of this chapter is to examine the ways in which the concepts of human security were in evidence in the Ottawa Process, and how that process predicted many of the features of the human security agenda. What led a majority of the world's states to support a ban on a weapon which had been in widespread use for decades? This chapter will highlight the innovations which occurred in the Ottawa Process and its possible foreign policy implications.

"For the first time, the majority of the nations of the world will agree to ban a weapon which has been in military use by almost every country in the world. For the first time, a global partnership of governments, international institutions, and nongovernmental groups has come together – with remarkable speed and spirit – to draft the treaty we will sign today. For the first time, those who fear to walk in their fields, those who cannot till their lands, those who cannot return to their own homes – all because of landmines – once again can begin to hope."

Prime Minister Chrétien, Signing of the Treaty Banning Antipersonnel Landmines, 3 December 1997

THE ORIGINS OF THE PROCESS

The Ottawa Process was a fast-track process led by Canada to develop and conclude in the space of fourteen months a global ban on antipersonnel mines (APMs). There were only 424 days between Canadian Foreign Minister Axworthy's dramatic 5 October 1996 call for an international convention banning antipersonnel mines and the 3 December, 1997 signature of that instrument. Only fifteen months later, the Ottawa Convention entered into force, becoming the most rapidly implemented multilateral convention of its kind in history. What enabled the process to achieve its objectives so quickly? The answer lies in the dynamic mix of public conscience, new actors, new partnerships, new negotiating methods, and a new approach to building security – making the safety of people a central focus of international attention and action.

Basing themselves on the principle of international humanitarian law that the right of the parties to an armed conflict to choose methods or means of warfare is not unlimited, on the principle that prohibits the employment in armed conflicts of weapons, projectiles and materials and methods of warfare of a nature to cause superfluous injury or unnecessary suffering and on the principle that a distinction must be made between civilians and combatants.[2]

The banning of a weapon system is not unprecedented. Total bans had been achieved before, for example, in the 1925 Geneva Protocol on Poisonous and Asphyxiating gases which banned the use of chemical and bacteriological warfare. Indeed, there was a preexisting principle of international humanitarian law (noted above) under which APMs should have been deemed illegal. The basis of these principles goes back to the Geneva Conventions of 1949, and were finally enshrined in the 1977 Protocol I addition to the Geneva Convention. Nonetheless, between 1949 and 1997, antipersonnel landmines – arguably a clear violation of these principles – were in the possession of most of the world's militaries and deployed by tens of millions in more than sixty countries. Clearly, the interests of the militaries had taken precedence over the security of individuals.

What happened to impel the global community to rise up and insist that the interests of the military take a backseat to the concerns of civilians, and that this neglected principle of International Humanitarian Law be enforced? The answer lies in the cumulative humanitarian tragedy occurring as a result of the widespread use of APMs, and the opportunities afforded by the end of the cold war.

As the cold war came to an end, many regional conflicts, often fought by proxies, began to die out. Into these postconflict environments flowed peacekeepers, aid, and development workers. What they saw was a humanitarian tragedy unfolding in slow motion: the deadly impact of buried APMs. They were appalled and felt compelled to act. Without the constraints of cold war ideology, new partnerships were forged between North and South around a common humanitarian goal and with the participation of nongovernmental organizations (NGOs). This effort coalesced in The International Campaign to Ban Landmines (ICBL).

THE CHALLENGE

The challenge is to see a treaty signed no later than the end of 1997 ... The challenge is to the governments assembled here to put our rhetoric into action ... The challenge is also to the International Campaign to ensure that governments around the world are prepared to work with us to ensure that a treaty is developed and signed next year.[3]

In Ottawa on 5 Oct 1996, while addressing the closing session of the International Strategy Conference: Towards a Global Ban on Antipersonnel Mines, Canadian Foreign Minister Lloyd Axworthy challenged the world to negotiate a mine ban treaty and return to Ottawa by December 1997 to sign it. The Ottawa Process was the expression coined by the international community to describe a new approach to global human security norm-building.

Behind the scenes, however, major decisions were being taken that involved untried and risky diplomatic initiatives. The intergovernmental make-up of the Conference on Disarmament – with its consensus based decision making and the entrenched positions it reflected – meant that there was little likelihood of progress. Throughout the day on 4 October and in the morning of 5 October, Axworthy held a series of discussions with the members of his staff and officials which focused on two key issues: (1) whether to take the negotiation of a landmine ban outside the usual United Nation's (UN) disarmament machinery; and (2) whether to jump-start the negotiations by attaching an ambitious deadline.

It was clear that any such an initiative would be strongly opposed, particularly by the major powers (the US, Russia, China, the UK, and France), at least until real momentum began to build. At the same time, the Ottawa conference had shown that there was a growing critical mass of support for immediate action within a cross-section of developed and developing countries. Axworthy came to the conclusion that if this energy could be captured and channelled, there was a real chance of success.

Still, when the minister stunned his audience with his call for a treaty-signing convention within fourteen months, few (even many supporters) thought the effort would produce the desired outcome. As expected, there was widespread opposition in several corners to Canada's plan. In a number of capitals around the world, there was both anger and skepticism: anger at the way in which the challenge was announced (i.e., without prior consultation), and skepticism that a ban could be negotiated in such short order, and in a forum that did not even exist.

Nonetheless, the Ottawa Process partners – governments and NGOs and international organizations such as the International Committee of the Red Cross (ICRC) and the UN – offered an open invitation: join as a like-minded partner with the clear goal of achieving a total ban on APMs within the coming year, or, step aside. The tactics were more ad hoc, as befitted a ground-breaking diplomatic process:

- develop an open-ended, dynamic, and continually expanding community of self-selected, like-minded states;
- build an intimate partnership with international organizations and NGOs;
- use every available means – diplomatic, public, political, technological, – to generate public and political will in support of the overarching strategic goal of achieving a ban;
- establish a credible political process and negotiating forum to conclude a legally-binding treaty;
- ensure the legitimacy and credibility of the new instrument by returning it to the UN secretary-general for long term custodianship.

What followed was characterized by improvisation, dynamism, and commitment on the part of the key players in the process. Canadian officials faced the daunting prospect of developing a process which would bring about the ban treaty in little more than one year. The objective was clear, the deadline was clear, but everything else about the process was undefined. How could an idea – promoted by a small group of countries (none of them major powers), catalysed by the challenge from Canada's foreign minister – be transformed into something to be taken seriously by governments around the world?

In the initial weeks after 5 October, reaction to Axworthy's challenge ranged from rage and skepticism to polite (and frequently impolite) dismissal. And while the UN secretary-general and the president of the ICRC pledged support for Axworthy's goal, few countries were prepared immediately to commit to this adventure. In fact, the proposal was met with outright hostility by the world's most powerful countries, the permanent five members of the UN Security Council.

THE STRATEGY

Canadian officials, in partnership with their most robust proban partners (Austria, Norway, South Africa, Switzerland, New Zealand, Mexico, Belgium, the ICBL, ICRC, and the United Nations Children's Fund (UNICEF)) ultimately agreed on a two track approach. Track One: to generate an unstoppable impetus of global public support and political will for total the prohibition of APMs. Track Two: to create a formal negotiating process leading to the conclusion of an internationally-recognized treaty instrument.

The partnership between NGOs and governments became a common front for advocacy of the ban. The global choreography of the campaign was complex but, at its heart, consisted of a series of carefully plotted political and public opportunities to promote the ban. These ranged from the strategic use of traditional diplomatic settings to promote, cajole, encourage, and entice governments to join the ban, to the more innovative (and, apparently, enervating) tactic employed by various national NGO campaigns to phone members of Parliament on their cell-phones – repeatedly – with a single message to support the ban. It was this unique combination of relentless bottom-up and top-down pressure that generated the political will necessary to achieve success.

However, governments were still required to deliver the necessary legal instruments to ensure a ban. Thus, it was essential to establish, in parallel, an effective state-led process that would: (i) enable the negotiation of a draft text; (ii) ensure the kind of full examination of an issue befitting a complex and technical international instrument; and (iii) lead to the formal adoption of a treaty by states.

To this end, a "Core Group" of countries was created in which political movements and substantive policy positions were carefully choreographed, coordinated, and placed along a continuum of clearly-established actions designed to achieve a mine ban treaty within a year. Led by Canada, Core Group countries – particularly Norway, Austria, and South Africa – worked in concert to ensure that no international opportunity was left unexploited.

Whether in the context of bilateral relations, specific regional settings (from the Organization of African Unity (OAU) and the Organization of American States (OAS), to the North Atlantic Treaty Organization (NATO) to the European Union (EU) or the Organization for Security and Cooperation in Europe (OSCE), the UN system, or the process of ad hoc negotiations that characterized the Ottawa Process itself, this small group of countries worked on a daily basis – by phone, e-mail, and frequent meetings – to prepare their common approach. The Core Group agreed upon tactics, developed strategies, undertook joint diplomatic efforts, and coordinated policies working as a single diplomatic team, integrated, and completely interoperable. The Core Group developed a unique quadrilateral relationship through its diplomatic representatives around the globe, who captured the Ottawa Process spirit and worked in extraordinary ways, together, to deliver the goal of a ban.

With the key Core Group partners working with a broader group of like-minded countries such as Switzerland, Mexico, Belgium, and New Zealand (expanding over time to include a comprehensive and diverse range of governments cutting across traditional north/south boundaries), it was possible to establish a plan of action and a series of desired outcomes for each specific event on the Ottawa Process agenda. This work was carried out in partnership with international organizations and NGOs to ensure that steady progress was made at every step along the way.

A series of carefully designed meetings, hosted and chaired by proban governments were held, to prepare the formal legal framework and political ground for a ban treaty. Little was left to chance in this process, which began in Vienna where the draft discussion text prepared by Austria was first reviewed, article by article, and became the working text for the eventual treaty. A meeting in Bonn, hosted by Germany, was dedicated to a focused review of the issue of verification. The Brussels conference produced a ringing political declaration which upped the ante for those governments still standing on the sidelines.

Prior to each of these meetings, the broader Core Group would meet, discuss strategies, ensure coordination, and complementarity with the ICBL, ICRC, and activists within the UN system such as UNICEF, in lobbying and applying political and public pressure to encourage support for the ban. By the time the international community gathered in Oslo for the formal round of negotiations, the momentum was undeniable.

Complementing this series of negotiating-track gatherings, the Ottawa coalition – ICBL, ICRC, and committed governments – worked together to stage a diverse series of regional events designed to build popular understanding and support for the ban. Meetings were held in Ottawa, Brussels, Maputo, Tokyo, Manila, Ashkhabad, Stockholm, Sydney, Harare, New Delhi, Senegal, Sanaa, and Kempton Park. Each gathering drew together unlikely combinations of NGO activists; serving and former military officers; medical practitioners; survivors; field workers; technical experts and diplomats. These events produced a dynamism of open debate and discussion which galvanized regional political and media attention and local commitment to act, and often changes in government positions.

TILTING THE PLAYING FIELD

One of the key determinants of success for the Ottawa Process was its proponents' ability to change the substantive discourse around, and ultimately the procedural treatment of, the landmines issue. Under the Certain Conventional Weapons Convention (CCW) (Convention on Prohibitions or Restrictions on the Use of Certain Conventional Weapons which may be Deemed to be Excessively Injurious or to Have Indiscriminate Effects, Geneva 10 October 1980), landmines had been treated largely as a traditional arms control and disarmament issue, handled by disarmament and military experts in the closed disarmament fora of the UN, with little space for public input or impact.

Under the Ottawa Process, the humanitarian aspects of the issue predominated, though almost all the negotiators at the table continued to be drawn from traditional arms control and disarmament fields. Those trying to oppose the ban on conventional grounds found themselves quickly at a disadvantage. There was a definitive shift in the focus of the landmine debate – away from discussion on how to control and regulate the use of a weapons system, (until then considered a legitimate instrument of war) and toward the determination of how to definitively ban APMs from the world's military arsenals.

The reason for this shift was the growing awareness that, whatever the residual military utility of APMs, it was far outweighed by the humanitarian cost of these weapons, responsible for upwards of 25,000 victims each year, not as a result of active war, but as a consequence of an incomplete and destructive peace. Public pressure drew the attention of governments to the humanitarian horror of these weapons. The result was growing global understanding that the impact of these weapons on the safety and well being of individuals was unacceptable. The basic concept of human security – putting people first – had, thus, begun to take hold.

The combination of the humanitarian argument and a stand-alone negotiating fora, designed to achieve the highest common denominator in negotiations (as opposed to the usual 'lowest common factor' approach), ensured that an influential minority of antiban governments could neither define the process nor effectively derail progress by using traditional UN consensus-based negotiating and blocking procedures.

During the tumultuous fourteen-month period of the Ottawa Process leading to the conclusion of the treaty, Canada was accused of many things – including running a self-appointed club of "true believers." Those who made the accusations missed the point. The process itself was completely open-ended – to those who subscribed to the ultimate goal of a ban on APMs. In this sense, it was far more inclusive than, say, the limited membership Conference on Disarmament with its fifty-one self-selected members whose rules – including for admission – could only be changed with the consensual agreement of the current membership. Negotiation by consensus, in the Conference on Disarmament, often resulted in a single delegation preventing progress, or defining objectives based on its own narrow interests.

Beginning with the first Ottawa meeting, governments were invited to change their national practices and policies to enable them to join the growing community of like-minded ban supporters. It was for this reason that the negotiations – difficult though they were – were not characterized by the destructive divisiveness of some other diplomatic negotiations. Indeed, with its empowerment of people, from victims in Cambodia and Mozambique to some of the world's leading political and public figures, it was arguably one of the most truly inclusive diplomatic processes up to that time.

Some major countries tried to suggest that an APM ban treaty without their participation was of no or limited value. While all agreed that it would have been ideal to have all major powers within the regime, it was recognized that the process embraced the vast majority of mine-affected states, most of the users and many producers, and all NATO allies with the exception of two (Turkey and the US). Thus, the regime had considerable reach, weight, and credibility.

Universality remains the goal of most international regimes. With an initial slate of 122 signatories and entry into force only fifteen months after being opened for signature, the Ottawa Convention established a new international norm. The fact that countries formally outside the regime – such as the US, China, Russia, India, and Pakistan – felt compelled by the weight of public opinion to take unilateral steps to put in place their own national moratoria on specific dimensions of the APM cycle (from production and transfer bans to stockpile destruction), demonstrated the universal character of the new norm.

THE PROCESS AND THE UN

One of the most serious criticisms of the Ottawa Process was that, in choosing a stand-alone negotiation outside traditional UN fora, the landmines treaty would undermine the credibility of the UN and its disarmament forum, the Conference on Disarmament. This was argued despite the fact that successive secretaries-general, Boutros-Boutros Ghali and Kofi Annan, had lent their early and full support to the Ottawa Process.

The Ottawa Convention is now cited by UN officials as one of the success stories on the global arms control and disarmament agenda, as well as in humanitarian law, and has brought credit to the UN. The secretaries-general understood that a multilateral success – demonstrating that political leadership can lead to change – no matter where negotiated, would increase the confidence of the international community in the multilateral efforts of the UN. For Secretary-General Kofi Annan, the Ottawa Process had the added benefits of engaging, as full partners, civil society and bridging the North-South gap. These attributes could only be welcomed by the custodians of an international system in transition. In inviting the UN secretary-general to act as treaty depositary (the UN has already assisted in the organization and staging of the First Meeting of States Parties of the Ottawa convention), the convention is firmly under the UN wing – which was always the intention of the drafters.

THE ROLE OF CIVIL SOCIETY

Stressing the role of public conscience in furthering the principles of humanity as evidenced by the call for a total ban of anti-personnel mines and recognizing the efforts to that end undertaken by the International Red Cross and Red Crescent Movement, *the International Campaign to Ban Landmines* (emphasis added) and numerous other non-government organizations around the world.[4]

Perhaps one of the most celebrated aspects of the Ottawa Process was the unprecedented degree to which international organizations and NGOs were partners with the coalition of states leading the ban movement. Indeed, paragraph eight of the preamble of the Ottawa Convention gives formal recognition to the ICBL and the ICRC for their efforts, an honour not normally granted in a treaty instrument developed by a state-focused international community. However, the fact is that it was civil society which made the treaty possible, and through the ICRC and ICBL, contributed to the drafting of its provisions.

The Nobel Prize-wining ICBL appeared to many as a finely-tuned, international juggernaut, sweeping more than 120 countries into a fast-track decision to sign the treaty. In fact, the ICBL itself was little more than a loose network of 1200 organizations worldwide, whose power derived from a combination of dedication and new technology.

The ICBL headquarters was a computer in a Vermont farmhouse, the home of then-ICBL Coordinator, Jody Williams. But the speed of e-mail, the Internet and faxes – and the carefully researched and documented messages conveyed across them – were the main ingredients in the ICBL's ability to mobilize civil society across the world at every stage of the process. Indeed, the ICBL routinely beat its government partners (and opponents) in getting information on key announcements or decisions to its members. As a result, ICBL's members were almost always better prepared to debate the issues than those who opposed the ban.

Traditionally, international norms have been established using a top-down approach. State representatives sat in the chambers of international organizations, and negotiated until consensus was reached. Legally-binding action to enforce the norm had to wait until all states were ready to sign on. This often meant inordinate delay and inaction.

The landmine campaign started from the premise that civil society can play a decisive role in establishing norms, and states can be brought along gradually to adopt them. That is why, when Lloyd Axworthy announced his challenge in October 1996, the principle concern was not *how many* states would sign the treaty in the initial stage but rather, the need to establish a *clear, new norm*. The Ottawa Process was based on the premise that universality would not be the enemy of the good. The force of public opinion would be the engine to move the landmine norm towards universal adherence.

The campaign also attracted the support of a many world figures, most notably, Princess Diana, Pope John Paul II, Bishop Desmond Tutu, and Queen Noor of Jordan. The human security dimension of the APM crisis was obvious to these leaders – as was the compelling need for governments to offer vision and take action. The reference in the convention to the "role of public conscience" in the ban movement was clear recognition of the part played by eminent people who lent their status to the humanitarian cause.

IMPLEMENTING THE OTTAWA CONVENTION
Signatures: 137
Ratifications/Accessions: 99
(as of 28 June 2000)

Banning Antipersonnel Mines
• Since the beginning of the Ottawa Process, thirty states have destroyed approximately 17 million landmines.
• The number of producers of antipersonnel mines has dropped from fifty-four to sixteen. Of the sixteen states that are still considered producers, many have not actually manufactured antipersonnel mines in recent years.
• Up to thirty-four states have been exporters of antipersonnel mines. Today, all but one of these states has made a formal statement indicating a ban or a moratorium on exports.

Clearing Land
• In Nicaragua, between 1993 and 1999, more than 1,200,000 square metres of land suspected to be polluted with mines were declared safe.
• Of the mined land cleared in Cambodia by the nongovernmental organization (NGO) HALO Trust between 1992 and 1998, 91 percent has been put into productive use, mainly for agriculture and the resettlement of displaced persons.
• In Afghanistan, between 1990 and 1998, over 329 square kilometres of mine areas and unexploded ordnance (UXO) contaminated battlefields were cleared. Almost one-third of this area has been made available for agriculture and grazing.
• Since 1993, eighty-eight minefields have been cleared in Jordan, freeing up more than 7 million hectares of land for cultivation.

Reducing Casualties
• Since 1993, the daily casualty rate in Afghanistan has dropped by half.
• Between 1996 and 1998, the casualty rate in Cambodia dropped by more than 50 percent. Preliminary figures for 1999 indicated another drop in casualties.

Source: Department of Foreign Affairs and International Trade
(For more information, please consult the Department of Foreign Affairs and International Trade SafeLane Website at www.mines.gc.ca)

IMPLICATIONS FOR THE FUTURE

The landmines campaign was a major success in terms of establishing an important new humanitarian norm. It was also an early example of governments sublimating their state/military concerns to those of human security. The resilience of that norm must be tested over time. This will be the measure of success for the techniques and assumptions on which the Ottawa Process was based.

However, the human security approach, as reflected in the landmine campaign, provides a new perspective on how international diplomacy can be conducted and new norms established. The human security focus implies that while military/strategic arguments are still relevant, they are not always decisive. And finally, the human security rationale means that the first measure of success is in the human life protected.

The Ottawa Process has not obviated the need for traditional multilateral diplomacy. However, it is clear from subsequent initiatives, such as the establishment of the International Criminal Court (ICC), or the negotiation of a Protocol on the Use of Children in Armed Conflict, that the mechanisms employed in the Ottawa Process may increasingly complement traditional diplomatic techniques. Moreover, what is clear is that it was an experience in international diplomatic relations that will have implications for both the practice of diplomacy and the humanitarian agenda for years to come.

NOTES

1 *Convention on the Prohibition of the Use, Stockpiling, Production and Transfer of Anti-Personnel Mines and on their Destruction, Ottawa, 1977* (Preambular Paragraph 1).
2 Ibid., preambular paragraph 11.
3 Lloyd Axworthy, Closing Session, International Strategy Conference: Towards a Global Ban on Antipersonnel Mines, Ottawa, 5 October 1996.
4 Convention, preambular paragraph 8.

REFERENCES

Axworthy, Lloyd. "Address to the Opening of the Mine Action Forum." Ottawa, 3 December 1997.
Axworthy, Lloyd. "Address at the Closing Session of the International Strategy Conference Towards a Global Ban on Anti-Personnel Mines." Ottawa, 5 October 1996.

Cameron, Maxwell A., Robert J. Lawson, and Brian W. Tomlin, eds. *To Walk Without Fear: The Global Movement to Ban Landmines.* Toronto: Oxford University Press, 1998.

Convention on the Prohibition of the Use, Stockpiling, Production and Transfer of Anti-Personnel Mines and on their Destruction. Oslo, 18 September 1997.

Convention on Prohibitions or Restrictions on the Use of Certain Conventional Weapons Which May be Deemed to be Excessively Injurious or to Have Indiscriminate Effects (and Protocols). Geneva, 10 October 1980.

International Campaign to Ban Landmines. *Landmine Monitor Report 1999: Toward a Mine-Free World.* New York: Human Rights Watch, 1999.

2 The Evolution of Peacekeeping

PATRICIA FORTIER

Every Canadian school child learns that Canada is a peacekeeping nation. Our Peacekeeping Monument rises within sight of our Parliament. There is consistently strong support for peacekeeping in all Canadian opinion polls. Yet the peacekeeping which is usually celebrated hardly exists anymore, except in the Middle East where it all began.

The Canadian monument exemplifies the classic model of peacekeeping. The military observer stands high on a plinth representing the cease-fire line, supported by other military, and looks toward Parliament Hill. There is also evidence of the need for constant negotiation and the inherent danger and bravery in standing between two opposing sides.

What would a monument to today's peacekeeping missions look like?

First, the platform would be crowded. The lone observer would be joined by combat pilots, combat troops, police, doctors and nurses, engineers, field diplomats, forensic specialists, human rights and electoral specialists, corrections officials, customs officers, humanitarian workers, judges, lawyers, and urban planners (among others). To add to the potential confusion, the military might be performing all or some of these roles, or vice versa. There would be no clear dividing line between antagonists or even a cease-fire. There would, however, be empty places on the monument scattered in inconvenient locations on which signs would indicate "awaiting logistical support" or "civilian police on order." A tin cup would be permanently affixed to the base with a polite but patently desperate request to donate to the worthy cause.

Peacekeeping is a unique expression of the operation of political will. Peacekeeping is based on a military model, and yet reflects the ideals and the habits of cooperation traditional to the international community, and particularly the United Nations (UN). Peacekeeping is dependent on volunteer national capacity, and remains rooted in the reality of field operations. It has evolved and changed, sometimes dramatically, sometimes incrementally, but always as a function of the dynamic between objective, local context, and capacity. The first task of any military commander is to define the objective. But the most essential information is what is happening on the ground. The key to action, then, becomes the operation's capacity: what resources are available to achieve the objective on this particular ground? This equation defines the operation.

The concept of human security is changing this operational equation, and the norms that animate it. Indeed, our definition of peacekeeping now includes peace enforcement, peace support, and peacebuilding, sometimes grouped under the rubric of "peace support operations." It increasingly reflects the interests of individuals under threat from conflict as well as the balance of state interests. But as our ambitions for peacekeeping have grown, the needed capacity has been available sporadically, and sometimes not at all.

CLASSICAL PEACEKEEPING

The 1956 Suez model of peacekeeping for which Lester B. Pearson won a Nobel Prize was built on the concept of the neutral observation of agreed behaviour, and military resources in support of diplomatic agreements. The aim was to stall conflict between nation-states, thereby avoiding direct involvement by Great Powers. The basic premise for all peacekeeping operations was that states were the forces to be dealt with, and that the insertion of a recognized global authority backed by neutral military was acceptable to them. Since no reference to peacekeeping exists in the UN Charter, the great diplomatic achievement of this period was the creation of the UN peacekeeping mandates and mechanisms based on Chapter VI of the UN Charter (Pacific Settlement of Disputes).

This classic model of peacekeeping flourished for close to thirty-five years (with the violent exception of the most deadly UN mission so far, the 1960 mission to Congo, ONUC). Canada and its Nordic and South Asian partners made a proud profession of it. Generations of military cycled in and out of observation posts on the Green Line in Cyprus, on the Golan Heights, and elsewhere. The aim of these missions was to maintain a state of reduced or no-conflict between nation-states. Conditions on the ground were predominantly static, with bursts of violence only between defined antagonists. There was a clear chain of command. The resources required were limited, predictable, and almost exclusively military. The exit strategy, if any, existed separately, in the diplomatic realm.

CIVILIAN POLICE IN PEACE SUPPORT OPERATIONS

Police have proven to be valued contributors to peace support operations, particularly in carrying out their two principal functions: overseeing the maintenance of public security by monitoring, mentoring, and advising local police forces; and reforming police organizations, including necessary training. They have been instrumental in building the capacity of local police to uphold the rule of law.

Police peacekeeping has changed considerably since the first large missions were established some ten years ago. In earlier missions, unarmed international police monitored local police and recorded human rights abuses they committed. They did not begin their work until the mission had established fairly secure local conditions. Police training programs, if any, were carried out by bilateral aid donors outside the United Nations (UN) mission. Increasingly today, international police enter the mission area almost simultaneously with the military peacekeepers, when the security situation is quite unstable. Police training and restructuring (whether in an academy or through field training and mentoring) is integral to the work of ensuring the new police have the skills for modern policing in accordance with international human rights standards. International police also work closely with military, judicial, penal, and customs/border control officials to ensure that all elements of the security sector are developed to work together in an appropriate, integrated way. Depending on local conditions, international police may also fill a temporary law enforcement function until a new police service has been trained to take over their proper duties. In certain cases, they may also support the forensic work of international criminal tribunals to help bring war criminals to justice.

In addition to their more "traditional" policing tasks, international police have played important roles in ensuring neutral environments during postconflict electoral campaigns; have monitored the disarmament and demobilization of police and security forces; carried out human rights investigations linked to the conflict; overseen the security and human rights of returned refugees and displaced persons; acted as a liaison between factions, nongovernmental organizations (NGOS), and UN agencies; and assisted humanitarian activities.

- Current UN missions with police elements: ten (BONUCA, MINUGUA, MINURSO, UNAMSIL, UNFICYP, UNMIBH, UNMIK, UNMOT, UNOA, UNTAET). There is also one OSCE mission with police monitors (Eastern Slavonia).
- Number of police authorized for current UN operations: 8,900
- Number of police actually deployed: 6,000
- Number of countries providing police: 68
- Largest police contributors: US (769), Jordan (678), Germany (421), Pakistan (320), Ghana (263), India (240)
- Canadian ranking: 12th (126)

Diane Harper

Source: The United Nations Department of Peacekeeping Operations

SHIFTING GROUND

Peacekeeping today looks and is different. The involvement of Security Council Permanent Members on the ground is considered key to a successful mission. Military resources are part of a package which is often weighted towards civilian aspects, particularly police (see figure 1). At the same time, the military remain the backbone of any mission in which they play a part because they can deploy more quickly, have varied resources, a chain of command, and, if necessary, use of overwhelming deadly force. Diplomatic agreements (where they exist at all) are often between factions within a state, as are the conflicts. Peacekeepers (military or civilian) are impartial in pursuit of their mandate, but never neutral. Regional powers are often involved. Mandates go far beyond observation to engagement or even enforcement, and are intended to create and sustain new behaviour and institutions. Mandates are creative compendiums of chapters of the UN Charter: Chapters VI (Pacific Settlement of Disputes); VII (Action with Respect to Threats to Peace, Breaches of Peace, and Acts of Aggression); and VIII (Regional Arrangements).

On the ground, the plethora of organizations involved means that the single most important function in any peace operation is often coordination. Some mandates are authorized posthoc by the UN, after the involvement of other organizations. Regional organizations play different roles at different times. Effective coordinating mechanisms within multilateral institutions such as the UN, and even within contributing countries, are beyond existing capabilities. The new missions are expected to bring peace, build the institutional capacity of receiving states, and sometimes fulfil all the functions of government while being responsive to people's wish to govern themselves. Peacekeepers

Figure 1
Civilian Police in Peace Support Operations

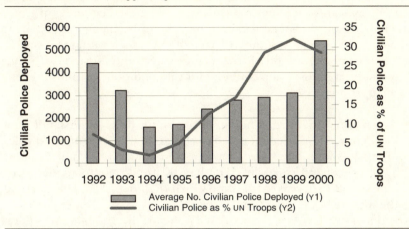

Note: Figures after August 1999 include nonpeacekeeping missions coordinated by DPA.
Source: UN Department of Political Affairs.

are held to the highest standards of accountability in both the contributing and receiving states. At the same time, resources are scarce to the point of debilitation, particularly money, police, and other civilian expertise, while the military building blocks of any mission – logistical support, equipment, and communications – are the object of constant pleading.

The change is radical not only in terms of mandates and mechanisms but mind set. The definitive break with the past occurred in 1989–90, when the new missions flowered and then seemed to have failed by 1995. Only in the last few years do we seem to have taken another step forward.

THE LESSONS OF THE 1990S

The 1990 Gulf War was a crucible of new aims and operations, and created a new standard in terms of the capacity which could be mobilized when there was sufficient will. Although the Iraq crisis started with a traditional security trigger, the invasion of one country by another, it changed into something quite different. The Chapter VII enforcement mandate of the UN charter released overwhelming force to prosecute a successful war that, in accordance with UN Resolutions, stopped short of inflicting total defeat. In its immediate aftermath came Resolution 688 which aimed at protecting the Iraqi Kurds as well as regional stability. But this resolution also forged a clear link between humanitarian impulse and international security, side-swiping sovereignty in the process. Sanctions also are authorized under Chapter VII and were applied vigorously before and after the Gulf War. From the beginning in 1991, the application of sanctions raised the issue of balancing enforcement action against a state and the suffering of individuals within that state.

Then came the period of lessons unlearned, and missions with confused aims, a poor understanding of local conditions, and insufficient or inappropriate capacity:

- Somalia in 1992: Initial humanitarian aims, little understanding of local context, an overresourced multinational force, confused rules of engagement, bifurcated chain of command, and erratic Chapter VII enforcement capability. The heavily armed multinational force handed off to a weaker UN force which then departed, after feeding the hungry but leaving a failed state;
- UNPROFOR (UN Protection Force)/Bosnia in 1992–5: An operation vacillating between the promotion of regional stability and the provision of humanitarian aid in the midst of a war marked by a UN-observed massacre, plagued by weak and constantly changing Chapter VI mandates/aims, and void of even cursory attempts to match mandates and resources. It was subsequently handed off to a heavily-armed regional military organization, the North Atlantic Treaty Organization (NATO); and
- Rwanda in 1994: An attempt to apply classic peacekeeping aims and therefore capacity to the overwhelming demands of widespread ethnic conflict. The Security Council's decision to leave was resisted, and the mission carried on through genocide and war and then dragged to a close a year after.

Canada participated in all these missions and learned its lessons painfully. In Somalia, the failure of a few obscured the positive contribution of many other Canadians. In Rwanda, Canadian General Dallaire commanded his inadequate UN forces in the face of political apathy and genocidal horror and became, in his own words, "a casualty of Rwanda, an injured officer of the Rwandan war."[1]

In all of the above cases, the exit strategy was still defined militarily. The missions failed to take into account the new human security equation – that the fate of ordinary people and their society was also crucial to mission success. The lack of credibility of the traditional approach was made clear with the world-wide revulsion to the events of 1994 in Rwanda. Here the withdrawal of all peacekeeping troops was the UN Security Council's considered decision in the face of genocide.

The nadir of global peacekeeping was 1995. The failure of countries to pay their peacekeeping assessments, particularly the USA, starved both traditional international peacekeeping and the new missions. The Security Council deliberated with an eye to the financial, not the human, costs. At the beginning of the decade, UN Secretary General Boutros Boutros-Ghali had envisioned the UN as the leading military peacekeeper and nation-builder on a monumental scale. Toward the end of the decade, however, the prevailing wisdom was that someone else would play that role, perhaps regional alliances under the newly-found application of Chapter VIII of the UN Charter, or wide-ranging powerful multinational forces under Chapter VII. The UN Security Council would retain its broad authorizing role, including the use of force by non-UN multinational forces, but would revert operationally to what it knew best – modest UN blue beret missions based on Chapter VI. Surprisingly, this forecast proved to be an overcorrection that failed to take full account of developments in peacekeeping's basic assumptions.

HUMAN SECURITY AND COMPLEX PEACE SUPPORT OPERATIONS

In the midst of gloom, there were examples of full or partial success, in Central America, Mozambique, Bosnia, Haiti, Namibia, and Cambodia. As the decade moved on, there was growing willingness and even a compulsion to embark on new missions in the Central African Republic, Sierra Leone, Guinea-Bissau, Kosovo, East Timor, and Zaire/Congo. The new objectives and norms inculcated partly by past failures and often by mass communication demanded that people be protected, that the root causes be addressed, and that justice be done. There were also demands that the international community pick up its collective burden again, partly in support of humanitarian workers who had died in increasing numbers when the Security Council had quit the field.

These high aims were tempered by the humbling lessons learned from the perils of vaulting ambition and limited knowledge, the reality of scarce resources, the necessity of engagement of those in conflict, and extreme caution regarding the use of force. Exit strategies became long work-out sessions requiring many partners and multiple benchmarks, many of them civilian rather than military. The first incursions into areas considered off-limits because of the principle of national sovereignty were permitted. These were gradually expanded until, with Kosovo and East Timor, UN peace operations became the effective local government. At the same time, Sierra Leone became a test case for the UN's ability to use force in pursuit of its wide-ranging internal mandate.

The aims of the new missions included stability, protection, human rights, justice, and development. The tools were:

- the use of either military or police force when necessary;
- the disarmament, demobilization, and reintegration (DDR) of former combatants, particularly children;
- the reform of the security sector (particularly military) and institutionalization of the rule of law, particularly police, justice systems, corrections, but extending to customs and border guards;
- the investigation and documentation of past abuse through forensic experts, Truth and Reconciliation Commissions, or criminal tribunals;
- the promotion of democracy, through the international support of elections;
- the establishment of human rights norms through observers and institutions; and
- the funding for social development and reconstruction.

The new tasks required that: (i) both civilian and military missions be planned and deployed in an integrated manner; (ii) all aspects be present from the beginning; (iii) the mission be deployed rapidly; (iv) mandates match resources; (v) flexibility be built in; and (vi) long-term commitment be understood. No mission has yet met all of the requirements, but the model reflects a new sense of purpose.

In Central America, the regional mission, the United Nations Observer Group in Central America, (ONUCA), began as a mission aimed at political stability. It required the disarmament, demobilization, and reintegration (DDR) of ex-combatants. Canada provided key headquarters and logistical support to this far-flung operation. Canada also continued to provide new types of military and civilian support as the mission evolved into other discrete peace operations in El Salvador and Guatemala. All were aimed at peaceful political integration, public airing of past abuses, human rights, democracy, and the rule of law. Problems remained, but peace began to be accepted as irrevocable, as the military reoriented, the police became stronger, and democracy was bolstered.

In Haiti, the US-led multinational force gave way to a Canadian-led UN operation that relied on military and police for stability, but included, in its initial phases, the seeds of a future emphasis on the rule of law, human rights behaviour, and development. Through a series of missions in Haiti, UN the military component maintained its residual enforcement capabilities while shifting its emphasis to the creation and support of indigenous police. The international police (including a major Canadian contribution) progressed through the stages of protection, training, mentoring, and advising, with the aim of achieving their own redundancy and exit. However, internal political struggles created paralysis and, therefore, threatened to undermine progress toward a democratic state where rule of law was observed.

In Bosnia, the reduced UN role and the expanded Organization for Security and Cooperation in Europe (OSCE) role, within the complicated civilian apparatus backed by NATO, responded to the needs of people by focusing on demining, police, refugee return, democracy, and human rights within a secure environment. Canada participated in both the civilian and military aspects, through the UN and NATO, including the initial contributions to the Mine Action Centre.

In the Central African Republic, a predominantly military UN mission replaced a multinational force to provide stability, the necessary space for elections, and a start to financial and security sector restructuring. Canada was the only non-African nation which provided troops to the end of the peace operation in late 1999, when it was replaced by a UN peacebuilding effort aimed at security sector reform. In April 1999, the overwhelmingly civilian UN mission in Guinea-Bissau was created with the specific aim of restructuring the security sector, particularly the military and police, and by the year 2000 it looked to be a real success story. And finally, the mandates of the latest UN mission in Sierra Leone, East Timor, and the Democratic Republic of Congo include provisions for the protection of civilians, with force, if need be.

The emerging pattern is one where complex military-civilian UN peace operations replace or support regional multinational forces (MNF) and organizations. These are followed by civilian-oriented missions aimed at long-term institution-building. There are several reasons for this development: (i) countries have staggered under the costs of voluntarily-funded MNF operations; (ii) the missions have required international legitimacy; or (iii) the missions needed access to a broader set of capabilities.

The difficulty with this elegant pattern soon became obvious in Spring 2000 in Sierra Leone. The departure of ECOMOG troops, the failure of disarmament programs, and the slow arrival of poorly equipped and trained UN troops led to renewed hostilities by armed groups, which started with the taking of hundreds of UN troops hostage. This ignited a debate similar to that in 1995, as to the UN's capacity to field robust peace operations. Could developing countries engage in effective enforcement action in the absence of developed country willingness to deploy troops on the ground?

In East Timor and Kosovo, the international community embarked once more on grand experiments in enforcement, peacekeeping, and peacebuilding. These missions went beyond anything contemplated in the early 1990s: the conduct of war followed by the creation of an international "protectorate" under the direct governance of the UN. In contrast to the 1989–95 missions, the immediate objectives focused on alleviating the suffering of people. While a non-UN military capacity was used for peace enforcement, the transition to a UN umbrella and the integration of civilian expertise was taken as a matter of course. There was little discussion of quick military-oriented exit strategies. Postenforcement conditions on the ground in both cases required extended partnerships with various institutions, from the United Nations High Commission for Refugees (UNHCR) to the World Bank, as well as with the people on the ground. This was necessary to achieve the aim of creating a peaceful reconstructed society where human rights were respected. In both of these grand experiments and in the case of the oft-delayed mission to the Democratic Republic of Congo, the weak link between the objective, and conditions on the ground, increasingly became capacity.

In the African Great Lakes region, failure to prevent genocide in 1994 did not lead the international community to look to understand the complex of issues that linked fragile regional nation-states, massive human rights abuses, and immediate human needs. These elements converged when the genocidaires turned border camps into armed launching pads and refugees into hostages or warriors. The humanitarian rationale behind Canada's role in leading a Chapter VII multinational force in 1996 was blunted by powerful interests in the field and a lack of multilateral capacity. The negotiation of the UN mandate for the Congo in February, 2000, was marked by greed and ethnic hatred as well as legitimate international security concerns. The result was a weak UN response. Even troops from willing countries required support from others to deploy. No organization or group of countries could summon either the will or the capacity to cover the geographic expanses required and accept the great risks posed by a war on so many fronts, by so many unrestrained actors, with such daunting social and institutional challenges.

Sanctions operations are also linked to political will, and capacity, in addition to peace operations, is the other operational tool which the UN Security Council has at its disposal. Sanctions policy and enforcement became an increasingly important adjunct to peace operations as greed rather than political power was identified more clearly as the mainspring of many conflicts, particularly in Africa. However, the capacity to formulate and to enforce sanctions within the UN system was even more undeveloped than for UN peace operations and relied heavily on bilateral capacity. Sanctions regimes experienced a similar trajectory to UN peace operations during the past decade. There was vigorous enforcement in the early 1990s (Iraq, Haiti), pro forma imposition in the mid-1990s, and, towards the end of the decade, insistence on credibility, targeting, and enforcement in Sierra Leone, the Balkans, and particularly Angola. With regard to Angola, Canadian chairmanship galvanized action in the Security Council Sanctions Committee and provided a model for future analysis and action.[2]

FUTURE CHALLENGES

As stated at the beginning of this paper, when faced with broad objectives and difficult local conditions, the challenge becomes the generation of sufficient capacity to carry out the mission. While the UN has its limits, it has a global mandate and field experience that includes both military and civilian operations. Although NATO and the Organization for Security and Cooperation in Europe (OSCE) are strong partners, they cannot provide all the capabilities required for comprehensive peace missions, such as in Kosovo. In Africa and Asia, all peacekeeping missions have eventually required the support of the broader international community in the guise of the UN. The experience in Haiti and Latin America shows the value of a global approach through the UN in partnership with regional actors and institutions.

However, neither the UN nor any other organization can reliably fulfil the requirement to plan and deploy rapidly in an integrated fashion. The 1995 Canadian study, *Towards a Rapid Reaction Capacity for the United Nations*, identified both the problem and some solutions, notably an integrated headquarters which would plan and deploy when needed. Although the analysis has been accepted within the UN, the capacity has not been created, and, in fact, overall planning and training capacity in the UN has declined. The creation of bilateral training programs such as the US or French African training initiatives or the Danish-initiated Standby High Readiness Brigade (SHIRBRIG) are potentially useful tools, but they have not filled the gap. At the same time, demands for rapid deployment have increased throughout the conflict resolution spectrum, particularly for enforcement, the establishment of norms, and institution-building.

For enforcement and stability, highly qualified, well-equipped armed forces are necessary. However, the supply is low. Cutbacks in Western military spending, the unwillingness of many countries to place their soldiers in jeopardy, and the concentration of NATO and other troops in the Balkans have all been cited as contributing factors for this situation.

GENDER TRAINING FOR PEACE SUPPORT OPERATIONS

Virtually every activity within a peace support operation has a gender dimension because women and men, girls and boys experience conflict situations in different ways and often face different opportunities and obstacles in working to build peace. Understanding gender relations in different cultural, political and social contexts and ensuring respect for women's human rights can lead to more effective peace support operations. For example, failure to recognize women's roles and responsibilities can mean food and other resources do not reach target populations. The United Nations High Commission for Refugees (UNHCR) discovered this in northern Iraq in 1991, when their decision to recruit local male community leaders to distribute food, resulted in malnutrition among female headed households.

Without clear policies and practices based on respect for women's human rights and understanding the role of women in different contexts, peace support operations can have a negative impact on the lives of the people they are meant to help. For example, as a direct result of the thousands of foreign troops deployed to Cambodia by the UN peace support operation, prostitution rates more than quadrupled, accompanied by a dramatic rise in HIV/AIDS infection and child exploitation.

With this in mind, the Department of Foreign Affairs in Canada and the UK Department for International Development have developed a gender training package for civilian and military participants in peace support operations. The course is designed to train peacekeepers and others involved in peace support operations to develop a practical understanding of the gender dimensions of peace and conflict, which they can factor into all aspects of modern peace support operations. A first draft of the course was tested in February 2000 by Canada's Pearson Peacekeeping Centre with a group of experienced peacekeepers, from Canada, the United Kingdom, the United States, and the United Nations. Participants came from the military, police forces, foreign ministries, development agencies, universities and humanitarian nongovernmental organizations (NGOs).

Jennifer Loten

Meanwhile, the establishment of new norms and the building of institutions has shifted the emphasis in many new missions to civilian tasks, and placed new demands on nations to provide both military and civilian resources. While troop contributors have demanded a seat at the table to discuss the new risks and requirements of increasingly robust and sophisticated military peacekeeping, civilian contributors are trying to determine just where the table is. Military training must now include not only traditional military tasks, but the new realities of military-civilian partnership in such areas as human rights, gender issues, and war crimes investigations. Responsibility for training the new civilian experts is a quandary for both multilateral organizations and the nations who send them. Military contributions often require enhanced logistical support, whereas civilian contributions always require total logistical support. Military capacity is at least measurable to some degree, including the capacity to deploy. Civilian peacekeeping capacity is a function of money, ad hoc deployment mechanisms, and individual choice.

New international and national structures are required for the funding, identification, training, and deployment of a variety of experts such as community police, forensic investigators, judges, lawyers, corrections officers, human rights experts, deminers, trainers, health practitioners, and city managers. The response from member states has been very uneven. International organizations such as the UN and the OSCE were similarly unprepared for their new role as governmental authorities within a peace operation. Nongovernmental organizations who have been called into service for these new needs are trying to determine the shifting lines of responsibility. Meanwhile, the individuals deployed need support, but are often not part of a national system which could provide that support. The barely suppressed chaos that accompanied the deployment of military, police, and human rights experts to such missions as the OSCE Kosovo Verification Mission in 1998–9 has been replaced by chronic gaps in fielding civilian police and other civilian experts in such missions as the UN Interim Administration in Kosovo (UNMIK) and the UN Transitional Administration in East Timor (UNTAET) in 2000.

Then there are the people on the ground – in need and in conflict. The key to success lies ultimately in their commitment, their capacity, and their willingness to work toward sustainable peace and security. In the Democratic Republic of Congo in 2000, for example, the UN mission was urged to deploy rapidly by all parties on the ground, and was criticized for not doing so, even as the host government hampered the mission's freedom of movement, and neighbouring countries opposing the government engaged in battles which threatened UN observers. When a mission does deploy, it then becomes subject to the high expectations which follow the end of conflict, i.e. the "politics of decompression." For example, in East Timor, the genuine good will toward incoming peacekeepers and UN administrators was soon strained by an understandable desire for self-government and a frustrating lack of indigenous capacity. In Kosovo, a similar dynamic applied with the added dimension of the attempt put into effect impartial human rights norms in the context of continuing interethnic tensions.

By the year 2000, the world community continues to view peace support operations and UN sanctions regimes as the primary vehicles for dealing with the varied faces of conflict. While the nature of conflict, and the make-up of the new operations, has evolved, this renewed political consensus as to the viability of peace support operations is the principal outcome of the turbulent years of the 1990s. But this renewed engagement is also the product of a shift in the orientation of peace operations from the monitoring of interstate cease-fire agreements to the promotion of agreed values and the protection of human security. It is the relevance of the human security agenda that has provided a better understanding of the complex needs that underlie a durable peace, and hence a new impetus to international peace support operations.

NOTES

1   "Lt.-General Roméo Dallaire to leave Canadian Forces," DND Press Release, Ottawa, 12 April 2000.
2   The Canadian-funded study by the International Peace Academy, *The Sanctions Decade. Assessing UN Strategies in the 1990s*, (Boulder CO: Lynne Rienner, 2000), argued forcefully for effective, humane, and targeted sanctions regimes.

REFERENCES

Charter of the United Nations. San Francisco, 26 June 1945.
Department of Foreign Affairs and International Trade, *Towards a Rapid Reaction Capability for the United Nations*. Ottawa: DFAIT, September 1995.
George A. Lopez and David Cortright. *The Sanctions Decade: Assessing UN Strategies in the 1990s*. Boulder, CO: Lynne Rienner, 2000.
United Nations. *Security Council Resolution 1291*, 24 February 2000 (MONUC).
–. *Security Council Resolution 1270*, 22 October 1999 (UNAMSIL).
–. *Security Council Resolution 1272*, 25 October 1999 (UNTAET).
–. *Security Council Resolution 688*, 6 April 1991.

Peacekeeping in Sierra Leone[1]

ALAN BONES

As an illustration of the importance of the protection of civilians in armed conflict, Sierra Leone provides a dramatic case study. Its record over the last decade has been horrifying on a scale with few parallels. Since the beginning of the civil war in 1991, more than 75,000 people have been killed, mostly civilians. Sadistic butchery has physically and mentally scarred an entire generation. At one time or another since 1991, half of the population has been displaced. In the United Nations Human Development Index, Sierra Leone consistently ranks last.

Sierra Leone's government has historically been weak, the majority of its people politically and economically marginalized, and its revenue dependent on a single, easily exploitable high-value commodity – alluvial diamonds. This vulnerability to instability and conflict is complicated by its proximity to Liberia, a politically volatile smuggling route for weapons and diamonds. Yet, this combination of a weak government and a dependency on a single resource that lends itself to corruption and exploitation is replicated in other postcolonial states without the same tragic results.

Why, then, has Sierra Leone's recent history been so devastating? Though there is no single answer to this question, a strong argument can be made that the lethal factor was economic. Greed, in combination with political marginalization and weak governmental institutions, turned Sierra Leone into a battleground, preyed upon by rebels and an unprofessional and poorly paid army, unprotected by a demoralized police force. In economically-motivated conflicts in weak states, popular support for the parties in conflict is neither a means nor an end. When the objective is booty, terror becomes a useful tool, and sociopathic behaviour a comparative advantage. In this context, traditional diplomatic or political solutions such as negotiated settlements or political sanctions are less effective, while the further breakdown of governmental capacity and local society drive the downward spiral. Over the last decade, there were attempts to work across the political, security, and development divides to address the worsening situation. They failed, and with each failure the challenge became greater. By the fall of 1999, it was clear that a checklist of requirements included a political settlement; robust force with the protection of civilians as its core objective; disarmament, demobilization, and reintegration (DDR) on a concerted basis; focus for assistance on the weakest, particularly war-affected children; and security sector reform, including a professional, accountable army.

The establishment of the United Nations Mission in Sierra Leone (UNAMSIL) peacekeeping mission in 1999 marked the first time in a decade-long war of medieval squalor that the international community approached human security in Sierra Leone with something resembling an adequate combination of political will, mandate, and resources. It also gave the United Nations (UN) renewed credibility in the protection of civilians. In much the same way that the UN refused to abandon civilians to their fate in the UN compound in Dili, East Timor, at the height of the violence last September, the member states of the UN finally recognized the plight of the civilian population of Sierra Leone.

Three major events in Sierra Leone's recent history provide a graphic illustration of how the protection of civilians is vital to breaking the vicious circle of instability and violence.

1993 NATIONAL PEOPLE'S REVOLUTIONARY COUNCIL (NPRC) COUP

In March 1991, the Revolutionary United Front (RUF), led by Foday Sankoh, launched an insurgency aimed at unseating the corrupt regime in Freetown. Comprised mostly of ragtag youths, the RUF established early its reputation for viciousness and cruelty, intimidating the civilian population through indiscriminate torture, rape, mutilation, and murder. In March 1993, a group of disaffected young military officers overthrew the besieged government and established the NPRC. Unequipped, either by experience or inclination, to govern effectively, the NPRC perpetuated the corrupt status quo. They proved no more skilled at fighting the RUF, and, over time, began to imitate them.

The civil war and the coup had immediate and dire consequences for the fate of civilians. As with most internal wars, civilians became prime targets, in clear violation of international humanitarian laws and norms. The RUF targeted women and children for especially vicious treatment, frequently augmenting its meagre ranks with children – either abductees, or disaffected casualties of economic mismanagement.

Despite the horror of the Sierra Leone conflict (and the conspicuous success of the RUF in civilian intimidation), it went largely unnoticed by the media and the international community, still traumatized by the peacekeeping debacle in Somalia. Little interest was expressed in fostering a peace process; even less so in a peacekeeping operation or observer deployment. There was minimal attention at the UN Security Council, and no sanctions or arms embargoes against the RUF. Mass displacements of civilians went largely unnoticed or unheeded, and nongovernmental organization (NGO) access to the area was minimal. In short, the civilian population of Sierra Leone was left to cope on its own.

As the civil war dragged on through 1994, the NPRC adopted the RUF practice of press-ganging youths into service at the front. Penury left the army in the same position as the RUF, – foraging outside of the main cities, or preying on civilians to sustain themselves. It was at this time that combatants on all sides recognized the vast potential for personal profit in the conflict, both through diamonds and the looting of civilians. By 1995, the war had become a mechanism for profit for both the army and the RUF, and this coincidence of interest led them to undermine any potential political solution to the war.

1996–7: ELECTIONS/COUP/AFTERMATH

The use of diamonds to finance the conflict attracted the attention of mercenary groups. Without the engagement of the international community in any meaningful peace process, the NPRC employed mercenaries to return order to Sierra Leone. While the mercenaries did not have the fair treatment of civilians uppermost among their priorities, civilians, paradoxically, benefited from the temporary measure of peace they brought to the country, and this enabled elections to be held. In March 1996, the respected Ahmed Tejan Kabbah was elected president. A renewed cease-fire with the RUF in February 1997 provided for a regional peacekeeping force, the Military Observer Group of the Economic Community of West African States (ECOMOG); a DDR program; and funding from Britain to start the recovery process. The initial euphoria over this agreement evaporated quickly, however, as inertia and a lack of international engagement slowed implementation of the agreement, leaving rural civilian populations vulnerable to the foraging tactics of both the army and the RUF.

The army was not pleased with its systematic marginalization (by mercenaries under the NPRC and by the regional ECOMOG force under President Kabbah). In May 1997, a military junta overthrew Kabbah. Major Johnny Paul Koroma, the coup leader, and his Armed Forces Ruling Council (AFRC), invited the RUF to join the new government. The ARFC/RUF regime was characterized by systematic cruelty (especially against women), murder, torture, looting, rape, and the virtual criminalization of state functions and institutions.

The international community scarcely took note of the coup: six weeks after the event, a UN Security Council statement indicated that "appropriate measures" would be taken to restore the democratically-elected government. In September 1997, the Security Council passed sanctions measures (oil, arms, and travel) directed at the junta. RUF revenue generation was not targeted, despite the precedent of sanctions passed in 1993 against the National Union for the Total Independence of Angola (UNITA) rebel movement.

With little tangible support from the international community, President Kabbah turned to Nigeria, as the main power behind ECOMOG, to help restore his government. Within months, Nigeria sent a total of 1,600 troops plus naval vessels in support, and received UN authority to enforce the sanctions measures against the AFRC/RUF regime. This arrangement with the region's major power was not ideal – Nigeria's democratic credentials were poor, and its tactics often crude. For example, in executing its sanctions enforcement mandate, Nigeria shelled Freetown harbour and its vicinity, causing considerable civilian casualties. The AFRC/RUF, under ECOMOG pressure, retreated from Freetown in February 1998, characteristically leaving civilian casualties in their wake.

Kabbah returned to Freetown as president on 10 March 1998. By April, his supporters controlled about 90 percent of Sierra Leone, though significantly not the diamond fields in the east. Pressure from the International Monetary Fund (IMF) to balance the budget gave Kabbah an opportunity to disband what he saw as an incorrigible and unreliable army. However, there was no program of support for DDR, either for exmilitary or rebels. Within months, exmilitary and RUF forces reoccupied large parts of the country, brutalizing civilian populations in rural areas. Though under Article 53 of the UN Charter Security Council authorization is required for regional enforcement action, ECOMOG never did receive explicit UN authorization for its actions (though tacit approval came retroactively the following year). The international community offered concerned words, but little tangible assistance, to Kabbah's democratic government, and he was forced into a series of unappetizing compromises and alliances which did little to stop the war. Despite the dissolution of the military and the presence of ECOMOG troops, the use of child soldiers was unabated and atrocities against civilians continued.

THE LOMÉ AGREEMENT AND THE CREATION OF THE UN OBSERVER MISSION IN SIERRA LEONE (UNOMSIL)/UNAMSIL

In view of the worsening situation, the UN Security Council in July 1998 created a forty-member military observer mission, UNOMSIL. Its mandate was to monitor the security situation and ECOMOG's DDR activities, and was later expanded to include human rights observers as well. While UNOMSIL continued its work, 10 to 12,000 ECOMOG troops, as part of their mandate to protect the government of Sierra Leone, continued a losing battle against the ARFC/RUF.

In January 1999, AFRC/RUF forces entered Freetown, resulting in two weeks of arson, mutilation, murder, and dismemberment. Casualties were estimated at over 6,000 civilian deaths, and 2,000 children went missing, presumably conscripted into the AFRC/RUF. ECOMOG succeeded in pushing the AFRC/RUF from the city, but their tactics sometimes degenerated into brutality. With its casualties numbering about 1,000, Nigeria decided to withdraw from Sierra Leone soon after its return to civilian rule on 20 May.

Though ECOMOG's presence was never enough to end the war, it did deny the RUF outright victory. Faced, therefore, with the prospective withdrawal of the only force that was effectively preventing a wholesale bloodbath in Sierra Leone, the UN Security Council decided to act. Nigeria was persuaded to delay ECOMOG's departure until 2000, and the RUF recognized that this was a propitious time to secure a reasonably advantageous cease-fire. On 7 July 1999, the Lomé Agreement was signed, which effectively traded accountability for a tenuous peace. A coalition government including both President Kabbah and the RUF was established, with rebel leader Sankoh as virtual vice-president. The agreement decreed an amnesty for all excombatants, and provided for the establishment of a peacebuilding program, including Human Rights and Truth and Reconciliation Commissions.

On 22 October 1999, the UN Security Council established UNAMSIL, a peacekeeping force with a robust Chapter VII (peace enforcement) mandate and 6,000 troops to carry out that mandate. DDR implementation was integral to the mission, and for the first time, the protection of Sierra Leone's civilians under immediate threat was part of the mandate. The dynamics behind the creation of UNAMSIL reflected the mindset of the international community at that moment. Many felt a post-Kosovo moral imperative to prevent humanitarian tragedies from festering, and several events made further inaction on Sierra Leone morally unjustifiable.

Canada had assumed a two-year term on the UN Security Council in January 1999. During its council presidency in February of that year, Canada had asked the secretary-general to prepare a report on the protection of civilians in armed conflict. This exhaustive and well-received report, which included forty recommendations for specific action, was released on 13 September 1999. Against this backdrop, the United Kingdom on 28 September shared with other council members its draft resolution on the establishment of UNAMSIL. It specified a Chapter VI (peaceful resolution of disputes) mandate for the operation – which, in effect, would have permitted UNAMSIL to protect only itself, not civilians under direct threat.

Canada's position was that in establishing the mandate for UNAMSIL, the international community had to realize that this was not a traditional peacekeeping operation separating duly-constituted forces operating under modern rules of war. Sierra Leone was a manifestation of a much older kind of warfare: a gruesome internal war virtually without rules. To bring order in such circumstances required a much more ambitious mandate. Canada maintained that, given Sierra Leone's grisly track record, and the recommendations of the just-released secretary-general's report, a strong mandate, under Chapter VII of the UN Charter ("action regarding threats to peace"), was necessary. The threat to the civilian population was simply too dire, and peacekeepers could not be placed in a position of witnessing the beating or butchering of civilians by belligerents without being able to take action. During early discussions, Canada was alone in wanting a Chapter VII mandate for UNAMSIL, but subsequently, the nonpermanent members of the Security Council agreed to the merit of this position. However, the five permanent members of the UN Security Council (P-5) maintained that, since a peace agreement was in place, UNAMSIL would fall under Chapter VI of the UN Charter.

This, in Canada's view, was missing the point. The role of UNAMSIL was not to take over ECOMOG's mandate to protect the government and people of Sierra Leone at large. Rather, UNAMSIL's mandate was to assist the signatories in implementing the Lomé Agreement, and its DDR plan. Integral to making the peace agreement work, as the recent history of the country had shown, was the protection of civilians under direct threat.

The response by most of the P-5 was that a Chapter VI mandate was adequate, though it could be upgraded to Chapter VII later, should circumstances require. Canada was categorical: this was unacceptable, as upgrading a mandate is a time-consuming exercise at a juncture when prompt action was a necessity. It is far better, Canada maintained, to "go in strong" with a robust mandate and the resources to match, and be prepared to scale back should circumstances on the ground warrant. In one of the most volatile and vicious conflicts of the decade, it was vital to use this first opportunity to put the principles enshrined in the secretary-general's report into practice.

What probably tipped the balance in favour of a robust mandate for UNAMSIL was a coincidence of two events. The United Kingdom introduced, at this point in the debate, a draft peacekeeping resolution for East Timor, which specified from the outset a Chapter VII mandate. Though comparisons between the two situations are invidious, it was clear that the sheer scale of civilian horror in Sierra Leone required a response at least as strong as that contemplated for East Timor. Also at this time, two Canadian Armed Forces generals were in New York testifying before the UN enquiry into the events surrounding the Rwandan genocide in 1994. Their experiences spoke to the horrors than can result when UN peacekeepers are sent into a volatile situation with inadequate mandate and resources.

A Chapter VII mandate for UNAMSIL was agreed on 22 October 1999, three days before a similar mandate for East Timor was approved. A further encouraging development was the decision by the Security Council on 7 February 2000 to increase UNAMSIL's capacity to meet effectively its mandate by increasing its troop commitment from 6,000 to 11,000.

On 29 April Foreign Minister Axworthy met in Freetown with President Kabbah, Foday Sankoh, and Johnny Paul Koroma (who had become the chair of the Commission for the Consolidation of Peace) to pursue a number of the human security themes reflected in the UNAMSIL mandate. Minister Axworthy informed President Kabbah of Canada's intention to contribute to the creation of the National Commission for War-Affected Children, which was designed to address the needs of children in the national reconstruction process. In his meeting with Foday Sankoh, the RUF leader promised to instruct his commanders in the field to release abducted children (further details of the meeting can be found in Lloyd Axworthy's postscript on his visit to Sierra Leone).

These efforts notwithstanding, the viability of UNAMSIL, and of the Lomé peace Accord, was severely tested two days later when Sankoh took hostage more than 500 UNAMSIL peacekeepers and UN workers.

Although widely portrayed in the media as a UN failure, the events of early May were, in fact, a result of the unexpected (by Sankoh) success of UNAMSIL. Despite the comparative under-resourcing of UNAMSIL, particularly its vital DDR program, UNAMSIL was clearly bringing a measure of stability, however fragile, to a society that had not experienced it for more than a decade. The DDR program was proving attractive to RUF combatants, despite Sankoh's best efforts to keep RUF members out of the DDR camps. Sensing his political advantage slipping away, Sankoh gambled that the international community would continue its recent history of not coming through when the going was tough, and that taking the UNAMSIL soldiers hostage would therefore reestablish his political credibility among the local population and his RUF troops.

The international community did not ignore Sierra Leone. Swift action, through the UN Security Council (which increased UNAMSIL's troop strength to 13,000 and coordinated additional logistical support from member states), through the Economic Community of West African States (ECOWAS), (which provided political support to seek an end to the crisis), and through bilateral contributions (such as the military support offered by the United Kingdom, in coordination with the UN), resulted in Sankoh's arrest by the Sierra Leone government, the splintering of the RUF, and the release of the hostages.

This is not to imply that UNAMSIL's performance was flawless: deficiencies were noted in addition to the under-resourcing of the DDR process noted above. These include balancing the number of troops provided with their training and equipment. Robust mandates need robust response capacity, which implies that peacekeeping troops require the training in both interoperability and logistics to work smoothly with each other, and deal with the unexpected. The magnitude of the RUF success in capturing peacekeepers can in part be attributed to inexperience and insufficient training on the part of some contingents.

Nonetheless, the consequence of the international community's support for UNAMSIL in May 2000 was a comparative restabilization of the situation in Sierra Leone, rather than Sierra Leone's expected descent back into chaos. There is cause for optimism that at least one of the corners in Sierra Leone's road has been turned.

LESSONS LEARNED

Sierra Leone has become a test case for the protection of civilians, and a number of lessons can be drawn from the events of the last decade.

- Conflicts motivated by economic agendas are particularly dangerous to civilian populations because they are not necessarily conditioned by popular support. Terror can become a vehicle to attain acquiescence, which is often cheaper than support.
- Conflicts motivated by economic agendas are less susceptible to traditional political/diplomatic solutions. A political settlement is a necessary component to a solution, but on its own is not sufficient.
- International attention, and support for a peace process, is necessary. Without it, weak or isolated governments often find themselves forced into inappropriate or unpalatable compromises that undermine their legitimacy and effectiveness, and in the end, prolong the conflict.
- Peacekeeping missions sent into these situations need robust mandates – which specifically include the protection of civilians at risk. They also require robust response capacity, including adequate training and equipment, to live up to these mandates.
- Peacekeeping missions must be multidimensional, and must have the capacity to support DDR programs, to focus on the weakest, and to promote security sector reform – they must also have the resources to do so. It is important that these functions be integrated into the planning of peace support operations: the events of 1997 and 1999 show that the "window of opportunity" to make DDR and security sector reform work is sometimes open only a short time. If the opportunity is not seized quickly, the effectiveness of the operation can be compromised.

Sierra Leone demonstrates that, despite the missed opportunities of the last decade, the diligent matching of local conditions to mandates and resources, can make a positive difference to human security. This is not to suggest, by any means, that the "problem is solved" in Sierra Leone: the events of May 2000 provide dramatic illustration that peace process is precarious and its future far from guaranteed. But the lessons we have learned can make a practical difference to the security of civilians in future conflicts.[1]

NOTES

1 Patricia Fortier of the Department of Foreign Affairs and International Trade played a critical role in the shaping of this case study. The Author also wishes to acknowledge the invaluable contributions of Ulric Shannon and Michael Blackmore, also of the Department of Foreign Affairs and International Trade, to the drafting of this work.

REFERENCES

Douglas, Ian "Fighting for Diamonds – Private Military Companies in Sierra Loene." In *Peace, Profit or Plunder? The Privatisation of Security in War-Torn African Societies*, edited by Jakkie Cilliers and Peggy Mason. Halfway House, South Africa: Institute for Security Studies, 1999.

Pratt, David. *Sierra Leone: The Forgotten Crisis*. Report to the Minister of Foreign Affairs, the Honourable Lloyd Axworthy. Ottawa: DFAIT, 23 April 1999.

Reno, William. "Shadow States and the Political Economy of Civil Wars." In *Greed and Grievance: Economic Agendas in Civil Wars*, edited by Mats Berdal and David Malone. New York: International Peace Academy, 2000.

United Nations. *Report of the Secretary-General on the Protection of Civilians in Armed Conflict* (S/1999/957), 8 September 1999.

–. *Security Council Resolution 1181*, 13 June 1998 (establishes UNOMSIL).

–. *Security Council Resolution 1132*, 14 April 1999 (sanctions on the AFRC/RUF).

–. *Security Council Resolution 1270*, 22 October 1999 (creates UNAMSIL).

Shannon, Ulric. "Human Security and the Rise of Private Armies." *New Political Science* 22, no. 1 (2000): 103–15.

Smillie, Ian, Lasana Gberie and Ralph Hazleton. *The Heart of the Matter: Sierra Leone, Diamonds and Human Security*. Ottawa, Canada: Partnership Africa Canada, 2000.

The Challenge of Microdisarmament

JENNIFER LOTEN

In civil wars, civilians take up arms. Ending civil wars requires the disarmament, demobilization, and reintegration into society of combatants from all sides. This complex process is known by the acronym "DDR," and the success of DDR programs is critical to any process of postconflict peacebuilding.

DDR is made more difficult by the proliferation of small arms. Small arms are unlike other weapons systems, in that they can be operated by a single individual and can be used by children or adults alike. Because they are easily concealed, they can be transferred to, used, and concealed by civilians much more readily than more cumbersome or complex weapons. Decisions about the use of small arms can also be made by individuals, to meet their individual needs, regardless of what their military or political commanders might dictate. Small arms frequently circulate in society among civilians and noncombatants well beyond the control of state agencies. What motivates individual people, their actions, and allegiances must, therefore, figure in any small arms disarmament initiatives.

This case study will "reverse the sights" on most treatments of DDR by focusing not on the steps in the process, as conducted by peacekeepers or other external actors, but on the individuals being demobilized, whose human security is by no means assured in postconflict contexts. Using this human security perspective, it becomes apparent that the success of DDR programs depends upon the prospects they offer individual excombatants for a safe reintegration into postconflict society.

DDR FOR REGULAR FORCES

The techniques for disarming, demobilizing, and reintegrating regular forces are well described in the "Practical Manual of Guiding Principles and Best Practices" for DDR Programs, prepared for the UN Department of Peacekeeping Operations by the Canadian Council for International Peace and Security. The manual defines DDR as: "The process by which armed forces (government and/or opposition or factional forces) either downsize or completely disband as part of a broader transformation from war to peace. Demobilisation typically involves the assembly, disarmament, administration and discharge of former combatants, who receive some form of compensation package and/or assistance programmes."[1]

DDR operations are increasingly recognized as essential components of peacekeeping operations and are, as much as possible, encouraged at the earliest stages of peace processes. Standard steps and their sequencing include the assembly of troops in designated areas, recording of information and other administrative tasks, disarmament or some form of weapons control, and discharge to communities.

DDR operations for regular forces have not typically enjoyed a high rate of success. The experience of the UN Mission in Cambodia (UNTAC) illustrates some of the pitfalls. Under the terms of the UN brokered Paris Agreement (October 1991), the four recognized parties to the conflict were responsible for a phased and balanced process of disarmament that was to result in a 70 percent reduction of the estimated 200,000 soldiers of the combined military forces. Weapons and ammunition were to be turned over to UNTAC. Their ultimate disposition would be determined by the victor in elections mandated by the Paris Agreement to be held in May of 1993.

However, the disarmament process unravelled in the face of the steady erosion of confidence and trust between the government and the two Khmer forces. Among the factors contributing to this situation were: the refusal of the Cambodian People's Party (CPP) to include the 36,000 police and security forces solely under their control; the inability of UNTAC to provide what the Khmer Rouge considered a neutral political environment leading up to the election; the Khmer Rouge's control over an illegal timber and gem trade that afforded them an ample supply of weaponry; and UNTAC's inability to verify the withdrawal of the Vietnamese military from the north of the country. Moreover, neither the Vietnamese nor the CPP police and security forces constituted formal parties to the conflict. The decision not to destroy surrendered weapons fostered uncertainty and seems to have encouraged many Cambodians to retain their weapons as a measure of insurance against an unpredictable future. When the process of disarmament collapsed, only 10 percent of formal combatants had been disarmed. Small arms continued to circulate among the civilian population, linked to drugs and other kinds of illicit trafficking. These factors contributed to the climate of instability which continued after the UN withdrawal and the composition of a new, coalition government.

INDIVIDUAL INCENTIVES FOR DDR

The Cambodian case represents a failure in the design of the DDR component of a peace process, for which the leadership on all sides was to blame. But even when the leaders of belligerent factions are ready to make peace, their followers may not perceive that much has changed. DDR operations normally begin with the formal end of a conflict, once a peace agreement has been reached and signed. However, for the combatants, the social conditions familiar to them are likely to have altered during the course of conflict, while the road map for peacebuilding has yet to be drawn. This highly uncertain phase may be characterized by a war-ravaged economy; a displaced, disenfranchised, and demographically imbalanced population; traumatized and distrustful communities that may be marked by deep political or ethnic divisions; destroyed or weakened infrastructures; and security sector institutions that, where they exist at all, may have no credibility or connection to civilian populations.

Faced with this, excombatants might be tempted to ask: reintegration into what? Or worse, why disarm at all? No longer part of an "army," (which in modern conflicts may refer to a wide variety of armed groups), but now a member of an uncertain and possibly ill-defined community; not at the end of a crisis, but in the midst of transition; often in the absence of an accessible reliable security sector; and in search of an immediate livelihood, it is easy to imagine the temptation to retain some measure of control and security in the form of a weapon. After many years of violent conflict, as in El Salvador, Nicaragua, and Cambodia, a weapon may be the most obvious and respected symbol of power available to an individual, and thus very attractive to excombatants returning to uncertain futures. Under these circumstances, retaining their weapons may be a rational choice for securing life as a civilian, and would require powerful incentives to counterbalance.

This calculus has led to the recent development of "microdisarmament" alternatives. These programs are "micro" in the disarmament sense, since they focus on small arms and light weapons; and they are "micro" in the economic sense, since they concentrate on motivating individual behaviour. Microdisarmament programs can be delivered in the context of DDR operations conducted by peacekeeping missions; or as stand-alone programs in societies suffering from high levels of insecurity due to small arms proliferation. They may involve voluntary or incentive-based exchanges, offering cash, food, goods, equipment, or training in return for weapons. Increasingly, microdisarmament initiatives have focused on individuals as members of a community, designing programs and incentives that benefit communities as a whole, such as construction of roads, electricity, training for local police, or other community goods and facilities. Weapons collection programs in Albania, El Salvador, and Panama are current cases in point.

FORMAL VS INFORMAL COMBATANTS

Whatever success DDR operations in peacekeeping missions have had to date, most have occurred in contexts of increasing proliferation of small arms among the civilian population. This is due, in part, to the fact that DDR operations normally direct disarmament efforts solely at formal combatants. However, modern conflicts usually involve paramilitary groups, militias, private security bodies, female and child combatants, camp followers, and a host of other individuals who are not members of organized bodies considered official parties to the conflict. Most of these people are not characterized as formal combatants, and are often left out of the DDR processes. For example, in Mali, admission to DDR encampments was restricted to armed combatants, who alone were offered employment opportunities in the restructured security sector and civil service. They were further offered twice the financial incentive at demobilization as unarmed combatants. This contributed to resentment among civilian populations as the policy appeared to perversely reward violence committed during the conflict. Further, no attention was paid to the reintegration needs of nonformal, unarmed combatants. In the case of Somalia, no provision was made for a disarmament component in the original UN mission in the Somalia (UNOSOM) peacekeeping mission mandate. Efforts made through Special Representative to the Secretary-General Mohamed Sahnoun, and in subsequent mandates to the region (Unified Task Force (UNITAF) and UNOSOM II) to rectify this oversight ultimately resulted in a policy of confiscation that authorized forcible removal of any weapon on sight. While weapons may have appeared to decline in the 40 percent of the country controlled by UNITAF, the policy led Somalis to hide weapons in homes and to transfer them to outlying districts, resulting in an explosion of weapons in the hands of nonformal combatants and civilians, who fell outside of the parameters of the missions mandated search for weapons.

In overlooking the disarming and reintegration of informal groups, DDR processes risk creating imbalances that may lead to uncontrolled and on-going violence that will compromise the peacebuilding phase. Further, little or no attention is paid to high levels of weapons among noncombatants. It is telling to note that evidence from El Salvador, Cambodia, Nicaragua, Mozambique, and Somalia demonstrates this tendency. Clearly, this trend does not point to or encourage the creation of a climate within which disarmament appears a safe, let alone rational, option.

A further dimension of the problem of limiting attention to formal combatants is that incentives may be crafted in absence of the context in which they will be drawn upon. In other words, do the skills training, cash, or goods offered as incentive packages relate to or benefit the broader community? Reintegration necessarily implies the interaction and interdependence of combatants and noncombatants. The involvement of recipient communities and noncombatants in the design of disarmament incentives and reintegration programs would seem to be a necessary ingredient for their success. Among the questions that need to be asked are: are these programs compatible with current community sources of livelihood? Do they risk creating dangerous competition between former opponents or noncombatants within the same community? Are they relevant to postconflict community demographics? In Sierra Leone, Mali, and in Mozambique, returning excombatants have experienced resentment from civilians and communities who feel they are yet again the victims of excombatants, who, benefiting from incentives and reintegration programs may threaten shaky livelihoods of those who have coped precariously in their absence. In displacing community structures, coping mechanisms and strategies that have evolved to respond to conflict, excombatants may experience a host of resentments and resistance in their efforts to "reintegrate." Further, the presence of former opponents may be perceived as a threat to nascent local peacebuilding initiatives.

COMMUNITIES IN TRANSITION

During the conflict period, communities have not been static. DDR processes must give due consideration to their capacity to absorb formal and informal excombatants. Communities are deeply affected by conflict in obvious and less obvious ways. For example, they may be largely under the leadership of women who, during conflict, have assumed a variety of nontraditional roles. In the postconflict period, they may be unprepared or unable to reorient themselves along traditional gender lines to create space for and respond to the expectations of returning combatants. Who, for example, has been carrying out and perhaps making a living through means now being offered to excombatants? Will an (impractical and unlikely) return to preconflict gender roles compromise the ability of women-headed households to provide for themselves? Will they lose access to or control over essential resources upon the return of excombatants?

The identity of excombatants and their traditional role in a community will affect their prospects for reintegration. Women excombatants may face added challenges or be rejected altogether as a result of the culturally antithetical role they played during conflict. In 1991, at the end of Eritrea's thirty-year struggle for independence, their fighting force of an estimated 95,000 was almost one third women. During the conflict, women had experienced an equality with their male comrades unheard of in Eritrea's traditionally male-dominated society. The prospects of returning to an oppressive and limited existence at demobilization simply did not appeal to many excombatants. Many of these women had children as a result of wartime marriages to partners deemed unsuitable by families, who disappeared at the end of conflict, or had been killed. Women excombatants, returning as single mothers, require the creation of special mechanisms for survival and eventual reintegration. Moreover, women may have played or been forced to play a sexual role with male combatants, may have exchanged sex for protection or maintenance, or have experienced other forms of sexual violence as a result of conflict. These experience may also complicate their immediate reintegration, and their prospects for longer term survival in communities.

Child excombatants are another group with specific and frequently overlooked needs. They are often not formally demobilized, as their presence is in violation of international law, and this may result in the stigmatization of one or more parties to conflict in the eyes of the international community. Such children are thus ineligible to receive any benefits, incentives, or reintegration support. In Mozambique, child combatants received inadequate attention and support as neither The Front for the Liberation of Mozambique nor The Mozambican National Resistance were willing to risk stigmatization in the period leading up to the election. As a result of their role in combat, children may be disabled or suffer psychological instability which may affect their ability to reintegrate into community and economic life. Without provision of support and assistance, children are far more likely to be revictimized, to contribute to criminality, or to succumb to drug addictions, sexually transmitted diseases, or other illnesses acquired while part of armed forces. Further, conflicts may go on for many years, as in the case of Angola, Mozambique, or Cambodia, and many combatants who were children at the time of recruitment will have reached the age of eighteen by the time of demobilization. They stand very little chance of receiving attention for their special needs as a result of experiences as a child combatant, despite their role as combatants during their formative years.

As we have seen in Sierra Leone, child combatants may have been forced to commit brutal violence against civilians, members of their own communities, or even their families, in order to ensure that their return to civilian life would be nearly impossible. If ties to community and family can be severed, and loyalty transferred to military forces that have control over them, children can be among the most fearless, brutal, and obedient of combatants. It is an error to assume that child combatants will automatically see disarmament and demobilization as in their best interests. Their experience as a "soldier" may have afforded them the only kind of power they have experienced in their lives. The structure of conflict may represent the only structure or family-type existence they have known, and is thus difficult to renounce.

Such violations clearly call for complex and long-term reintegration strategies that grapple with the needs of both the alienated child and the traumatized community. In the face of mounting evidence demonstrating the special needs of child combatants and their potentially devastating impact on communities and prospects for peace, the UN Mission in Sierra Leone (UNAMSIL) is the first to make specific provisions for child combatants.

THE DISARMAMENT TRANSACTION

In turning in a weapon, an individual must be reasonably sure that he or she is not leaving themselves vulnerable to the wide variety of threats to human security that may have led to the conflict in the first place. For this reason, to an individual, disarmament is contingent upon the strength of prospects for reintegration. Disarming, though an imperative from the state or institutional perspective, is not a rational choice for the individual unless security, livelihood, and community have been addressed.

A focus on the individual allows us a new perspective on the nature of the microdisarmament transaction. The "transaction," handing over a weapon for any one of a variety of incentives, can be described as the exchange of one method or framework of security for another. The exchange is far more than a mere technical exercise. In handing over a weapon, individuals engage in a redefinition of security, and a reallocation of responsibilities vis-à-vis their communities. In disarming, they are deciding to reject a weapon as a means of individual security in favour of a different set of collective measures.

In recent years, a number of weapons collections programs have directed their efforts at individuals as community members, making explicit the reinforcing of community ties for security, and strengthening relations with security sector institutions as both means and ends of the weapons collection process. In Gramsh, Albania, the United Nations Development Program's pilot weapons collection project offers incentives to a community as a whole. Such incentives take the form of, for example, road work, communications improvements, or lighting, and are decided upon by the community as a whole. This has the combined effect of building community coherence through the identification of shared goals, and in physically enhancing community security. In El Salvador, the success of intermittent weapons collections days hinges upon a number of factors, not least of which is the transparency of cooperation of the police and military, who offer and deliver amnesty, security, and safe on-site destruction of collected weapons. An obvious spin-off benefit to the community of these exchanges has been an enhanced sense of trust and partnership between participant communities and security sector institutions.

In both Gramsh and El Salvador, individuals who turn in weapons are making a statement about community membership. They are acknowledging collective action as more likely to address their security, they are underlining their membership in a group with shared interests, and they are pledging their support to community action. This is of crucial importance as, for informal combatants such as children, the challenge of renouncing membership in a gang or armed group in favour of an unarmed community, with its uncertain and unfamiliar methods and mechanisms, should not be underestimated. This act is different, though not necessarily easier, for adult participants in protracted conflict, for whom years may have passed in a climate of conflict and insecurity, whose family may be internally displaced or refugees, and for whom little or no room exists to confidently and realistically conceive of anything other than life as a member of one side or the other, one faction, clan, or ethnicity, a victim or aggressor.

Evidence suggests that individuals' sense of control over their security can also be enhanced by the act of disarming. In the Mozambique Arms for Tools Project, participants reported that the surrendering of weapons gave them a sense of control and responsibility within their communities. In taking action to address what they considered to be a key source of insecurity within communities, and in enhancing personal security by removing the threat represented by the presence of a weapon in their home, participants felt empowered by the act of disarming. It is important to note that in the Mozambique case, microdisarmament was implemented by the Christian Council, a trusted and committed partner in community development. Incentives in this program were not financial, but skills and income related. Participants were given tools and equipment such as farming implements, improved housing, bicycles, or sewing machines in exchange for surrendered weapons, or for information related to the location of weapons caches. Surrendered weapons and caches were then publically destroyed. Thus, this initiative combined and acknowledged a variety of human security related needs to support participation and to transform the transaction from a technical exchange to a buy-in to new methods for security of livelihood and a strengthening of community ties through trusted partner institutions and public weapons destruction.

In September 1999, the Canadian and Norwegian governments supported a forum in Montreal that brought together practitioners of microdisarmament from Albania, Sierra Leone, El Salvador, and Mozambique. One of the conclusions of this forum was that microdisarmament was more likely to achieve success if carried out not by a technically proficient agency such as the military or other weapons experts, but by agencies that had a high degree of trust within the community. The most effective agencies are perceived as long-term partners with a stake in the community. External bodies or transitional authorities may create a security vacuum by removing weapons as part of an overall "exit strategy." Their inevitable departure may leave questions of long-term security unanswered, counteracting the confidence required to disarm. The measure of success of the exercise is expressed not in the quantity of arms collected, but in the degree to which the exercise strengthens interaction, transparency, and trust among community members and security sector institutions.

The point here is that the possession of small arms is not only a catalyst for social ills, it is also a reaction to them. Small arms proliferation is a symptom of many of the factors responsible for the onset of conflict in the first place. Since the same factors also influence the decision to disarm, curbing the proliferation of small arms must go well beyond immediate postconflict DDR operations. It is an essential component of multidimensional, long-term peacebuilding.

Human security is about freedom from fear, as experienced by individual people. The highly nuanced transaction embodied in the voluntary relinquishing of a weapon is perhaps the most poignant symbol of a truly successful social disarmament strategy.

NOTES

1 Canadian Council for International Peace and Security, *Disarmament, Demobilization and Reintegration (DD&R) of Ex-Combatants in a Peacekeeping Environment – Principles and Guidelines* (New York: Department of Peacekeeping Operations, United Nations, December 1999).

REFERENCES

Canadian Council for International Peace and Security. *Disarmament, Demobilization and Reintegration (DD&R) of Ex-Combatants in a Peacekeeping Environment – Principles and Guidelines.* New York: Department of Peacekeeping Operations, United Nations, December 1999.
Kaffel, Hasebenebi. "The Reintegration of Demobilized Fighters in Eritrea: A Gender Perspective." *World Bank Conference on Gender, Armed Conflict and Political Violence.* June 1999.
Malan, Michael. "Disarming and Demobilising Child Soldiers: The Underlying Challenges." Paper for West African Conference on War-Affected Children, 27–8 April 2000, Accra, Ghana.
Pike, Claire. *Facing the Challenges of Microdisarmament: A Case Study Review of Practices in Post Conflict Countries.* Ottawa, Canada: Department of Foreign Affairs and International Trade, March 1999.
Swords for Ploughshares: Microdisarmament in Transition from Conflict. Norway: FAFO Institute for Applied Social Science, May, 2000.

3 Peacebuilding
in Postconflict Societies

MICHAEL SMALL

Peacebuilding is the effort to strengthen the prospects for internal peace and decrease the likelihood of violent conflict. The overarching goal of peacebuilding is to enhance the indigenous capacity of a society to manage conflict without violence.[1]

The Canadian Peacebuilding Initiative had its origins in a confluence of intellectual and political trends in the early 1990s. A rapid succession of bloody, intrastate conflicts dominated the attention of international agencies in the immediate postcold war period, in Afghanistan, Angola, Bosnia, Cambodia, Croatia, El Salvador, Haiti, Guatemala, Liberia, Mozambique, Nicaragua, Rwanda, and Somalia (to name only the most visible cases). In dealing with these conflicts, different communities of international workers encountered the limits of their standard responses. Development agencies discovered that increasingly their core clientele in the world's poorest countries were also societies in conflict. An eruption of civil war, as in Rwanda, could wipe out years' worth of investment in economic development and human capital. Humanitarian workers found that delivering humanitarian assistance in conflict zones, as in Somalia or Angola, could provide protection and save lives, but could do nothing to bring the conflict to an end in the first place. Peacekeepers sent in to enforce an immediate postconflict settlement, as in Haiti or Bosnia, found that the provision of security could not, in itself, lead to an "exit strategy," and that responsible, accountable local security forces could not be expected to emerge to take over from the peacekeepers without a different kind of international stimulus. Finally, diplomats discovered that negotiating a peace agreement to terminate an intrastate conflict (as in Nicaragua and Cambodia) required not only external assurances of support for the agreement and an end of outside intervention in the conflict. It also required a package of positive incentives to keep the internal parties to the conflict committed to the terms of the settlement, and to give them new roles to play in a new national administration. Something clearly was missing from the standard arsenal of international responses to complex emergencies. The term used by the United Nations (UN) in the 1992 "Agenda for Peace" to describe what was missing was "peacebuilding."

In Canada, this concept captured the imagination of a cross-section of nongovernmental organizations (NGOs) and government policy makers who were groping to find a shared agenda at the intersection between security, diplomacy, and development. A coalition of Canadian development NGOs interested in peacebuilding formed a "Contact Group" in 1994 with the assistance of the Canadian International Development Agency (CIDA) to convene an informal government-NGO forum on peacebuilding issues. Within CIDA, several geographic programs – most notably those dealing with Haiti and Bosnia – made peacebuilding the over-arching focus of their programming (without formally using the term). The agency's policy branch became one of the principal advocates within the Organization for Economic Cooperation and Development (OECD) Development Assistance Committee of a new Task Force on Conflict, Peace, and Development, charged with developing a set of guidelines for development programming in conflict contexts. At the same time, within the Canadian Department of Foreign Affairs and International Trade (DFAIT), a Global Issues Bureau was created in January 1995 as a focus for emerging, transboundary issues that had no clear institutional home. Unlike its counterpart in the US State Department, the DFAIT Global Issues Bureau was given a mandate to consider emerging political and security issues through the creation of a small "Peacebuilding and Democratic Development" division.

The aftermath of the Rwandan genocide of April-June 1994 triggered Canadian government support for two major initiatives which laid the groundwork for a more proactive approach to peacebuilding. DFAIT conducted a major study of what would be required to increase the UN's rapid reaction capacity to respond to humanitarian crises such as Rwanda, which was tabled at the General Assembly in September 1995. At the same time, CIDA became one of the principal sponsors of the multidonor evaluation of Rwanda which (four years before the UN's own self-examination) comprehensively documented the failures of coordination by the international community to act in the face of genocide.

LAUNCHING THE INITIATIVE

Lloyd Axworthy came to the portfolio of Canada's foreign minister in January 1996 intrigued by the concept of peacebuilding. It resonated with his own experience following the tortuous evolution of the Central American peace process since his time as an opposition critic for external affairs in the late 1980s. His appointment as Canadian foreign minister coincided with the early implementation of the Dayton Accord in Bosnia, and the culmination of the Guatemala peace process – in which he took a direct personal interest, and which served in his mind as an early test case for the initiative. The recommendations of the multidonor evaluation of the Rwandan Genocide also made a deep impact upon him. Axworthy could see the political possibilities of peacebuilding as a cause which could tap into Canadians' well-springs of internationalism and idealism, and which could serve as a civilian counterpart to peacekeeping. Finally, peacebuilding fit the type of "niche diplomacy," which characterized his initial thinking about how and where "Canada could make a difference" in global affairs. Thus was born the idea of launching a Canadian Peacebuilding Initiative.

This vision was captured by Minister Axworthy in his October 1996 speech, which launched the initiative: "I see peacebuilding as casting a life line to foundering societies struggling to end the cycle of violence, restore civility and get back on their feet. After the fighting has stopped and the immediate humanitarian needs have been addressed, there exists a brief critical period when a country sits balanced on a fulcrum. Tilted the wrong way, it retreats back into conflict. But with the right help, delivered during that brief, critical window of opportunity, it will move towards peace and stability."[2]

As part of the initiative, a new $10 million a year Peacebuilding Fund was announced. It was to be managed by CIDA on behalf of the initiative; and two domestic initiatives were put in place: a roster of human rights and democracy experts, which would help identify Canadians with the skills needed for peacebuilding; and a new process of annual peacebuilding consultations would be convened with the Canadian NGO community, which would serve as a joint stock-taking and priority-setting exercise for the initiative between the Canadian government and the Canadian NGO community.

The public launch of the initiative was followed by an intensive process of internal negotiation between DFAIT and CIDA regarding a shared strategic framework for the initiative, and agreed project approval mechanisms for the Peacebuilding Fund. The fund, in its first year of operation, identified four geographic priorities: Guatemala, the Great Lakes of Africa, former Yugoslavia, and Cambodia. By the end of its first fiscal year, it had been able to support a number of innovative, largely NGO-led projects, in each of these regions. In the summer of 1997, DFAIT was able to put into operation a small complementary funding mechanism of its own, the Peacebuilding Program, intended to focus on areas that fell outside of CIDA's priorities, such as domestic capacity building in Canada, initiatives in non-ODA (official development assistance) countries, and multilateral mechanisms for peacebuilding led by diplomatic or political institutions. Both departments established a close policy dialogue with the International Development Research Centre, which had sponsored the early work of the Peacebuilding Contact Group, and which had decided to consolidate its activities in Cambodia, Palestine, Central America, and southern Africa into a new Peacebuilding and Reconstruction Program Initiative.

In parallel, a solid partnership was established between the Canadian government and the Canadian NGO community with the launch of a now annual process of peacebuilding consultations, and the provision of program funding to the Canadian Peacebuilding Coordinating Committee. An innovative government-NGO experiment in mid-1997 was a census of Canadian NGO peacebuilding capacity, managed by the coordinating committee with DFAIT funding. While the final results of the census were diffuse and hard to summarize – 135 Canadian NGOs reported that they were working in 86 different countries – it generated a useful by-product: a "Peacebuilding Activities Chart" (see below) which provided an "operational definition" of peacebuilding divided into eleven categories of activities which illustrated what the concept meant in practice. This chart was, in fact, widely used by Canadian government officials in the early months of the initiative to explain to other interlocutors what was meant by the term; and the definition of peacebuilding (quoted at the beginning of this chapter) and used in the chart went a long way to resolving time-wasting definitional debates.

PEACEBUILDING ACTIVITIES [1]
Definition: Peacebuilding is the effort to strengthen the prospects for internal peace and decrease the likelihood of violent conflict. The overarching goal of peacebuilding is to enhance the indigenous capacity of a society to manage conflict without violence. The definition covers peacebuilding in pre, mid, and postconflict situations.

Peacebuilding is a relatively recent term. Many organizations do not necessarily describe their activities as peacebuilding. The attached Peacebuilding Activities Chart is intended to list the range of activities that comprise a peacebuilding agenda, as the term is currently used by the Canadian government and nongovernmental organizations (NGOs).

Peacebuilding Activity	Examples
Early Warning	– intelligence and monitoring – data collection and analysis – transmission and early action
Environmental Security	– conflict assessment and resolution related to resource depletion, human migration, etc.
Physical Security	– demobilization, disarmment, and demining – protection of civic population – police and security force reform/ training
Individual Security	– gender-specific, sexual orientation-specific, and racial/cultural-specific violence
Human Rights	– field operations, investigation, and reporting – training and advocacy
Conflict Resolution	– community-based initiatives – second-track diplomacy – mediation and negotiation
Social Reconstruction	– psycho-social trauma counselling and social services (health, education) – reintegration of refugees/displaced persons/combatants – peace education and access to information
Governance and Democratic Development	– electoral assistance – civic education, judicial reform, media development, and training
Institutional/Civic Capacity Building	– government and NGO capacity building – implementation of peace accords – probity/corruption (transparency/ accountability)

Policy Development, Assessment, and Advocacy	– research, assessment/evaluation – lessons learned – public consultation
Training	– peacebuilding training in above activities and training of trainers

1 For further information on the Peacebuilding Activities Chart or the 1997 Peacebuilding Census, please consult the website of the Canadian Peacebuilding Coordinating Committee at:www.cpcc.ottawa.on.ca.

If 1997 was spent on internal consolidation of the initiative, the next two years focused on developing external contacts with comparable units in other donor agencies. Close working connections were established, in particular, with counterparts in the governments of Norway, Sweden, the United Kingdom, Japan, and with US Agency for International Development USAID, the United Nations Development Program (UNDP) and the World Bank. An informal network of bilateral and multilateral donor agencies engaged in peacebuilding and postconflict reconstruction was launched by USAID in late 1997. Meetings of the network revealed to the Canadian participants that, despite the intense inward focus in Ottawa of the first year of the initiative, other peacebuilding units in comparable agencies were facing identical problems. All of them were struggling to engage the main bilateral and geographic programs in their organizations with the imperatives of peacebuilding. There was a common search for policy frameworks and programming tools to deal with problems that routinely occurred in postconflict settings: such as the issue of small arms proliferation; dealing with the impact of conflict on children; assessing the gender dimension of peacebuilding; and the problems of building a free and self-sustaining media. The same kind of dialogue occurred in the annual peacebuilding consultations, which both the Canadian government and NGOs used as a forum for reciprocal learning about how to address the challenges of peacebuilding.

The two Canadian government departments involved in the initiative used their respective funding mechanisms to support a number of catalytic projects. Some projects involved quick response to international appeals, as for example, from the Office of the High Representative in Bosnia for budgetary support for a new pro-Dayton government in the Rpublika Srpska, or for a radio campaign to counter propaganda against the International Criminal Tribunal for the former Yugoslavia (ICTY). Other projects were more carefully designed through consultation with Canadian NGOs active in the field. One project, sponsored by two well-known Canadian human rights organizations and their Guatemalan counterparts, was designed to build the capacity of civil society groups that had been given a formal role to play in the Guatemalan peace process, but which lacked the organizational capacity to actually mobilize the social groups they were expected to represent. Other projects were intended to push the envelope of peacebuilding policy development, such as the drafting of the first set guidelines for the UN on how to conduct disarmament, demobilization, and reintegration (DDR) of excombatants.

NEW DIRECTIONS

The start of Canada's tenure on the Security Council in 1999 encouraged a fresh look at the challenges of peacebuilding in the context of peace support operations. A study was commissioned of the lessons learned from the new missions authorized since 1996.[3] An unintended side effect of the intense effort devoted to DFAIT/CIDA coordination under the initiative had been a diversion of both departments' peacebuilding units from any serious examination of the potential for collaboration with Canada's Department of National Defence or the Royal Canadian Mounted Police – both of whose roles were changing as the nature of peacekeeping missions evolved into multidimensional peace support operations. The experience, and limitations of using the ODA resources of the Peacebuilding Fund to staff civilian roles in the Organization for Security and Cooperation in Europe (OSCE) Kosovo Verification Mission highlighted the need for both DFAIT and CIDA to take a closer look at how to meet the growing demand for deployment of individual experts (both military and civilians) in modern peace support missions.

The early decision to make "the protection of civilians" the broad theme of Canada's Security Council presidency in February 1999, and the follow-up report requested from the secretary-general, also encouraged more thinking about how UN forces, both military and police, should be trained and mandated to protect civilian populations in the early phases of a peace support operation. Minister Axworthy's increasing emphasis on human security as the over-arching theme to many of his initiatives, including peacebuilding, encouraged the foreign ministry to use its Peacebuilding Program to support a greater range of multilateral instruments, such as the UN Special Rapporteur on Freedom of Expression, and the ratification of the International Criminal Court (ICC).

DEPLOYING CIVILIANS IN PEACE SUPPORT OPERATIONS

As peace support operations evolve into missions with broader and, increasingly, civilian-oriented mandates, the deployment of experts has taken on a greater importance. Modern peace support operations are often mandated to provide for free media, reconciliation, disarmament, demobilization, and reintegration (DDR), judicial reform, civil administration, and human rights monitoring. These and other activities together form the continuum of peacebuilding which not only fosters security, but also provides the underpinnings for institution-building and the growth of civil society.

Canada has responded to the changes in peace support operations by taking a leading role in developing new mechanisms to identify and deploy civilian expertise. Unlike the deployment of military force, the deployment of civilians has often lagged behind peace agreements, thereby threatening the success of the entire mission.

The main difficulties are in ensuring availability of civilian expertise for rapid deployment, while providing for training standards, personal security, etc. Internationally, Canada has taken an active role in promoting the effort of the United Nations (UN) and the Organization for Security and Cooporation in Europe (OSCE) in improving their responsiveness. Domestically, one of Canada's main tools for identifying civilian candidates for deployments is the Canadian Resource Bank of Democracy and Human Rights (CANADEM). CANADEM, funded by the Canadian foreign ministry, was established in early 1997. Its mandate includes maintaining a roster of qualified Canadians who could fill nongovernmental organization (NGO) and multilateral requests for personnel. Since 1998, the Canadian government has been using CANADEM to help identify personnel to form part of the Canadian contribution to international peace support operations, most notably in Kosovo.

Barry Parkinson

One issue which had been on the peacebuilding agenda from the outset – the impact of armed conflict on children – was effectively elevated to the highest priority for the initiativein 2000. The decision by Foreign Minister Axworthy and his Ghanaian counterpart, Victor Gbeho, to host a regional meeting of West African foreign ministers on war-affected children in Accra in April 2000 became a focus for a broader dialogue among developing countries on interconnected human security issues. The agenda ranged from early warning and conflict prevention, strategies for engaging armed groups to respect humanitarian standards, disarmament and demobilization of child soldiers, to using the West African moratorium on small arms as a template for joint action on war-affected children. In September 2000, an international conference on the issue, hosted by Canada, involving youth, NGOs, international organizations, and developed and developing country governments is being held in Winnipeg. In its agenda and diverse participants list, the Winnipeg conference promises to be the closest approximation to the broad call to arms envisioned in Lloyd Axworthy's original 1996 speech, launching the Peacebuilding Initiative.

LESSONS LEARNED AND FUTURE TRENDS

Over the past four years, there has been a maturing of the Peacebuilding Initiative, from an intense focus on the "brief critical period when a country sits balanced on a fulcrum"[4] to a broader vision of the international architecture required to promote human security. The challenges of that brief crucial period remain no less critical for those societies, such as Kosovo, Sierra Leone, and East Timor, in making the difficult transition through the first phases of postconflict peacebuilding. But the degree of confidence that marked the inception of the initiative – that with the correct peacebuilding "tools," applied in the right sequence, and with appropriate sensitivity, peacebuilders could cast "a lifeline to societies struggling to end the cycle of violence, restore civility, and get back on their feet"[5] – now seems overstated. There is a natural tendency for outsiders to overestimate the degree to which local political actors, who "own the conflict," share outsiders' perceptions of what should constitute peace. Local political realities will always assert themselves, despite the international community's best intentions: as in Liberia, when the population democratically elected the country's biggest warlord, Charles Taylor, in order to end seven years of civil war; or in Kosovo, when the Kosovo Liberation Army (KLA) took advantage of the North Atlantic Treaty Organization's (NATO) imposed peace to create "parallel structures" to the UN mission in Kosovo (UNMIK); or in Guatemala, when the landowning elite refused to support the government's measures to raise taxes and increase social spending to meet the social provisions of the peace accords; or in Cambodia, when it took a brief, bloody putsch by the Deputy Prime Minister, Hun Sen, to restore a degree of governability to the unworkable power-sharing arrangements created after the 1993 UN sponsored elections.

Looking ahead, five trends can be identified which will shape the direction of our peacebuilding efforts in 2000 and beyond. The first is a shift in time-scale, from an exclusive focus on postconflict peacebuilding to earlier points in the conflict continuum. In the past four years, donors have become much more concerned with conflict prevention and what might be called preconflict peacebuilding, in order to find ways to intervene long before they are called to pay for postconflict reconstruction. In the diplomatic/political arena, this is reflected in a closer look at the different institutional methods which the UN and regional organizations can use to find an "early entry-point" to mediate a rising intrastate conflict. In aid and development circles, a focus on conflict prevention has led to a new interest in the methodology of peace and conflict impact assessment. This analytical approach brings a much wider range of development activities under the peacebuilding lens than the kind of postconflict reconstruction tasks captured in the Canadian peacebuilding chart. It is based on an awareness of the negative as well as the positive incentives for mitigating conflict that outside assistance can generate.

The second trend is a shift in scale, from an exclusive focus on peacebuilding in small, insular societies, often with failed or failing states, such as Cambodia, Bosnia, or Haiti, to the challenges of peacebuilding in larger, more robust states, which are nevertheless marked by significant degrees of internal conflict – such as India, Pakistan, Indonesia, and Nigeria. In these countries, externally mandated peace support operations are not an option, and will not provide a focus for initial peacebuilding efforts. A much greater reliance has to be placed on local institutions for conflict resolution: within political parties, traditional political councils, municipal levels of government, in the private sector, and the diverse institutions of civil society. For example "peace dialogues" led by local elites have flowered in South Asia, even in the aftermath of the nuclear tests. These constitute indigenous peacebuilding strategies. Even in areas without large robust states, it has become evident that regional strategies are essential for peacebuilding, to take into account the cross-border linkages with neighbouring states. The chronic regional war in the Democratic Republic of Congo provides one clear example of this problem; the impact of the conflict in Afghanistan on all of its neighbours, in terms of drug trafficking, arms sales, and the export of fundamentalism, is another case.

A third trend is a greater appreciation of the role of international architecture needed to support incountry peacebuilding. One important strand of work includes international disarmament and arms control measures to curb the proliferation of the weapons used in civil conflicts, such as the Ottawa Convention banning antipersonnel mines, and the various efforts to develop codes of conduct on small arms transfers. Another important strand includes the efforts to develop the instruments of international law, such as the ICTY and the International Criminal Tribunal for Rwanda (ICTR), and the ICC. A third strand includes the various human rights instruments and their monitoring and enforcement mechanisms, through Special Rapporteurs on Freedom of Expression or Internally Displaced Persons, or the Special Representative of the Secretary-General on Children and Armed Conflict. All of these strands come together in a human security approach. Their importance for peacebuilding is that they offer other avenues, besides direct intervention in a conflict, for the international community to reinforce respect for the indigenous institutions for conflict resolution.

A fourth trend is the growing realization of the limits of aid as an instrument for peacebuilding. "The Influence of Aid in Situations of Violent Conflict," prepared for the OECD by Peter Uvin,[6] is eloquent on the ineffectiveness of aid alone as a tool of conditionality in conflict situations. The study documents the difficulties of actually achieving donor coordination, especially at the strategic or headquarters level, in sending consistent messages to the parties in a peacebuilding situation. This trend has encouraged governments to look more widely at the variety of other instruments they have to influence conflicts, such as: providing and withholding political recognition; arms embargos and other targeted sanctions; military-to-military cooperation and training; encouraging codes of conduct for foreign investment in conflict-affected countries; and debt relief and easing of access to international financial flows from the multilateral lending institutions. The use of a broader range of instruments is particularly important when undertaking peacebuilding in the midst of conflict, where the scope for providing ODA is limited, and other measures are required to bring parties to the negotiating table. The microeconomic "incentives and disincentives" analysis which the OECD has pioneered in its study of the impact of aid can be equally well applied to this much larger universe of policy instruments for peacebuilding. Unfortunately, the prospect for achieving "policy coherence" among donors across the totality of instruments that can be used to influence a conflict is relatively low. This represents as much of an institutional, political challenge within donor governments as it does between them. The G-8 Foreign Ministers' focus on conflict prevention in the current cycle of G-8 meetings, from Cologne in 1999 to Miyazaki in 2000, is beginning to address this challenge. But we are still a long way off from finding the right kind of institutional fora which will compel outside donors to harmonize the full range of their policies towards specific countries in conflict.

A final trend is a growing appreciation of the impact on peace of a people's need for security. For example, Canadian-sponsored work on microdisarmament programs demonstrate that what is needed to make these "goods for guns" buy-back schemes work is a sufficient level of trust between the local populace and the security forces encharged with protecting them once they disarm. People have to be convinced that their personal security will be increased, not diminished, before they engage in these kinds of transactions. Canadian-sponsored work on the gender dimensions of peace support operations has also shown the very different impact of conflict on men and women, as they try to rebuild family support networks and resume normal economic activity. In every society, the family is the basic unit of personal security. Participants in peace support operations need to be more aware of the impact that massive influxes of foreign aid and foreign personnel can have on traditional gender roles – ranging from creating new opportunities for women to participate in political councils, to setting new positive military role models for young boys, to generating new markets for prostitution by young women. For most people in a postconflict context, the greatest threat to their personal security is not a resurgence of political violence, but violent crime, which usually takes off once formal combatants have been disarmed and the social and economic constraints of wartime are relaxed. Frustration with rising crime levels can rapidly diminish popular perceptions of the benefits of peace – as has occurred in Guatemala, El Salvador, Mozambique, and South Africa in the aftermath of their various peace processes.

Probably the most difficult challenge for peacebuilding anywhere is the process of "security sector reform," which amounts to making the security institutions of a society more accountable to the needs for personal security of local citizens. This is a major challenge in many stable, high income developing countries, such as Mexico or Brazil. It is even more daunting in postconflict societies, such as Kosovo or East Timor, where local security forces have to be built from scratch. Security sector reform cannot just be a top-down process – which is how security institutions naturally organize themselves. It requires the engagement and trust of the local communities, which frequently have no history of respect or protection from the security institutions of the state. Security sector reform represents the long-haul challenge for peacebuilding – both in robust states and failed ones, in preconflict and postconflict settings.

This final observation reveals how Canadian thinking on peacebuilding and its relationship with human security has come full circle in the past four years. In Lloyd Axworthy's speech in October 1996, peacebuilding was posited as a means to build human security in societies torn by conflict. After four years of reflection and action, the essential insight of human security – that people have their own security needs, which are identifiably different from the security needs of states – has become a touchstone for effective peacebuilding. An excessive reliance on donor-driven, institution-building strategies marked the early phase of the Canadian Peacebuilding Initiative. A greater appreciation of the locally driven, personal, social, and psychological dimensions of peacebuilding is now required. There is a need to reexamine, at the level of individual people, one of the essential insights of peacebuilding: that intrastate conflicts are cyclical if nothing is done to address their root causes in inequality, injustice, and insecurity. Only on the basis of these insights will we be able to move towards sustainable strategies for building peace in societies that have lost the capacity to manage conflict without violence.

NOTES

1 *Strategic Framework for the Canadian Peacebuilding Activities* (Ottawa: Department of Foreign Affairs and International Trade/The Canadian International Development Agency, 1997).
2 Lloyd Axworthy, "Building Peace to Last: Establishing a Canadian Peacebuilding Initiative" (Speech delivered at York University, 30 October 1996).
3 Robin Hay, *Peacebuilding During Peace Support Operations: A Survey and Analysis of Recent Missions* (Ottawa: Department of Foreign Affairs and International Trade, 1999).
4 Axworthy, "Building Peace."
5 Ibid.
6 Peter Uvin, *The Influence of Aid in Situations of Violent Conflict* (Paris: OECD/DAC, 1999).

REFERENCES

Axworthy, Lloyd. "Building Peace to Last: Establishing a Canadian Peacebuilding Initiative." York University, 30 October 1996.
Hay, Robin. *Peacebuilding During Peace Support Operations: A Survey and Analysis of Recent Missions.* Ottawa: DFAIT, 1999.
OECD Development Assistance Committee (DAC). *Guidelines on Conflict, Peace and Development Co-operation.* Paris: Organisation for Economic Co-operation and Development, 1997.
Strategic Framework for Canadian Peacebuilding Activities. Ottawa, Canada: Department of Foreign Affairs and International Trade. The Canadian International Development Agency, 1997.
Uvin, Peter, *The Influence of Aid in Situations of Violent Conflict.* Paris: OECD/Development Assistance Committee, 1999.

Bosnia and Herzegovina

SAM HANSON

The supposedly ancient ethnic hatreds of the Balkans are often cited to explain why international engagement in the Balkans is not working, cannot work, or should never have been tried. The interethnic tensions of the Balkans are, in fact, of relatively recent date.

It was the economic and then the political upheavals of the 1980s that created conditions for the revival of ethnic nationalism and ethnic conflict. In 1980, when the sirens sounded and broadcasts were interrupted with the announcement "umro je drug Tito" ("Comrade Tito has died"), people who had held Tito in contempt all their lives stopped in the street and wept at the news of his death – not in mourning, but because they knew that a geopolitical switch had been thrown and their lives would never be the same again.

The post-Tito leaders of the former Yugoslavia had no remedy to mend the disintegrating fabric of their Communist state. They had no intention, however, of relinquishing power, and their means of keeping it was to divert popular fear away from social and economic ills and into ethnic channels, so that blame for the failure of the state was laid not at the doors of failed politicians, but at those of other ethnic groups.

The disintegration of the former Yugoslavia was attended by several different kinds of conflicts. Those in Slovenia and Croatia were primarily wars of secession. In Bosnia and Herzegovina (BiH), the conflict initially took the form of a similar attempt at independence by the Bosnian Muslims, or Bosniacs. Very rapidly, however, it became more than a struggle for control of the territory of BiH. For the other two conflicting parties, the Bosnian Serbs and the Bosnian Croats, with the active assistance of the Federal Republic of Yugoslavia (FRY) and Croatia, the objective became the destruction of one or more of the other two ethnic communities, in all or part of the territory of BiH. The Bosniacs were also the target of an attempt by the others to deny and destroy their ethnic identity. Hence the atrocities: the mass killings, the systematic rapes, the mass expulsion of civilians. The suffering of the civilian population was not collateral to the war aims of the conflicting parties: the civilian population was directly targeted for what soon became known as ethnic cleansing.

The initial response of the international community was a decision by the Security Council to expand the UN Protection Force (UNPROFOR), its peace support operation in Croatia, into BiH, in order to protect the delivery of humanitarian assistance to the civilian population. Subsequently, it sought to defend the civilian population by declaring several "safe areas." The eventual result was a debacle, which was made inevitable by the failure of the Security Council, if not to recognize ethnic cleansing for what it was, then to respond appropriately. UNPROFOR was thus described by one UN official as an "armour-plated meals-on-wheels service," attempting to hold a humanitarian safety net under ethnic cleansing. The safe areas were not safe, and the council authorized neither the mandate, the rules of engagement, nor the troop levels that would have been necessary to make them safe. Troop contributing countries then failed to provide sufficient troops to meet the inadequate levels established by the council. Without the mandate or the means to intervene in the conflict, UNPROFOR could do little more than bear witness as the atrocities continued, culminating in the massacre at Srebrenica in July 1995. Those accused of these atrocities are beginning to answer for them at the Hague. The responsibility for the international community's failure to respond was mainly that of the Security Council, especially its permanent members, but it was the UN as an institution that suffered lasting damage to its good name and authority.

During the summer and early autumn of 1995, the military situation in both BiH and Croatia turned against the Serb forces. This, together with North Atlantic Treaty Organization's (NATO) air strikes, created the opportunity for a USA-led diplomatic initiative that resulted in the negotiation of the General Framework Agreement for Peace at Dayton. It established BiH as a state composed of two entities with limited common institutions. The status of the Brcko District was negotiated subsequently; it was set up in 2000 as a separate district, held in common by both entities.

THE DAYTON PROCESS

Dayton provides both for a cease-fire and a peacebuilding process. The latter involves political, economic, and institutional reforms, including, among other things, free and fair elections, the constitution of BiH, human rights, the return of refugees and displaced persons, and the apprehension of persons indicted for war crimes. Its implementation involves a large cast of international actors. Military implementation is assigned to a NATO-led force, SFOR (Stabilization Force, formerly IFOR, Implementation Force). Civilian implementation is led by a high representative, with specific roles for the Organization for Security and Cooperation in Europe (OSCE) (elections), a UN mission, the United Nations Mission in Bosnia and Herzegovina (UNMIBH) (police and judiciary), and a UN High Commissioner for Refugees (UNHCR) (return of refugees). The trial of persons indicted for war crimes is carried out independently by the International Criminal Tribunal for the Former Yugoslavia (ICTY), located in the Hague.

The high representative, currently Austrian diplomat Wolfgang Petritsch, receives political guidance from the Peace Implementation Council (PIC),[1] the successor to the International Conference on the Former Yugoslavia. Originally assigned little more than a coordination and monitoring role, the high representative's mandate has been augmented by successive declarations of the PIC, and he now has the authority both to impose legislation and to dismiss BiH officials who obstruct the implementation of Dayton. In recent months, for example, the high representative acted to dismiss twenty-two local officials, and imposed legislation on the establishment of a state border service and on property ownership.

Progress has been slow, and what has been achieved is by no means irreversible. Four years after it was signed, Dayton is more successful as a cease-fire than as a peace agreement. This has enabled some reconstruction, some return of refugees and displaced persons, and some reform of the judiciary, the police, and the economy. But at the level of the common institutions of the state, deadlock continues on crucial matters: BiH has no cabinet, due to the Parliament's inability to adopt new legislation on a Council of Ministers; similarly, there is no progress on the adoption of a new electoral law.

BiH has been described as one of the most highly assisted counties in the world. In the four years since Dayton, some $5.1 billion (US) in reconstruction funding has flowed in, and has been a major factor in economic growth. These levels cannot be sustained, however, and economic instability will ensue if BiH does not achieve transition from donor-dependent to self-sustaining growth. BiH will have to make the fundamental economic reforms necessary to attract foreign investment and establish a market economy.

There are approximately 300,000 BiH refugees in other countries, and about 800,000 internally-displaced persons in BiH. The right of these people to return to their prewar homes is the major human rights issue in BiH. A major obstacle has been the difficulty of adopting, harmonizing, and implementing property legislation in BiH's two entities. Individual human rights cases typically involve disputes over title to properties from which people have been ethnically cleansed. Progress has been made in resolving thousands of property claims, and 2000 is expected to be a major year for a return of refugees and internally-displaced persons, of which there are approximately 1.2 million.

Disarmament and demobilization have been hindered by the fact that BiH has two defence ministries and effectively three armies. Each of the three armies has received financial and material support from abroad: from Croatia, Yugoslavia, and the United States. Reductions have been achieved, however, despite the obvious complexities: 15 percent in 1999, with a further 15 percent pledged for 2000. Work is also under way with the World Bank on a program to reintegrate demobilized soldiers into civilian society.

One benchmark for progress is BiH's ambition to be admitted to the Council of Europe. In a statement to the Council of Europe Political Committee on 5 April, High Representative Petritsch suggested that priority be given to three preconditions for admission:

- the basic functioning of the common institutions at state level, i.e. the presidency, the council of ministers with one prime minister, and the State Parliament.[2]
- adoption of the draft Election Law.
- implementation of preconditions governing human rights.

However, of forty human rights-based preconditions for admission, only seven have been met so far – and four of those had to be imposed by the high representative.

The current high representative is promoting the concept of "ownership" in an effort to persuade local politicians to assume responsibility for their own country's governance and peace process. There is a tendency for local politicians, when they reach a deadlock on an issue, to appeal to the international community for an imposed solution. It is perhaps symptomatic that "ownership," in the sense intended, does not translate very well into the local language: if there is no word to express the thought, the very idea may be hard to imagine. The main reason for the continuing dysfunctionality of BiH's institutions of government, however, is the continuing predominance of ethnic nationalist parties and politicians for whom the governance of the country comes well behind the interests of their particular ethnic group – or, indeed, their own self-interest.

Both BiH and our allies have expectations of us, Canada, as a leading member of the international community. Canada is assuming a larger role in SFOR, including the largest area of responsibility of any contingent and rotational command of a multinational division, and thus a larger role in the international community's peacebuilding efforts in BiH. We cannot do everything, but we are well placed to do some things. Canada provides a successful example of a society that manages to transcend ethnicity, while still accommodating it. Canada is assisting divided communities to move past the recent horrors through conflict resolution techniques, as no future can be forged without addressing the past. We encourage the development of human security by supporting that which upholds and promotes the rule of law, such as indigenous human rights institutions. We are working with local communities to build a stronger civil society which seeks cooperation, not division. And we are assisting BiH academics, officials, and institutions to build a better future through the reform of the primary health care system. Many evils remain hidden, including the thousands of mines scattered throughout the country. Canada is committed to the development of an integrated approach to mine clearance. Our efforts to develop the media will hopefully make it less likely that it could be used as a tool of the unscrupulous and ill-intentioned. Only with concerted, consistent, and coordinated effort will the coming decade be more promising than the last.

LESSONS LEARNED

Looking back on the past decade in the Balkans, one is tempted to conclude that healthy societies produce healthy leaders, and vice versa. BiH today is far from being a healthy society: its institutions are largely nonfunctional. It would be a brave citizen, indeed, who put his faith in the government, the legislature, the courts, the police, the banks, the schools, or the public utilities. No domestic politician has thus far come forward with a program for making these institutions work. BiH today is still a place where ethnic nationalism works. Politics is still dominated by Serb and Croat parties that would gladly see BiH divided between Serbia and Croatia, and by a Bosniac party that would have BiH become a Bosniac nation-state with the others (as they fear) reduced from the status of constituent nations to ethnic minorities.

It must be acknowledged that Dayton itself is part of the problem, precisely because it enshrines ethnic division. This was an essential pre-requisite for a cease-fire, but it is an obstacle to peace. It divides the country into ethnically-based entities, provides for an ethnically-composed house in the state Parliament, and creates a collective presidency defined in ethnic terms. In each institution there is effectively an ethnic veto. Getting beyond ethnic politics in BiH, therefore, will eventually require getting beyond Dayton. It would be perilous, however, to embark on such an enterprise while the scene is still so dominated by the politics of ethnic division, or to assume that any "Dayton-Plus" that could be negotiated would represent little improvement on the present agreement.

Removal of ethnically-based institutions would not remove ethnic division itself. Part of the solution must be to encourage cooperation and bridge-building across ethnic lines, not only in politics, but in other fields of endeavour. The leaders of the four religious communities have set a positive example: the Muslim Reis-ul-Ulema, the Serb Metropolite, the Catholic archbishop, and the president of the Jewish community have formed an interreligious council devoted to combatting interethnic hatred and promoting interreligious tolerance. Organized crime, on the other hand, has set a negative example: when the language is money, there appear to be no interethnic obstacles to understanding or cooperation.

There has been some debate about possible options for the international community in BiH. Ranged from least to most interventionist, they include the following:

- complete and immediate withdrawal;
- cease-fire maintenance only;
- maintain the present approach;
- enforce Dayton more robustly;
- rewrite Dayton;
- impose an international protectorate.

Some of these options are more practical than others, and some are not practical at all. The discussions, moreover, tend to analyze the international community's options without sustaining a focus on the purpose of international involvement in BiH. They sometimes appear to be premised on the belief that the international community's primary objective in BiH is to extract itself. Even if that were so, we are now relearning the same lesson that the Romans, the Ottomans, the Austro-Hungarians, and the Axis powers all learned the hard way: it is easier to get into the Balkans than it is to get out.

Much of this discussion is also influenced by the premise that nothing can be done about the "ancient ethnic hatreds" of the Balkans. The situation would indeed be hopeless if the solution required politicians and diplomats somehow to get Serbs, Croats, and Bosniacs to love each other. Ethnic hatred, unfortunately, is quite common: so much so that its existence does not explain why conflict breaks out on some occasions and not others. Elsewhere in Europe, a Seven Years War, a Thirty Years War, and a Hundred Years War have been fought – yet today the English, French, and Germans are cooperating within the framework of the European Union (EU), the Organization for Security and Cooperation in Europe (OSCE), and NATO. This is possible not because they now love each other, but because they have developed institutions on which they can all rely so that they no longer need to fear each other.

THE WAY FORWARD

The problem in the Balkans is not hatred, but fear – due to lack of human security and the institutions that provide it. The solution is to restore human security through a process of peacebuilding to rebuild and create the necessary institutions and engender popular confidence in them. If we consider the international community's options from this perspective, and ask what approach is best for establishing sustainable human security in BiH, the choice becomes clearer.

Withdrawal would result in renewed conflict. Merely maintaining a cease-fire is necessary, but insufficient for peacebuilding. Calls to rewrite Dayton do not address the principal obstacle to implementation: the ethnic factor will remain for the foreseeable future, whether or not it is written out of Dayton. The challenge is to transcend it while still accommodating it. The best prospect for establishing human security in BiH is to implement Dayton, as robustly as necessary, as an essential precondition for moving beyond it.

In practical terms, implementing Dayton means maintaining military security, establishing functional political institutions, the return of displaced people and refugees, a police and judiciary constituted to protect human rights and maintain the rule of law, a reliable banking system, and a free market economy. None of these will be quickly or easily achieved.

In the case of BiH, human security is a question not just of individuals, but of ethnic groups and ethnic identity. Human security for individuals means not only confidence that their economic needs, physical security, and individual rights will be protected. It also means security for their ethnic identity. In BiH, where the recent conflict involved attempts to deny the existence of certain ethnic identities and extinguish them, ethnic security will have to be accommodated as a component of human security.

NOTES

1 The PIC has a steering board composed of the European Union EU (represented by the EU presidency, the European Commission and individual EU member states), the US, Japan, Russia, Canada, and the Organization of the Islamic Conference. Other PIC members are BiH, Bulgaria, China, Croatia, the Czech Republic, the Federal Republic of Yugoslavia, the Former Yugoslav Republic of Macedonia, Hungary, Norway, Poland, Romania, Slovakia, Slovenia, Switzerland, and Ukraine.
2 The Standing Committee on Military Matters, the Central Bank, and the Constitutional Court, are working reasonably well, although they need continued support from the international community.

REFERENCES

Bosnia and Herzegovina: Essential Texts. Sarajevo: Office of the High Representative, 1998.

Glenny, Misha. *The Fall of Yugoslavia: The Third Balkan War.* New York: Penguin, 1993.

Gow, James. *Triumph of the Lack of Will: International Diplomacy and the Yugoslav War.* New York: Columbia, 1997.

Holbrooke, Richard. *To End a War.* New York: Random House, 1998.

Malcolm, Noel. *Bosnia: A Short History.* New York: New York University Press, 1994.

Owen, David. *Balkan Odyssey.* New York: Harcourt Brace, 1995.

United Nations. *The Fall of Srebrenica.* Report of the Secretary-General pursuant to General Assembly resolution 53/35 (A/54/549), 15 November 1999.

CASE STUDY

Haiti

DAVID LEE

This year marks a decade of active involvement of the international community with Haiti, in seeking to prevent conflict, build peace, foster democracy and the rule of law, and encourage political, economic, and social development. Looking back, we can see this engagement embodies, to one degree or another, all the elements of *An Agenda for Peace*, the landmark document produced in June 1992 by United Nations Secretary-General Boutros Boutros-Ghali in response to the call from the Summit Meeting of the Security Council of the previous January. In articulating for the new post cold war world "an integrated approach to human security," Boutros-Ghali laid out a five-fold set of aims. They involved: preventive diplomacy, peacemaking, peacekeeping, postconflict peacebuilding, and tackling "the deepest causes of conflict – economic despair, social injustice, and political oppression."[1]

In the real world, of course, including in Haiti, the several sets of activities do not necessarily take place in neat sequence, but get mixed up together – the practical diplomatist (or secretary general) pulling off the shelf whatever tool seems best suited to the immediate situation, utilizing it as required, then shifting back to an earlier technique, or choosing (or creating) a new one, or a portfolio of techniques, as circumstances change. Nevertheless, there has been a trend in Haiti to progress along this spectrum towards the peacebuilding and development end. To attain sustainability, the trick is to enhance indigenous capacities in each of these areas of activitiy, recognizing that the responsibility for Haiti rests with Haitians.

PEACEBUILDING IN HAITI

During the period of de facto rule by the military and their front men from 1991–4, the efforts of the international community were concentrated on various aspects of preventive diplomacy and peacemaking, trying to bring about a return of legitimate government. A civilian mission, known as the International Civilian Mission in Haiti (MICIVIH), led throughout by Colin Granderson, was despatched in 1993 jointly by the Organization of American States (OAS) and the United Nations (UN), partly as preventive diplomacy, partly to observe the human rights situation, build confidence, and facilitate agreement within Haiti. With President Aristide's return in October 1994, most attention was devoted to peace support operations, including the Security Council-authorized Multinational Force (MNF, October, 1994) led by the United States, and the Security Council-mandated peace support operations from March 1995, which included large military components plus small civilian police elements.

At the same time, aid donors met under the auspices of the World Bank and agreed upon arrangements for a strong program of quick-disbursing loans and grants to kick-start Haitian employment. Longer-term plans were put in place, sector by sector, and to address the problems of absorptive capacity, governance, and growth. In addition, the international community provided considerable electoral assistance and observers to a series of Haitian elections from 1995 on. In November 1997, the United Nations Security Council ended its military peacekeeping missions and launched the International Civilian Mission in Haiti (MIPONUH), of which the mandate was essentially to reflect the changed circumstances in Haiti, and mentor and train the fledgling Haiti National Police (HNP). Moreover, MICIVIH's mandate was broadened to include democratic development and human rights training, as well as human rights observation.

In summer 1999, the UN Economic and Social Council (ECOSOC) adopted a resolution (for the first time pursuant to Article 65 of the UN Charter, regarding cooperation between the Security Council and ECOSOC), cosponsored by Haiti, the Group of Friends (see below), and others, which inter alia called upon the secretary-general to prepare a report on ways to promote and coordinate Haitian long-term development. It was understood that close coordination was required with parallel work within the World Bank and the International Monetary Fund (IMF), given their emphases on poverty reduction. Building upon this effort, in late 1999, in a further move to reflect the evolving situation in Haiti, the UN General Assembly (with leadership from the Group of Friends) assumed the task of working out and agreeing upon a resolution to establish a new kind of mission. Elements of this mission's mandate came from both MIPONUH (police training) and MICIVIH (human rights matters), which were to be wound up. Justice reform and training were added; and stress was laid on the link to longer-term development and the institutions related thereto. The new International Civilian Support Mission in Haiti (MICAH) went into effect on 16 March 2000, under a representative of the secretary-general, and is due to terminate 6 February 2001, at the end of the term of Haiti's President René Préval.

Increasingly from the fall of 1999 on, the efforts of the international community focused on the holding of credible legislative and local elections in Haiti as soon as practicable in the first half of 2000, with presidential elections due later in the year. Considerable technical and financial assistance was provided along with international observers. Successful elections and the establishment of a functioning Parliament were seen as crucial to reestablishing international confidence and cooperation, including the processing of several hundred million dollars (US) of available loans for peacebuilding and development.

CANADA'S INVOLVEMENT

Given its longstanding relationship with and interest in Haiti, Canada has been actively involved as part of the international community's efforts in regard to that country. Canada has provided intellectual and diplomatic leadership as a member of the Group of Friends of the UN Secretary-General for Haiti throughout the period. It worked at the Organization of American States (OAS) in the early days and contributed to the UN/OAS International Civilian Mission (MICIVIH), and has always favoured the closest feasible collaboration between the UN and the OAS. It has provided leaders at different levels to the various UN missions, along with considerable numbers of troops and police – as well as voluntary financial contributions as required. All of this has been supplemented by a large bilateral aid program (the largest Canadian program in the western hemisphere), which has included important elements of support to the police and justice reform in Haiti, as well as institutional and other development projects. Canada has engaged directly with the Haitian authorities and the public to encourage them on their path toward democratic political, economic, and social development, recognizing that responsibility rests with the Haitians, and that the magnitude of the effort required will take time to implement.

THE POSITIVE LESSONS LEARNED

The effort in regard to Haiti represented an interesting collaboration between the UN and the OAS. In fact, at the beginning, the latter took the lead, although as time went on the initiative largely shifted to the UN. For a while, the two secretaries-general appointed the same special envoy. The civilian mission, MICIVIH, was jointly led and funded. This kind of cooperation, though it ultimately ran into financing difficulties when the OAS's voluntary funding for MICIVIH largely dried up, could serve as a model in future cases.

The UN secretary-general early on established a group of "Friends of the Secretary-General for Haiti" with whom to consult and who could be counted upon to take a lead. The group has varied in membership, but seems for now to have stabilized around Argentina, Canada, Chile, France, the United States, and Venezuela. In Port au Prince, the group is frequently convened by the representative of the secretary-general (RSG), though it also meets on its own. It may issue statements, or consult with the Haitian authorities and other political figures. Other interested representatives are sometimes invited informally on an ad hoc basis, e.g. from the European Union (EU) or Japan. This group has cosponsored resolutions on Haiti in UN bodies (UN Security Council, UN General Assembly, Human Rights Commission), increasingly although not necessarily in conjunction with Haiti. It is clear that the Friends Group has played an important role in reflecting the views of the international community in regard to developments in Haiti, and that more generally, this mechanism is a useful tool in peacebuilding.

Similarly, the RSG can play a very positive role. As well as being the head of the successive missions, representatives in practice, and in response to a clear need, have generally operated on a broader basis, both reflecting to the Haitian authorities and people the evolving views of the international community, and also convening consultations among the friends and facilitating coordination of international actions. The representative's relationship with the highest Haitian authorities can greatly assist the achievement of Haitian and international community objectives, particularly if the representative is working closely with the friends and the donor community. Further reflection, however, should be given to the arrangements at UN headquarters for managing the relationship with such missions and the RSG in order to break down the stovepipe mentality found in some quarters of the secretariats, and to improve functional cooperation among secretariat departments, and with agencies. This should also have a positive influence on field cooperation, which in Haiti has depended significantly on the individuals who have headed up the different offices.

Progress along the spectrum from traditional peacekeeping missions, through a civilian police mission (all under the UN Security Council) to a peacebuilding mission (MICAH, set up in late 1999 by the UN General Assembly), reflected the change in circumstances in Haiti. The last step, in particular, called for a strategic approach, which began in a small way among the friends about a year prior to UN General Assembly agreement on MICAH. The approach recognized that the UN Security Council was increasingly of the view that the situation on the ground no longer represented a threat to international peace, yet that international involvement with Haiti on security, justice, and human rights matters was still needed. It also acknowledged the evolution of views within Haiti, which were opposed to the presence of very visibly armed and uniformed foreigners. It was decided that, with a boost from the ECOSOC, the UN General Assembly would best meet the requirements as the locus for authorizing a mission which focused on political questions, but which was clearly heading toward a goal of handing off responsibility to development bodies over the longer term (as the UN General Assembly Resolution recognized). The resolution laid out a comprehensive mandate for the mission, as well as the RSG. It also integrated the role of the United Nations Development Program (UNDP), for example, specifically continuing the practice of naming the UNDP Resident Representative as the UN RSG's Deputy. It also established a committee of local representatives of the international community to advise and assist the RSG.

Increasingly, as the international community's involvement in Haiti evolved, it became more apparent that the long-term developmental aspects needed to be included more fully. Although the formal meetings convened by the World Bank and involving the government of Haiti had to be suspended because of the political stalemate in Haiti, periodic informal consultations took place among donors at World Bank headquarters. These included aid and, on occasion, foreign affairs representatives from interested governments and the UN RSG, as well as multilateral donor institutions, and proved very helpful in facilitating coordination of the political and developmental aspects of the international community's involvement in Haiti. Similarly, the initiative in the ECOSOC to look at Haiti's long-term development, for the first time invoking UN Charter Article 65, in practice was carried through by the combined work of the political and economic wings of the friends' UN Missions. The secretary-general's report called for by ECOSOC has yet to be considered, and discussion will have to take account of the political situation in Haiti over this year of scheduled elections. Nevertheless, it represents a further recognition that the involvement of the international community through its various interventions in Haiti has as its goal assisting the Haitians to establish a democratic regime, based on the rule of law and respect for human rights, and to set the country on the path to long-term economic and social development.

SOME NEGATIVE LESSONS

The international community did not fully appreciate at the time the impact on Haiti of the economic sanctions adopted during the de facto period. In fact, they had a devastating effect on Haiti's economy, on the already poor, of course, but also on such light industry as existed. The situation, unfortunately, will not be put right overnight with peacebuilding and with the simple infusion of the substantial donor funding anticipated once Haiti's Parliament and government function as they should. Ironically, it was not so much the effects of the embargo, but rather the readiness of the UN Security Council to provide for the sending in of foreign troops which finally swayed the well-off military rulers in September 1994 to depart peacefully.

Also, the international community, for a variety of reasons, failed to take advantage of the opportunity provided by the arrival of the 20,000 strong, well-equipped, multinational force (MNF) in October 1994 and the disbandment of the military by Aristide, to disarm the former military and other groups. The result is that Haiti is replete with small arms, augmented by those of drug dealers and others.

Although not formally part of its various mandates, the international community, through its missions, has not found a way to assist Haiti to counter adequately the growing pressure of the drug cartels, whose use (notably but not only) of Haiti's south coast as an entrepôt is having a markedly deleterious impact on Haiti's political culture, institutions, and security. And apparently, local drug use is also increasing.

Financing has proved a weak point in the missions in Haiti, both for the UN and for the OAS. Unpalatably, the Security Council mandated missions had increasingly to rely upon large amounts of voluntary funding. The loss of sufficient voluntary funding for MICIVIH led to its demise and incorporation of its mandate into MICAH. In turn, the discussions of funding in the lead-up to the MICAH Resolution of December 1999 were difficult and protracted. The saw-off was that approximately 40 percent of the money was to come from the regular budget of the UN, with the remainder to be provided through voluntary contributions. The latter were generally so slow in arriving that the secretary-general had officially to draw the matter to the attention of the UN General Assembly, observing that if the gap continued MICAH should be wound up. Fortunately, adequate funding was subsequently assured. However, it is clear more broadly that, if the international community wishes to persevere on the path of peacebuilding missions, it will need to address seriously the issue of funding. In the author's view, funding for most elements of the "peace agenda" should normally come from the appropriate mandated UN budget.

CONCLUSION

As these words are written, the jury is out on the success of efforts by Haitians, assisted by the international community, to bring about democratic reform and promote development. There has been some progress, but the pace of reform has been slower than hoped (perhaps unrealistically). There remain many difficulties and problems, not least the increasing impact at all levels of society of the drug trade through Haiti. Governance remains weak, and real justice reform has not progressed very far. Legislative and local elections scheduled for spring 2000 were delayed several times. However, on 21 May the first round in most of the country was held in relatively calm conditions and with a welcome 50–60 percent turnout – albeit with the announced results remaining controversial at the time of writing. The second round is mooted for late July, with presidential elections due before the end of the year.

Evidently, there are limits to what the international community can and should do. Haitian history is for Haitians to write. Successful foreign involvement can only be to encourage and assist. It is legitimate for this to be forceful at times, but it is neither appropriate nor effective if the steps are such that duly constituted Haitian authorities are unwilling to take ownership of the course of action – or blame foreigners for their ills. Haitians have a term, "marronage," for the avoidance of responsibility. The offer by various international donors of several hundreds of millions of US dollars in loans has been pending for several years – lacking the necessary legislative and other approvals – despite the desire of most Haitians to achieve democracy and its anticipated benefits.

These factors underline the differences between the situation of Haiti and that, for example, of Kosovo or East Timor, where the international community has intervened and effectively taken over. In Haiti this has not been the case. During the de facto period of military rule, the principle was upheld that the recognized government of Haiti remain under President Aristide. And even after Aristide's return, even with some 20,000 American and other troops on the ground, the international community did not purport to govern in Haiti. The international community may try to persuade, but must recognize what the authorities actually do – and do not do. The international community, and its individual members, then have a responsibility to assess the extent to which they are in a position to continue to accompany Haiti, and in what fashion. In the end, however defined, establishing human security in Haiti would require an optimal combination of principle, planning, resources, diplomacy, cooperation, flexibility, and patience.

NOTES

1 United Nations, Boutros Boutros-Ghali, *An Agenda for Peace: Preventive Diplomacy, Peacemaking and Peace-keeping*, Report of the Secretary-General to the Summit Meeting of the Security Council (A/47/277-S24111), 17 June 1992.

REFERENCES

Malone, David. *Decision-Making in the Security Council: The Case of Haiti*. Oxford: Clarendon Press/Oxford University Press, 1998.
United Nations, Boutros-Ghali, Boutros. *An Agenda for Peace: Preventive Diplomacy, Peacemaking and Peace-keeping*. Report of the Secretary-General to the Summit Meeting of the Security Council (A/47/277-S24111), 17 June 1992.

Guatemala

DANIEL LIVERMORE

Guatemala is, in many respects, a fascinating model of "peacebuilding." In part, this is because of the length of its recent internal conflict – almost four decades – and, in part, because it emerged from conflict as "peacebuilding" and "human security" began to form part of the lexicon of international relations. At the same time, caution needs to be exercised about case studies. A fundamental tenet of "peacebuilding" is that, while there might be common frameworks for "peacebuilding," every peace process follows its own path, with its own dynamics and internal logic. The significance of Guatemala is the lessons we can draw from experiences in helping to "build the peace" – especially issues of pace and direction – and what those lessons can tell us about "peacebuilding" as a distinct aspect of a longer-term process of consolidating fragile countries.

In the Guatemalan situation, in which I was an observer and participant from 1996–9, four issues essentially determined whether a peace process could successfully conclude a racial, class, and ideological conflict which began in the early 1960s. In brief, those issues were: the "timing" or synchronization of political will among the actors involved in the peace process; the existence of effective, internal conflict-resolution mechanisms; the nature of international support for peace; and the economic underpinnings of peace.

While these four issues allow generic conclusions to be drawn about peacebuilding as a concept, another corollary may be more contentious. Simply put, the success of peacebuilding in Guatemala, and possibly in other situations, is largely determined by indigenous factors in which the international community has only a limited margin of manoeuvre. In Guatemala, the international community provided at best 5 to 10 percent of the political capital invested in the peace process. While this support was significant and at times even decisive, it is important not to exaggerate international influence at the expense of domestic issues. When peacebuilding succeeds, it does so because it addresses the tensions within a society and the factors which have precipitated conflict in the first place.

SYNCHRONIZATION IN THE GUATEMALAN PEACE PROCESS

With respect to the question of "timing" or synchronization, the Guatemalan peace process finally began to succeed in the early 1990s because key parties developed a shared interest in ending a long and bitter conflict. The four insurgent movements which had formed the Unidad Revolucionaria Nacional Guatemalteca (URNG) were defeated militarily by the mid-1980s, although they still carried on low-level conflict aimed against the economic elite. Changing international conditions in the 1990s, especially the decline of Cuban support for revolutionary movements, further eroded the military assistance the Guatemalan insurgency could summon from abroad. At the same time, the Guatemalan armed forces, which had virtually single-handedly borne the government's burden of a dirty struggle for supremacy, had gradually become convinced of the need to sue for peace and seek a different role if they were to survive over the long run as a credible national institution.

Successive governments of Guatemala following the restoration of civilian rule in 1985 were also anxious to finalize a peace agreement. Peace offered the prospect of reversing Guatemala's quasi-pariah image, while opening the country to increased foreign investment. When one looks at the rough correlation of political forces in Guatemala, the three key actors – the insurgents, the armed forces, and the political elites – at roughly the same time, became convinced of the desirability of peace, albeit for varying motives. They therefore embraced a negotiating process which led eventually to finalizing the peace accords on 29 December 1996 and initiating a follow-on phase in the "peacebuilding" area.

The conjunction of forces favouring peace was the result of domestic pressures, namely, exhaustion after decades of conflict. Strong international pressure played a role, especially after peace was achieved in neighbouring El Salvador in 1992. The Contadora Group, the "Group of Friends" and the US worked behind the scenes for its conclusion. But, as visible as international pressure was, it affected the Guatemalan peace process in only small, complementary ways. Had the pace of domestic change been forced prematurely, or had new directions been imposed on key players, an eventual peace might have lacked the domestic support required to sustain it over time. In Guatemala, this did not happen, because the pace and direction of negotiations reflected the political realities of Guatemala's domestic situation.

CONFLICT-RESOLUTION MECHANISMS

With respect to a second important factor underpinning successful peacebuilding, "conflict-resolution mechanisms" were a relatively new concept in Guatemala. These processes engage actors in a peace process, and allow them to resolve disputes which bedevil any path to longer-term peace. These mechanisms vary from country to country, process to process. Guatemala's long and bitter internal conflict had been triggered, in part, because the country had never enjoyed the type of political system where conflicts could be resolved, or interests brokered, based upon broad social engagement and a commitment to compromise. Its return to democratic government in 1985 was an important step in the right direction. But a true peace demanded more in the way of engagement, particularly between the poor, largely illiterate Mayan majority and the nonindigenous minority which controlled the land and the economy.

In the Guatemalan case, although the peace process was negotiated between the insurgents and the government (including the armed forces), its conflict-resolution mechanisms were developed as part of an "inclusive" approach to peace. A Peace Commission was headed by a cabinet-level official capable of speaking authoritatively on the part of the government, and a "comision de acompanimento" (accompaniment commission), consisting of representatives of the government, the guerrilla movement, the nongovernmental sector, the business community, and the international community. Implementation of the peace accords fell to some nineteen other "comisiones," structured according to the issue at hand. These mechanisms were mandated by accords signed between 1990 and 1996, supplemented where necessary by national legislation. Their legitimacy rested not so much on any legal basis (there was none in most cases), but because they reflected national realities and real political exigencies.

Guatemala's conflict-resolution mechanisms are not a template solution for all peacebuilding efforts. Its structures suffered from many deficiencies, including inadequate representation from the small but powerful business sector to an unduly large number of commissions, which inhibited effective participation by the nongovernmental sector, particularly indigenous organizations. These mechanisms worked more or less effectively, however, even in a peace process so broad and encompassing that no single person or institution could manage its agenda. The Guatemalan case illustrates the importance of "process" issues, which are often underappreciated in a peace settlement. Bad processes exacerbate even the smallest substantive difficulty and invite problems on their own, while good, inclusive, functional processes facilitate surmounting obstacles of all kinds.

INTERNATIONAL SUPPORT FOR PEACE

International support for peace, the third pillar of successful peace-building, can be very helpful, as in the case of Guatemala between 1985 and 1996. Effective international support has to be organized. In the early years of the Guatemalan peace process, the "Group of Friends" (which included the US, Norway, Mexico, and Spain, among others) provided, at difficult stages of negotiations, the necessary support and resources to move negotiations forward. Their contributions ranged from holding meetings in neutral countries, to underwriting the expenses of the insurgents, to developing programs to facilitate implementation of the peace accords. Once the final accord was signed in 1996, the international community was largely represented through the UN Development Program and the UN Verification Mission in Guatemala (MINUGUA), although the "friends," which by this time included Canada in an informal way, continued to function behind the scenes.

In the Guatemalan case, it was vital that influential and capable neighbouring countries and international institutions lent their political will to the pursuit of peace, neither pushing beyond the realm of the attainable nor injecting extraneous concerns into an already complicated process. At critical times, the international community was able to provide resources for the peace process, sometimes rapidly, often flexibly, at times in situations in which there was a high risk of failure. Peacebuilding rarely allows for the classical approach to funding projects through careful assessment of objectives and results. Situations are often volatile and the outcomes highly unpredictable. The purposes to which funds are deployed are often unusual – such as supporting military demobilization or the destruction of munitions. In Guatemala, many donor countries deployed funds flexibly and relatively quickly to unblock sudden obstacles or to pave the way for the successful resolution of small disputes.

ECONOMIC UNDERPINNINGS OF PEACE

The issue of the economic underpinnings of peace is a simple, but sometimes overlooked proposition. As a peace process moves forward, there must be some basic, fundamental consensus about the directions of national economic policy and the maintenance of a stable economic environment in which peace can survive and flourish. In Guatemala, economic problems have delayed implementation of the peace accords, but they have not been the cause of crisis. The international community helped set the scene for productive national debate on economic issues by sponsoring seminars, forums, and professional gatherings which have built better political consensus on potentially divisive economic and fiscal questions, from taxation to land reform to social spending. Other projects helped the government of Guatemala with trade promotion programs or trade negotiations in order to facilitate Guatemala's more effective integration into regional and global markets.

The process of economic change in Guatemala was facilitated, in part, by the absence of divisive ideology in much of this debate. The peace accords mapped out a mainstream economic blueprint for the future. Even the former guerrilla movement recognized the importance of regional trade agreements and the need to promote a more vigorous private sector in the country. The peace process survived some buffeting in the economic area. It surmounted one crisis in which the congress, led by the influential business community, rejected higher taxes to fund implementation of the accords. One could imagine, however, what might have been the case had the Guatemalan economy been in recession, or had the debate on economic policy been more divisive, or, in the worst-case scenario, had Guatemala gone through the economic calamities which befell some of the former Soviet republics. Guatemala largely benefited in the late 1990s from a basic level of economic stability, essential to successful peacebuilding.

THE PRACTICAL LESSONS OF
THE GUATEMALAN PROCESS

Building peace in Guatemala is a work in progress. But, since the early 1990s, it has produced a number of practical lessons, particularly about flexibility in programming, the need to accept risk, and the requirement for rapidity in decision making. Canada was fortunate in having diplomatic and developmental tools appropriate to the peacebuilding process, through the Canada Fund for Local Initiatives and the highly-lauded Democratic Development Fund (DDF), both Canadian International Development Agency (CIDA programs). The latter was created as the Guatemalan peace process began to take hold, and was aimed at supporting initiatives promoting respect for human rights, participation of aboriginal people, and activities to sustain democratic principles, practices, and values.

The flexibility of the DDF was its chief advantage at a time when the political landscape was rapidly evolving. It supported a variety of useful initiatives at precisely the right time in the evolving peace process: seminars with the government, professional organizations, unions, the nongovernmental community, and selected political leaders on future directions in social and economic policy; training in the conflict-resolution area; an educational campaign undertaken by the Guatemalan law society promoting the peace accords; and a dialogue between the government and interested organizations on tax reform.

Larger programs funded by Canada addressed aspects of the peace accords as diffuse as assisting in the resettlement of refugees and internally-displaced persons, to launching a major geographic information systems project, to grappling with the massive land question in Guatemala. In charge of "donor coordination" and acting as a focal point between the government and the international community were the United Nation's Development Program (UNDP) and MINUGUA, which mended the "disconnects" and coordination difficulties inevitable to a process as large and complex as the Guatemalan case.

BEYOND GUATEMALA

The Guatemalan case helps to set in perspective some of the practical problems of advancing a wider peacebuilding agenda. The role of the international community, although necessarily a limited one in countries whose histories are as complex as Guatemala's, is nevertheless vital. The international community establishes the example, the model of change, and it is largely with the help of the international community that negotiating parties arrive at a program for change. The international community also provides some or even most of the bridging resources to help the recipient country on the path to change. Underpinning any peacebuilding effort is the assumption that change in any country can be a slow process. Even with broad consensus on a peace agenda, a large part of any civil society will remain unconvinced, actively or passively resisting the directions of change.

In the end, there is inevitably a wide gap between expectations of change and what can realistically be delivered, both nationally and internationally, in the immediate aftermath of peace. Indeed, managing expectations in constructive directions is a basic challenge which only domestic politicians can address. The key to establishing peace is a partnership between the international community and domestic actors in which national processes, informed by local circumstances, can be played out. This, in the Guatemalan case and in most situations, is the ultimate formula for successful peacebuilding.

REFERENCES

Castellanos, K.P. *El rol de la Sociedad Civil en los processos de paz de Guatemala y El Salvador.* Guatemala: Panorama Centroamericana, 1996.

Guatemalan Peace Accords. Acuerdo de Paz Firme y Duradera and Acuerdo sobre Cronograma para la Implementacion Cumplimiento y Verification, de los Acuerdos, 29 December 1996.

International IDEA. *Democracy in Guatemala: The Mission for an Entire People.* Stockholm: IDEA, 1998.

Torres-Rivas, Edelberto and Gabriel Aguilera. *Del Autoritarismo à la Paz.* Guatemala: FLACSO, 1998.

4 Humanitarian Military Intervention

DON HUBERT AND MICHAEL BONSER

Civilians are increasingly targets in violent conflicts, representing 80 percent of all casualties. Their injuries, fatalities, and displacement often constitute deliberate war aims. This is why future peace support operations must make the protection of civilians one of their primary objectives.

Efforts to build a culture of conflict prevention are welcome. No approach can be more effective in reducing the human costs of war than preventing the outbreak of war in the first place. Yet, in spite of the vigour which we bring to the challenge of effective preventive action, there will be cases where prevention does not succeed, where the spiral into violent conflict cannot be constrained. In these instances, the international community should be prepared to step in to protect civilians and avert a humanitarian crisis. This chapter will set out the broad objectives and practical considerations that will require the attention of policy makers on this topic.

Humanitarian military intervention can be defined as the use of nonconsensual military means to fulfil humanitarian objectives, including the provision of physical protection. It is a concept that has received growing support within the international community as a means of halting human suffering and/or bringing an end to wilfully committed atrocities within the borders of a sovereign state. While sovereignty will continue to be a guiding principle of international relations, the international community is less and less willing to ignore massive violations of human rights resulting in widespread and acute suffering within state borders. The Commission on Global Governance, for example, in its 1995 report, *Our Global Neighbourhood*, asserted: "Where people are subjected to massive suffering and distress ... there is a need to weigh a state's right to autonomy against its people's right to security."[1] It is within this context, including the considerable body of international humanitarian and human rights law (notably the Convention on the Prevention and Punishment of the Crime of Genocide), that intervention can be contemplated.

During the 1990s, the United Nations (UN) has undertaken or authorized a series of operations in response to humanitarian crises, including Northern Iraq, Somalia, Haiti, the former Yugoslavia, Rwanda, and East Timor. Yet these operations have often proved too little, too late in providing safety for people at risk. Srebrenica and Rwanda are only the most egregious examples of the chequered will of the international community to intervene in a timely and effective manner to protect civilians.

North Atlantic Treaty Organization (NATO) action in Kosovo sparked an intense debate regarding current legal and political frameworks for humanitarian military interventions. In the wake of NATO intervention, Canada began to call for a more systematic debate on the conditions and circumstances where the principle of sovereignty could be overridden, and where outside military intervention to halt violations of human rights and humanitarian law resulting in massive human suffering (see Minister Axworthy's speech to G-8 foreign ministers below).

The secretary-general further intensified the debate when, in his speech opening the fifty-fourth session of the UN General Assembly in September 1999, he proposed the "core challenge to the Security Council and to the UN as a whole in the next century: to forge unity behind the principle that massive and systematic violations of human rights – wherever they may take place – should not be allowed to stand."[2]

This challenge extends beyond the confines of the UN organization. It is a challenge to which the members of the international community must respond, by:

• strengthening norms and practices regarding the protection of civilians;
• mobilizing the political will necessary for swift action where warranted; and
• developing the military and other capability necessary to succeed.

Over the past few days, we have, together, brought about the beginning of the end of the Kosovo conflict. Kosovo is a good illustration of the human security crisis that the world is facing at the end of this century, and marks a turning point in global affairs, where the security of people figures prominently as an impetus for action ...

As it gains a new weight in international affairs, human security raises contradictions with existing norms ... Human security is going to have to be reconciled with the principle of nonintervention in the internal affairs of states. Kosovo illustrates this particular contradiction well. None of us around the North Atlantic Treaty Organization (NATO) table saw, or sees, any strategic advantage to intervening in Kosovo. No oil or other vital minerals are at stake. No commanding height or ocean choke point is at issue. There is no scientific knowledge to control. All there is, is a relatively poor population in a relatively poor part of Europe being abused by its own government – that, not some cold calculus of realpolitik, was the reason for action ...

No one, least of all the country with the smallest population represented here, is promoting a world in which the strong intervene where they will and the weak suffer what they must. The norm of noninterference in the internal affairs of other states remains basic to international peace and security, and the intervention in Kosovo must not be held up as a precedent justifying intervention anywhere, anytime, or for any reason.

However, in cases of extreme abuse, as we have seen in Kosovo and Rwanda, among others, the concept of national sovereignty cannot be absolute. Clearly, tests and standards need to be established by which the necessity, or not, of international enforcement of a human security standard can be judged. And these tests must be very demanding. One obvious standard is the perpetration of genocide or other crimes against humanity.

The point is that times are changing, and the UN Security Council cannot stand aside in the face of the outrages we have seen in a variety of violent disputes – for example, Sierra Leone, Sudan, and Angola. In states that have failed due to the oppression of a dictator or the actions of a warlord, there must be a new test of accountability, and that new test is human security. The new norm exists – now the United Nations and other international organizations must rise to the challenge of enhancing and enforcing that norm.

Address by Lloyd Axworthy, Minister of Foreign Affairs, G-8 Foreign Ministers' Meeting, Cologne, Germany, 9 June 1999

STRENGTHENING THE NORMS

Beyond addressing threats to international peace and security and/or for reasons of self-defence, the key determinant for multilateral humanitarian military intervention in the affairs of a state must be to prevent or stop genocide or acute suffering and widespread loss of life, caused by massive and systematic violations of human rights. Protection of civilian populations is a core norm of international behaviour. In extraordinary circumstances, an effective response will require the use of coercive measures, including military force. It should be underlined that humanitarian military intervention is not undertaken against the integrity or political independence of any state or to seize territory. Rather, it is aimed at stopping the suffering and destruction of people living within the borders of that state when the governing authorities of that state are unable or unwilling to do so themselves. The UN secretary-general's report, *Protection of Civilians in Armed Conflict*, which was adopted by the Security Council in September 1999, urges nations to further strengthen the legal and physical protection of civilians, explicitly calling for enforcement action to stop massive and ongoing abuses of human rights and international humanitarian law.

The arguments justifying intervention take numerous forms. The UN Charter was issued in the name of the peoples, not governments, of the UN, aiming not only to preserve international peace and security, but to reaffirm faith in fundamental human rights, in the dignity and worth of the human person. Furthermore, crimes against humanity, war crimes, and violations of the Genocide Convention constitute grounds for humanitarian military intervention. Article 1 of the Genocide Convention, for example, affirms that contracting parties confirm that genocide, whether committed in time of peace or in time of war, is a crime under international law which they undertake to prevent and punish.

In addition, the Security Council has, at times, relied on a broad interpretation of the question of what constitutes a threat to international peace and security under Chapter VII of the charter, in order to justify military interventions for humanitarian purposes. Genocide, mass killings, the interference in the delivery of humanitarian assistance, and mass civilian displacement, have all, at various times, been cited by the council as justifiable reasons for enforcement action.

Finally, principles and practice regarding humanitarian military intervention are evolving over time. States that once rejected any international discussion of human rights on the grounds that it was exclusively a matter of domestic jurisdiction now engage in discussions, respond to allegations, and challenge other states to meet accepted norms. Recent developments, including the creation of international tribunals on the former Yugoslavia (1993) and Rwanda (1994), as well as the International Criminal Court (ICC) (1998), serve to reinforce the position that those responsible for massive and systematic violations of human rights such as genocide, war crimes, and crimes against humanity within state borders are not immune from international law. In extreme cases, the international response has taken the form of forceful military action.

BASIS FOR TAKING ACTION

Building and strengthening a norm based on the protection of civilians will require policy makers to address a number of fundamental factors pertaining to the issue of whether and when intervention represents an appropriate course of action. These factors should not constrain our ability to act in support of affected populations. At the same time, they must be stringent enough to protect against illegitimate interventions.

- *Urgency: Has time run out on other peaceful dispute resolution instruments?*

The goal is to prevent and/or stop acute and widespread human suffering and loss of life. Forceful humanitarian military intervention should be undertaken when it is clear that all reasonable peaceful efforts to prevent and/or resolve an internal conflict either have failed or will not prevent massive human suffering and loss of life. While a credible threat to resort to force may be an important component of diplomatic efforts to achieve peace, the actual use of force should be employed judiciously.

- *Prevention: Is there a danger that an intrastate conflict will proliferate and threaten regional/international security?*

Preventing the spread of conflict across borders, of course, continues to be an accepted international objective, and has proven to be an important justification for Security Council action in the past. In building political support for the use of humanitarian military intervention, it should be clearly stated that nonintervention can have a destabilizing effect on regional/international security. Nonintervention in Rwanda, for example, has contributed to the spread of atrocities and civil conflict in central Africa. Protecting people from massive atrocities is in the general interest and is an important factor in ensuring long-term regional/international stability. This is not to suggest that humanitarian military intervention should only be approved when a clear threat to regional/international security exists, but merely to reiterate that such concerns must be considered in order to clarify the objectives of the intervention itself.

THE RWANDA CRISIS AND ITS CONSEQUENCES

In what was an historic failure by the international community, between April and July 1994, the United Nations (UN) Assistance Mission for Rwanda (UNAMIR) found itself without the mandate or means to stop the massacre of some 800,000 ethnic Tutsi and moderate Hutus. In the wake of the genocide and following the military victory of the Tutsi-led Rwandan Patriotic Front, almost a million Hutu refugees fled to camps along Zaire's eastern border. The camps quickly came under the control of so-called "intimidators," former Rwandan army soldiers and members of the Interahamwe Hutu militia who were implicated in the genocide. Although much of the international community recognized the destabilizing effect which the armed camps would have on the region, there was little willingness to see the UN intervene to effectively disarm the Hutu militias.

By November 1996, the Rwandan refugees were facing dire conditions in crowded camps in eastern Zaire. The Hutu militia refused to return to Rwanda to face possible retribution for the 1994 genocide and prevented refugees in the camps from leaving Zaire. As conflict in eastern Zaire between the Zairean armed forces and an alliance of rebel forces led by Laurent Kabila intensified in late 1996, the humanitarian situation for the Rwandan refugees deteriorated significantly. Tens of thousands of refugees under the control of the Hutu militia had been forced to flee their camps, aid agencies' efforts were hampered by the fighting, and relations between Zaire and Rwanda, which Kinshasa accused of backing Kabila's rebels, degenerated to a near state of war.

In response to the deepening crisis, the UN Security Council, on 15 November, adopted resolution 1080, authorizing the deployment of a multinational force to eastern Zaire with a mandate to facilitate the delivery of aid and the voluntary return of refugees and displaced persons. The adoption of the resolution was made possible in large part by Canada's declared willingness to lead the multinational force. In the days leading up to 15 November, Canada had been meeting with potential troop contributing nations, discussing the size, composition, and control of the force. The international response was encouraging.

By the time the Security Council adopted resolution 1080, however, the situation on the ground had been fundamentally alterred. Kabila's rebel forces attacked the Mugunga refugee camp on 13 November routing the Hutu militia. Thousands of refugees, freed from the control of the Hutu militia, began moving east towards Rwanda. In light of these changed circumstances, many countries (including Rwanda itself) began to question the need for a robust international mission. Debate over the number of refugees left inside Zaire and the requirement for a mission soon divided many potential troop contributors. Although it was clear that not all the refugees had returned to Rwanda, the international consensus which had existed on 15 November quickly dissipated. Debate over the numbers of refugees left in Zaire, and whether those remaining were members of the Hutu militia who would never return to Rwanda, continued for several weeks. Finally, on 13 December, it was decided that the mission would wind down. Canada, the only county to actually deploy troops under the multinational force, decided to withdraw its forces by the end of December.

In the aftermath of the crisis, Zaire, and much of central Africa, was convulsed by conflict. Kabila's rebel forces eventually marched on Kinshasa and overthrew the Mobutu regime. Along the way, the rebels were reported to have massacred hundreds of Hutus who had fled westward from the refugee camps. Now Kabila's Democratic Republic of Congo is engulfed by one of Africa's largest and most complex conflicts. The instability which stemmed from the presence of the armed Hutu militias in eastern Zaire's refugee camps after the Rwandan genocide has persisted ever since 1994. Had the international community acted decisively in 1994 or in 1996, the destabilizing effects of the situation in eastern Zaire may have been averted. Instead, the movement of refugees and displaced persons, and the continued presence of armed ethnic militias has resulted in a wave of crisis which has cut a swathe of war from Sudan to Angola.

Mike Elliot

- *Consistency: When and where should the international community take action?*

As a matter of principle, all civilians are inherently equally worthy of protection. The international community has a moral obligation to come to the assistance of people experiencing widespread and acute suffering as a consequence of massive violations of human rights, wherever they are found. In practice, this principle raises the issues of the international community's will and capacity to act. It does not now dispose of the requisite means to intervene everywhere.

MOBILIZING THE WILL TO ACT

Strengthening the emerging international norm on humanitarian military intervention requires strengthening the disposition to act. The Security Council, as the preeminent global body tasked with the maintenance of international peace and security, must rise to the challenge of humanitarian intervention. Even while authorizing interventions on humanitarian grounds, some council members have been unwilling to apply consistently a broader definition of the charter peace and security mandate that responds to the character of today's conflicts. What happens when a majority or even an overwhelming majority of the council is frustrated by the threatened or actual exercise of a veto? If the council is paralysed, particularly by recourse to a veto that is regarded by a majority of council and even General Assembly members to be inappropriate and abusive of the intent of the framers of the charter, who authorizes international humanitarian military intervention? The need for effective Security Council action was highlighted in the secretary-general's recent UN General Assembly speech where he stated, speaking about Rwanda: "Imagine for one moment that, in those dark days and hours leading up to the genocide, there had been a coalition of states ready and willing to act in defence of the Tutsi population, but the Council had refused or delayed giving the green light. Should such a coalition then have stood idly by while the horror unfolded?"[3] In the case of Kosovo, that community of states that make up NATO decided to act.

Interpretations of the charter must be more in step with the changing nature of conflict and the new challenges it poses, not only to international peace and security, but to fundamental values. Intrastate armed conflicts are matters for council action. Human rights and humanitarian responsibilities should be given greater weight in the Security Council's calculus of when to act. These are the pressing challenges before the council today. Yet, in the face of unspeakable atrocities, all too often we see council paralysis instead of council engagement. In these circumstances, should the General Assembly engage itself, under the Uniting for Peace procedures, when the council cannot? Does the obligation to act devolve upon regional organizations when the Security Council itself is unable to do so?

A key to mobilizing the political will for the UN to act is to lay out a critical path enabling governments to decide when intervention is warranted and how it should be carried out to prevent and stop widespread and acute human suffering and loss of life caused by massive and systematic violations of human rights. Five important considerations stand out.

- *Independent Corroboration: Is the scale of the crisis corroborated by credible third parties?*

A corroboration by credible third parties (e.g., regional intergovernmental organizations or international humanitarian agencies) that a crisis is generating or will generate massive and systematic violations of human rights causing acute and widespread suffering should be a prerequisite.

- *Practicability: Can the humanitarian military intervention achieve its goals and generate a positive outcome for victims?*

Humanitarian military intervention should be undertaken when it is clear that, with adequate resources, a clear mandate and a broad base of international support, it could bring an end to acute and widespread suffering and loss of life. Sufficient international commitments of finances, human resources, and political support are key elements in ensuring that humanitarian military interventions can be undertaken successfully. The question of whether or not the international community has sufficient capacity to intervene requires the attention of its members.

- *Scale: Is the force appropriate to the circumstances?*

The ethics of using violence to prevent or stop violence can pose difficult dilemmas. Efforts, therefore, must be made to ensure that the military strategies selected are appropriate to the tasks at hand, and proportionate to the objectives envisaged, targeting primarily the perpetrators of violence and the infrastructure on which they depend with due regard to civilians and the environment.

- *Multilateral: Is the intervention multilateral in nature and widely supported?*

A multilateral humanitarian military intervention requires a collective decision and, as such, helps to ensure that such action has a strong degree of international support. Unilateral interventions, on the other hand, raise questions of abuse and/or self-interest by the intervener.

- *Sustainability: Is the intervention part of a longer-term strategy to build and sustain peace?*

Humanitarian military intervention should not necessarily be viewed as a stand alone activity. The promotion of good governance, democratic institution building, and respect for the rule of law are key components of a longer-term strategy to help build sustainable peace and prevent further conflict. In extreme instances, where massive human rights violations are taking place, humanitarian military intervention may represent the first step in this long-term process. Clearly, its goal is to bring an end to massive and systematic violations of human rights causing acute and widespread suffering. Where possible, however, this should be seen only as the first step in sustained multilateral efforts to help ensure long-term stability and prevent the outbreak of renewed violence.

BUILDING THE CAPACITY TO SUCCEED

Mobilizing political will is closely linked to the availability of adequate military capacity to undertake humanitarian military intervention rapidly and effectively. At a time when requests for troops to help keep the peace or resolve conflicts are growing, the capacity of many countries is shrinking, as is the capability of the UN itself to manage complex missions.

Efforts that have been underway to develop a rapid reaction capability within the UN have not yet succeeded. The peacekeeping capacity of the UN over the same period of time has also diminished. Moreover, as indicated in the 1995 *Supplement to the Agenda for Peace*[4], the UN lacks the military capacity to organize enforcement operations. With the decision to eschew gratis staff, the secretariat has become still less capable of planning timely action. Increasingly, the task of humanitarian military intervention falls by default to coalitions of the willing and/or regional organizations. But the strong preference remains for a UN mandate, even by ad hoc coalitions. A well-coordinated and integrated approach is required at our respective national levels as well as internationally in order both to obtain workable mandates and effective military resources. Such mandates need to build in military and civilian cooperation from day one.

Events in the past decade have left us very well aware of the high human cost of inaction or delayed response. The basis for action set out above, though not a doctrine governing humanitarian intervention, clarifies the decision-making framework for a timely response.

NOTES

1 The Commission on Global Governance, *Our Global Neighbourhood* (New York: Oxford University Press, 1995), 71.

2 United Nations, Secretary-General, *Report of the Secretary-General to the Security Council on the Protection of Civilians in Armed Conflict* (S/1999/957), 8 September 1999.

3 Ibid.

4 Boutros Boutros-Ghali, *Supplement to an Agenda for Peace* (New York: The United Nations, 1995).

REFERENCES

Annan, Kofi. *Address to the United Nations General Assembly.* New York, 20 September 1999.

Commission on Global Governance. *Our Global Neighbourhood.* New York: Oxford University Press, 1995.

United Nations. *Report of the Secretary-General to the Security Council on the Protection of Civilians in Armed Conflict* (S/1999/957), 8 September 1999.

The Kosovo Air Campaign

PAUL HEINBECKER AND ROB MCRAE

While the Gulf War was fought to uphold the principle of sovereignty and territorial integrity in the name of Kuwait, the Kosovo air campaign was conducted, in large part, to defend universal principles of human rights and international humanitarian law. The mass exodus of refugees from Kosovo into neighbouring states, and the incipient threat to regional stability, galvanized publics and leaders alike. For an organization based on collective defence and deterrence, the air campaign was both a major departure for the North Atlantic Treaty Organization (NATO) and an entirely new phase in its decade-old determination to bring peace to the Balkans. A lot of lessons have been learned, and it will take time to digest them. However, one thing is sure: the Kosovo air campaign was unique in the annals of air wars. That campaign was large-scale, yet carefully attuned to political standards that were so high as to be virtually unreachable. The Supreme Allied Commander Europe, General Wesley Clark, was daily asked to wage an air campaign which destroyed Milosevic's war machine, while (i) incurring minimal Allied losses; (ii) inflicting the least possible number of civilian casualties; and (iii) synchronizing the campaign with a multitrack diplomatic effort. In other words, the military campaign was never wholly in the hands of the military to run: there was constant political and diplomatic oversight the whole way. Hence the lessons learned are necessarily complex.

Unlike the short, sharp air campaign in Bosnia that brought Milosevic to the table at Dayton, the air strikes in Kosovo were actually preceded by a Dayton-like process. It failed, of course, though parts of

Rambouillet lived on in the UN Resolution authorizing the civil and security missions in Kosovo. In October, 1998, US envoy Richard Holbrooke had obtained what might have become the essential underpinning of such a deal, by providing for the deployment of an international civil presence (the Organization for Security and Cooperation in Europe's (OSCE) Kosovo Verification Mission) and setting out rules of disengagement (which were to be backed up by air strikes). But when Milosevic began reneging on his commitments, nothing happened. Because his transgressions were not flagrant, they did not catch the public eye. Milosevic's transgressions were incremental, and by January, 1999, he had almost doubled the number of his troops and police inside Kosovo. Just when this troop build-up, together with the Racak massacre, encouraged the US to start preparing Allies and the public for air strikes, the Europeans took another track altogether. They revived the Contact Group (which the US had declared dead in December), and took the lead in developing a political track. At the same time, the big European powers led the way in building up troops in the region to implement the deal when it was agreed. This gave the impression that it was part of a longer-term plan to enhance the European Union's (EU) security role in Europe. But it also gave Milosevic two more months to pursue ethnic cleansing in Kosovo.

THE AIR CAMPAIGN

Though it is possible to argue that we should have launched the air campaign in January, 1999, or even in late 1998, in fact it was necessary to explore every avenue for a peaceful solution. The UN's involvement, the UN secretary-general's statements, the Rambouillet marathon, the Russian engagement, the series of high-level visits to Belgrade, – all of this constituted a necessary prelude to the political decision to launch air strikes. NATO did not take this action lightly. On the contrary, many nations, like Canada, were very concerned about the lack of an explicit UN Security Council Resolution authorizing the use of force. But when the moment came, when every equitable political option had been pursued, there was surprisingly strong consensus around the table to take action in line with the demands of previous Security Council Resolutions.

Why was this so? No doubt, for many countries, there was lingering regret over the atrocities committed in Bosnia and the belief in some quarters that earlier, forceful action might have been able to prevent the deaths of many tens of thousands of civilians in that conflict. Secondly, a number of expressions of resolve on the part of the international community (including the legally-binding resolutions, statements by the UN secretary-general, the OSCE, the EU, the Council of Europe, and by NATO) were being ignored by the Federal Republic of Yugoslavia (FRY). UN Security Council Resolution 1199 from September, 1998, called on the FRY to cease all action by its military and security forces in Kosovo, and referred to "possible further action." The UN Security Council Resolution 1203 of October, 1998, made the Alliance an interested party in events in the FRY. By January, there was ample evidence that the FRY had broken all of its commitments to the OSCE and Richard Holbrooke, and then in February-March the Rambouillet Negotiations collapsed. Attempts by Canada and others to obtain an explicit UN mandate for action against the FRY to deal with the unresolved situation in Kosovo, which the Security Council had already found to constitute a continuing threat to peace and security in the region, were frustrated by Russian intransigence. But the majority views of the council were nonetheless clear. On 26 March 1999, a Russian-proposed resolution in the Security Council that condemned the air campaign was defeated by twelve votes to three. One of the other members of the Security Council pointed out at that time that the UN Charter itself confirmed that the Security Council had the primary but not the exclusive responsibility for maintaining international peace and security.

Finally, the evidence of human rights abuses, including atrocities committed against civilians, was both compelling and increasing. There had been the Racak massacre on 15 January, in which 45 ethnic Albanians had been killed in their own village, and additional rumours of other massacres from refugees who had fled Kosovo. Daily reports by the OSCE's Kosovo Verification Mission provided a catalogue of extrajudicial killings, oppression, and other flagrant human rights violations. On 23 March 1999, the day before the start of the air campaign, the UN High Commissioner for Refugees (UNHCR), Madame Ogata, reported to the UN Security Council that 410,000 ethnic Albanians had been pushed out of their villages by Serb forces, while 90,000 were already outside the country as refugees. Over 500,000 people had been forced from their homes before the bombing got under way, and the trend clearly demonstrated a pattern of increasing numbers of expulsions and mounting evidence of orchestrated and officially-sanctioned violence against civilians. The FRY was in clear breach of the established norms of international humanitarian law. Though all knew that the bombing itself could not stop abuses on the ground in the short term, its goal was to impair and destroy Milosevic's ability to wage war on the civilian population of Kosovo, and to pressure him into accepting a settlement that would be monitored and secured by the international community.

In other words, the crisis in Kosovo was perceived as a human security crisis. NATO's action became an instrument of human security, driven as much or more by values than by interests. But there were interests at stake too. The attacks by the FRY on its own citizens in Kosovo, and the resulting outpouring of hundreds of thousands of refugees, threatened the fragile democracies in Albania, the former Yugoslav Republic of Macedonia (FYROM), and Bosnia. The collapse of any of these states would have created a much larger regional crisis, a crisis that could have affected the security of NATO member states and others in the region. Moreover, if no action had been taken, the credibility of more than a few international organizations, including the UN, NATO, and the OSCE, would have been eroded in both the neighbouring countries and in other countries that had opted for western models of democracy and free markets after the end of the cold war. This, itself, would have contributed to future instability in the region.

While the loss of pilots, and the media's obsession with it, might have curtailed the military effectiveness of the air campaign, the issue of collateral damage became a much more potent challenge to western leadership. If this campaign was all about protecting human security, how could we justify incurring civilian deaths? Neither the Gulf War, nor the air strikes in Bosnia, had prepared allies for dealing with this issue. From the beginning, General Clark's priority was to avoid civilian casualties. But three considerations need to be borne in mind: (i) perfection in this regard is an impossible standard; (ii) international humanitarian law recognizes that, and acknowledges the possibility of collateral damage to civilian sites in the pursuit of legitimate military targets, provided the former is not disproportionate to the latter; and (iii) considering the number of sorties, ordnance used, and targets attacked, the number of civilian losses was – however regrettable – both astonishingly low, and legally and morally defensible. Furthermore, if our publics had been able to see on their televisions what was happening on the ground to the Kosovars, the debate about collateral damage might have been different.

But the fact was that NATO had taken on a dictator who could control the information flow about the conflict, and thereby shape western public opinion. In the end, NATO came to the conclusion that it would never win the propaganda war with Belgrade. It took the Alliance twenty-four to forty-eight hours to determine, via air surveillance and by satellite, where a bomb had actually fallen and the resulting damage. NATO was always in a reactive mode, and could rarely counter Serb claims about civilian deaths the day they occurred. The conclusion was that the best approach was simply to be as transparent and as credible as possible, by providing the facts known and by regretting casualties. The civilian casualties were of course tragic. But our publics were faced with the choice between accepting them or doing nothing. The result was that, for the most part, they stayed the course. Even at the end of the campaign, the solidarity of allied governments was unshakeable, something which surprised even those on the inside. It proved wrong those pundits who had argued that an alliance of democracies could not maintain cohesion in a conflict based on values. It was a reminder of how strong those trans-Atlantic values really are, and how significant in the broader global context.

While it is difficult to see how we could have improved the handling of collateral damage, much more could have been done in terms of the information war in the FRY. Months before the air strikes, NATO and the west could have devoted significant resources to providing FRY citizens accurate information about the conflict in Kosovo and western concerns. Though it would not have been decisive, this would have at least undermined one of Milosevic's power bases, the control of the media. When the air campaign began, an aircraft-based radio station beamed information into the FRY, but it was difficult to receive. The project of an air-borne television station never really got off the ground. It was only towards the end of the campaign that significant steps were taken: Hungary offered the alliance an unused radio station in the southern part of the country that was powerful enough to reach a significant part of the FRY. And the board of European Telecommunication Satellites (EUTELSAT), prompted by European governments, but only after much delay, banned the FRY from using the satellite network to broadcast its propaganda back into the country.

However, the suppression of state propaganda being broadcast via local antennas was more problematic. First, it was difficult for western governments to accept the idea of attacking the Serb media. It ran up against strongly-held views on free speech. Second, the destruction of state-run broadcast antenna led Milosevic to force non-state television stations to rebroadcast FRY propaganda. The alliance was then faced with the unacceptable option of attacking a much broader range of stations, with, no doubt, disproportionally more civilian deaths. The inevitable conclusion was that air power was not a useful tool for fighting the propaganda war inside the FRY.

Paradoxically, Western media provided the FRY propaganda machine ample opportunity to convey its message to western publics. We have become accustomed, at times of major western engagement in conflict, to view CNN as the only game in town. We have even created a name for it: "the CNN factor." What is meant is that television provides a real-time window on conflict anywhere in the world. The CNN factor can feed the public's demand for their governments to "do something" to bring war or suffering to an end, wherever it might be. During the air campaign, Serb television film of collateral damage was repeated three or four times during a ninety second journalist's report, often followed by a lengthy diatribe from a FRY deputy minister of Information. Soon, CNN was even relying on retired FRY deputy ministers of Information (for some reason living in New York) to fill in virtually nightly slots reserved for Serb propaganda. CNN even granted Arkan, by that time publicly indicted by the International Criminal Tribunal for the Former Yugoslavia (ICTY) for war crimes, a lengthy "up front and personal" studio chat. He went literally from CNN's studio to Kosovo where he was implicated in more war crimes. CNN's role and the FRY's successful propaganda war, both within and outside the country, demonstrate that there is a lot to learn about the so-called information revolution. We have not yet arrived at a time when the flow of information to global civil society is both responsible and available to all: globalization still has its limits.

The facts of the air campaign itself are now fairly clear. NATO adopted an incremental, phased approach, both because alliance consensus demanded it and because of the conditions imposed on it. Initially, the weather was largely unfavourable and improved steadily until the end of the campaign, when it was almost always favourable. Secondly, the tactics changed over time, evolving from predetermined targets to targets of opportunity. This change of tactics happened to coincide with a change in tactics by the Kosovo Liberation Army (KLA), which shifted from small-scale hit-and-run-operations to broader infantry-like assaults ideally suited to flushing out entrenched Serb armour and troops. The result was that in the last two weeks of the air campaign, NATO's ability to take out FRY targets, including armour and troops, increased exponentially. Still, though the numbers would have changed if the campaign had continued, the air campaign resulted in only moderate damage to the FRY war machine in Kosovo. It did, however, keep that machine pinned down for most of the conflict. However, if NATO had been authorized to act earlier, when FRY forces were still deploying and before they were dug in, the damage to Miliosevic's war machine would have been much greater. But it was precisely this period that was devoted to the Rambouillet peace negotiations, as the last chance effort to obtain a diplomatic solution.

On the other hand, the strategic air campaign was highly successful in that the supporting infrastructure for Milosevic's forces was largely destroyed. The soft bombs, the attacks on the private assets of Milosevic and his cronies, and the cumulative damage to the FRY economy no doubt put Milosevic in the mood to deal. The mounting damage to the military-economic infrastructure, combined with highly successful air attacks (with KLA help) on the FRY military and police inside Kosovo in the closing days of the campaign, contributed significantly to Milosevic's capitulation. But it would not have happened at all without the diplomatic efforts of Talbott, Ahtisaari, and Chernomyrdin, and the G-8. This effort coincided with a belated but significant shift within the Alliance on the issue of a possible ground campaign. Not only the UK and Canada, but apparently the US too had come to the conclusion that, if the diplomatic effort and the air campaign did not work, serious and urgent consideration had to be given to a ground incursion. Thus it is incorrect to say that NATO "won" by air power alone. Both KLA tactics and the diplomatic track proved to be essential ingredients, as did the growing determination to pursue the ground option if all else failed. The lesson here was that there is no such thing as an "air war" alone. Both force and diplomacy worked hand in glove to produce a successful outcome. Finally, although publicly ruling out the ground option might have reassured some hesitant publics, it probably prolonged the conflict.

The big unknown is what kind of resistance might have been mustered by the VJ (Vojske Jugoslavije, the Yugoslav Army) in Kosovo if NATO had indeed launched a ground offensive. There was no way to predict this without actually doing it, despite the various claims about VJ morale. The ground option remained risky because it was unpredictable. But most military planners here believed that if NATO troops could force the Serbs to manoeuver and to concentrate forces, the VJ would be destroyed. On the other hand, if the VJ remained spread out and entrenched, it would be a long and bloody clean-up operation. Given the unconventional nature of the VJ campaign to date, the latter seemed more likely, perhaps buttressed by the use of human shields. After all, this was the army that had used the expulsion of over a million people as a weapon of war designed to overwhelm NATO's military build-up in theatre. The VJ would never engage NATO in a way that enabled NATO to maximize its manoeuverability and speed. In the end, it turned out that the expulsion of the refugees was a public relations disaster for Belgrade. The story of what was going on in Kosovo began to trickle out. Even though "refugee fatigue" soon gripped the western media, it also provided NATO an opportunity to show how it could support and carry out humanitarian missions that had literally overwhelmed the UNHCR and other civil agencies.

Canada's role in the air campaign not only amounted to a significant contribution to the Allied effort. This commitment of "hard power" also lent credibility to our active role on the diplomatic front, both in NATO councils and in the G-8. Out of nineteen NATO member-states, thirteen countries contributed to Operation Allied Force. Canada contributed eighteen CF-18 fighter bombers (the sixth largest number), hundreds of ground crew, and airborne tankers for air-to-air refuelling. We were one of the principal contributors of air crew to the AWACS surveillance aircraft. In terms of our fighter-bombers, Canadian pilots flew 678 combat sorties, of which fully 558 were air-to-ground sorties, i.e., air strikes on FRY targets. The air strikes were conducted by means of "packages" of fifty aircraft each, with groups of aircraft carrying out various complementary roles. In all of the air strikes in which we participated, Canada was the package commander for half of them. This statistic reflects hugely on the quality of our air crew and our aircraft.

THE DIPLOMATIC TRACK

The diplomacy that ended this war was as unprecedented as the war itself. It was, in fact, conducted on a variety of tracks, with NATO negotiating with the Russians and the Russians negotiating with the Serbs. In fact, the American decision to engage Finnish President Ahtisaari to explain reality to both the Russians and the Serbs was decisive (apparently with some help from a Swedish businessman). This remote-control diplomacy proved ultimately both quite effective and very convenient, after the war crimes indictment made Milosevic an untouchable.

From the beginning, at the G-8 Political Directors' meeting, 7–8 April 1999, until the conclusion of the UN Security Council on 10 June, optimism and pessimism pursued each other relentlessly from Dresden to Moscow, Helsinki, Belgrade, Bonn, and New York. There was clearly an ongoing policy debate in Moscow, with its own version of doves and hawks familiar to those who were seasoned observers of the interagency process in Washington.

The Americans appeared the first to resist broadening the circle of participants beyond themselves and the Russians, but, in the end, could not resist the Russians' wish to use the G-8 and the German G-8 presidency's determination to do so. From the Dresden political directors' first draft of the principles for ending the war to the Bonn-Cologne ministerial negotiations of the UN Security Council resolution and its shepherding of that resolution doggedly to conclusion, the G-8 proved to be an effective operational organ. To be sure, it was the Chernomyrdin-Ahtisaari duo, coached from the background by State Department Deputy Secretary Strobe Talbott, that convinced Milosevic to yes.

Canada earned its way militarily, diplomatically, and legally. Militarily, Canada provided a relatively modest but highly effective air campaign contribution (leading approximately 10 percent of the strike sorties in the early going). Our pilots went in harm's way where some of our European allies had neither the capability nor the political stomach to follow. Their professionalism brought Canada NATO's respect and secured us helpful negotiating standing as well. Were membership in the G-8 based on military contributions alone, the bona fides of some of its larger members would certainly be questioned. Ours would not be.

At the same time, the diplomatic contributions of the G-8 members were equally chequered, with some of the larger countries clearly punching below their weights. Perhaps the G-8 format favours ministers from Westminster traditions and from cultures where ministers are expected to lead on policy development, not just on its expression.

The Canadian team worked long, hard, and effectively. Officials from Ottawa to NATO to Washington, Bonn, the UN Headquarters in New York and other "front line" posts conducted themselves with a professionalism and an indefatigability that did the foreign and public service proud. It was neither easy nor fun to push their way into the games the bigger powers play, but they had to do so and they did. Minister Axworthy provided the policy leadership, the political sensitivity, and the sense of the moment for Canada to play successfully in the major league of diplomacy. At the first G-8 ministers' meeting in May, he prevented the process from derailing and coined the key compromise on the crucial issue of the international security presence. At the ministerial meeting in June, he played a central role in drafting the UN Security Council resolution ensuring that the KFOR (Kosovo Force) would cooperate with the ICTY on war crimes. Defence Minister Eggleton very early recognized the stakes, spoke plainly about the dangers, and ensured that Canada carried its share of NATO's common burden. Prime Minister Chrétien, among the most experienced of NATO leaders, recognized from day one that ground forces might be necessary. He alone broached the issue at the NATO summit when others preferred the safety of keeping silent, even though they knew that taking this option off the table had been a mistake. The prime minister was steadfast in the face of too many Canadian pundits who too often seemed more preoccupied with posturing than principle and more comfortable with the nostrums of a familiar past than the risks of a potentially better future. This time it was the critics who were ready for the last war. Parliament decided early on to back the government and generally did so, albeit increasingly raggedly as time and the air campaign wore on. Last, but not least, the Canadian population knew evil when they saw it, and questioned not the necessity of fighting it but rather NATO's effectiveness in doing so. In the end, all share in the satisfaction of knowing that a great wrong was righted, and that Canada made a difference in the righting of it.

LESSONS LEARNED

It is too early to draw any definitive list of lessons learned from the Kosovo campaign, but already now some things seem clear. Every avenue to reach a peaceful solution had to be explored before resorting to the use of force. But once committed to act, the stakes for NATO and Canada were not small. In fact, they were staggering. Increasing human rights abuses in Kosovo, including atrocities committed against civilians, posed a direct challenge to the human security agenda. That agenda would have suffered a major, perhaps a decisive setback if the intervention had failed. NATO would have been discredited, with unfathomable consequences. Perceived Alliance fecklessness would have encouraged mini-Milosevics around the world. The UN's peace and security mandate would certainly have been made correspondingly irrelevant. Canada might well have been faced with a choice between ineffectual multilateralism and fortress North America. Not all of these dire consequences might have materialized, of course, but even if only some of them did, the consequences of failure would still have been dramatic.

In the end, justice prevailed because the intervention defended universal principles of human rights and international humanitarian law. Justice also prevailed thanks to an ICTY prosecutor whose independence of mind safeguarded her mandate. Judge Arbour acted when most "experts" wished she had not, and quite probably hastened the end of the war when Milosevic saw his retreat into an immunity deal blocked and heard the ever-louder drumbeat for a ground campaign. As for the Serbs, themselves, they will only get closure on this issue when Milosevic goes to the Hague. Western spokespersons repeatedly stated that the war was with Milosevic, not the Serbs, and this despite their apparent near total disinterest, at best, in what was happening to their Kosovar cocitizens.

The other major lesson was that traditional peacekeeping is no longer enough. The new peace support operations make and enforce the peace, while providing substantial support to the civil mission. Rather than being sloughed off by the military as add-ons, the military's support for the civilian mission is now taken as a standard of success by our publics and governments. In fact many of the supporting roles being played by KFOR are geared to human security objectives, which attests to the extent that the human security agenda has moved up the scale of public awareness since the Bosnia conflict and the landmines campaign. But the biggest challenge facing KFOR is the lack of a peace settlement. At the moment, there is no agreed exit strategy and no collective definition of success that would permit KFOR's eventual withdrawal. Even in the event of successful elections in Kosovo down the road, it is difficult to imagine an exit strategy for KFOR before democracy comes to Serbia. This is why Balkan reconstruction and support for the opposition in the FRY is so important. Recent positive electoral outcomes in Croatia and Bosnia validate NATO's strategy, but the future of the FRY, and the fate of Milosevic, remains key for the region.

History looks inevitable in retrospect, but those who live it know otherwise. NATO proved up to the task its members set for it, although there were and remain doubts that a coalition of democracies is well suited to wage war, particularly in cases where their strategic interests are not at stake. The very precariousness of the operation should chasten any allies who might have liked to see NATO as Globo-Cop. The uncertainty of whether NATO will act should nevertheless restrain some tyrants and warlords. Whether the Kosovo experience accelerates the realization of a European Security and Defence Identity (ESDI) remains to be seen. What the Kosovo experience does show is that NATO qua NATO remains an effective instrument of Euro-Atlantic security and stability. Would that Africa, in particular, and other regions had the same capacity.

For the UN itself, all's well that ends well, or so we can only hope. The resolution terminating the war on the conditions it was ended implicitly validated the decision of the nineteen NATO democracies to act when the Security Council was unable to do so. The resolution also amounted to an expression of hope that the UN would yet serve the peace and security purposes the world needs it to do. Whether it does so will depend upon the extent to which the more truculent Permanent Members of the Security Council and the less principled among the general membership come to understand that the human security issue is real. What is needed now is not a return to an increasingly shrill insistence on national sovereignty as absolute. We need an openness to both developing the rigorous tests, and strengthening the standards, that should govern other legitimate humanitarian intervention in the future (such as, for example, to prevent or stop genocide or crimes against humanity). As Kofi Annan has so eloquently put it: "in a world where globalization has limited the ability of states to control their economies, regulate their financial policies and isolate themselves from environmental damage and human migration, the last right of states cannot and must not be the right to enslave, persecute or torture their own citizens." Only governments reserving the right to oppress their own people need fear such an approach.

NOTES

1 United Nations, Kofi Annan. *The Effectiveness of the International Rule of Law in Maintaining International Peace and Security* (SG/SM/6997), The Hague Appeal for Peace, 18 May 1999.

REFERENCES

Charter of the United Nations. New York, 26 June 1945.
United Nations. Annan, Kofi. *The Effectiveness of the International Rule of Law in Maintaining International Peace and Security.* Speech at the Hague Appeal for Peace (SG/SM/6997), 18 May 1999.
–. *Security Council Resolution 1199*, 23 September 1998.
–. *Security Council Resolution 1203*, 24 October 1998.

5 Protecting the Most Vulnerable: War-Affected Children

CARMEN SORGER AND ERIC HOSKINS

In a world of diversity and disparity, children are a unifying force capable of bringing people to common ethical grounds. Children's needs and aspirations cut across all ideologies and cultures. The needs of all children are the same: nutritious food, adequate health care, a decent education, shelter and a secure and loving family. Children are both our reason to struggle to eliminate the worst aspects of warfare, and our best hope for succeeding at it.[1]

INTRODUCTION

The plight of war-affected children[2], in particular the emerging trend of targeting children both as victims and combatants, is one of the most disturbing human security issues facing the global community today. The devastating toll exacted on children is evident by the numbers over the past decade: close to 2 million killed; more than 4 million disabled; over 1 million orphaned; 20 million displaced; over 10 million children psychologically scarred by the trauma of abduction, detention, rape, and witnessing the brutal murder of family members; and over 300,000 girls and boys serving armies (as fighters, sexual slaves, minelayers, and spies).

In the face of this human tragedy, the global community has been compelled to take steps to further protect children from the inferno of war and extreme violence. In 1996, the UN secretary-general appointed Mme Graça Machel as his expert to carry out a comprehensive study of the impact of armed conflict on children. The Machel study detailed the vulnerability of children in wartime, including the plight of child refugees and unaccompanied children, child soldiers, and the special needs of girls. Mme Machel also described the heightened dangers for children during conflict, such as landmines, widespread sexual exploitation, and abduction. The study was based on a series of regional consultations which brought together nongovernmental organizations (NGOs), United Nation's (UN) agencies, regional organizations, and governments to determine the needs of children in the Americas, Africa, the Middle East, and Asia. In addition to bringing the situation of war-affected children in sharp focus for the international community, the study laid out a series of specific recommendations for action at the level of governments, institutions, and civil society. One of those recommendations was the creation of a special representative to the UN secretary-general to advocate on behalf of children.

In September 1997, the UN General Assembly created the position of Special Representative to the Secretary-General (SRSG) for Children and Armed Conflict and appointed Mr Olara Otunnu. Otunnu's appointment was timely. By early 1998, humanitarian and advocacy NGOs who played an active role in the Ottawa process on landmines were now looking for other issues which had stagnated within the UN system and which might lend themselves to a similar formula. Child soldiers and the Optional Protocol on the Involvement of Children in Armed Conflict seemed like an obvious choice. The challenge of the new SRSG would be to maintain a focus on the broader issue of war-affected children, in the face of a mounting global campaign to end the use of child soldiers. In particular, Otunnu was faced with the fact that his mandate was restricted primarily to advocacy. There was space for Canada to assume a leadership role in merging political action with operational standards and concrete initiatives, initiatives which could make a difference in the lives of war-affected children.

This chapter describes Canada's response to the plight of war-affected children, and how we helped shape and advance the issue of war-affected children both domestically and internationally. It also describes how Canada played a key role in mobilizing a small but effective *coalition of the willing* to advance the issue of children and armed conflict beyond merely a human rights issue, to make it a legitimate peace and security question.

THE POLICY CONTEXT

The issue of war-affected children came to the fore at a time when Canada started to give increasing prominence to human security. At the same time, the media began regularly broadcasting stark images of the situation of war-affected children: girls abducted by Uganda's rebel Lord's Resistance Army and forced into sexual slavery where sexually-transmitted diseases and HIV/AIDS infection rates were increasing exponentially; in Sierra Leone, infants with limbs hacked off, often by child rebels; children psychologically scarred by terrorism in Algeria and living with the trauma of witnessing extreme physical and sexual violence, including widespread rape, torture and abuse of family and community; refugee children fleeing persecution in Kosovo; street children in Colombia displaced by years of internal conflict; and the war against children in Bosnia, where the social fabric had been torn apart and children were directly exposed to intentionally-targeted violence, precisely because they were the children of opposing groups.

In light of the above, giving priority to war-affected children within a human security agenda made sense for several reasons. First, the changing landscape of internal conflict meant the decoupling of the traditional notion that 'women and children' as victims face the same vulnerabilities in war. Today, given the targeting of children in conflict, the experiences of children are increasingly different than those of adults. As a result, children require separate protection and responses before, during, and after conflict. Second, globally, one in every three people is a child under fifteen years of age, while in some parts of the developing world, it is closer to one in two. Giving priority to the rights and well-being of children today contributes directly to our long-term human security goals. Third, in situations of war and conflict, children represent the majority of civilians affected by exposure to extreme violence. As violent social change and turbulence are likely to continue, more effective and concerted child protection is required. Finally, children are the most vulnerable group in society. The priority given to the well-being and development of children is an excellent measure of society's commitment to human development in general.

For Canada, giving priority to this issue made political sense as well. At the most basic level, both domestic and international audiences, government and nongovernmental, young and old, can understand the vulnerability of children in situations of armed conflict, and the imperative for effective protection of this most vulnerable group. Furthermore, many of our human security concerns were centrally part of the war-affected children's agenda (e.g. landmines, small arms, gender, and peacebuilding). Finally, in putting people's needs at the heart of Canadian foreign policy, Foreign Minister Lloyd Axworthy had also placed a special emphasis on children, particularly on child labourers and sexually exploited children. Adopting the theme of war-affected children seemed a natural next step for Canada.

WAR-AFFECTED CHILDREN:
THE CANADIAN RESPONSE

In many ways, the children's agenda preceded even the Canadian government's involvement in the campaign to ban antipersonnel mines. Before Mr Axworthy became minister of Foreign Affairs, the prime minister had appointed him as minister of Human Resources Development. In that portfolio, Axworthy was responsible for many of the major UN conventions on social policy. It was during this time that he was exposed to the myriad of the threats facing children, including the issues of child labour and the sexual exploitation of young people. Mr Axworthy brought the commitment to safeguarding children's rights that he further developed at Human Resources with him when he came to the Department of Foreign Affairs.

What was missing in Canada's foreign policy when he arrived, and what the minister set out to establish, was a strategic framework aimed at establishing a comprehensive children's agenda. In time it became clear that this aspect of the foreign policy agenda should focus specifically, but not exclusively, on those children at greatest risk – war-affected children.

In developing a strategy on war-affected children, the Canadian government's goals were threefold: first, to raise domestic and international awareness about the issue; second, to tackle the specific problem of child soldiers through the Optional Protocol on the Involvement of Children in Armed Conflict; and third, to consolidate international efforts for child protection. As it developed, Canadian initiatives on war-affected children were shaped primarily by two factors: (i) domestic circumstances, and (ii) the international agenda.

(i) domestic circumstances
Within the Canadian government, the broad agenda of war-affected children provided a solid and sustained entry point for various government departments, most notably, Foreign Affairs, the Canadian International Development Agency (CIDA), and the Department of National Defence (DND). In the Department of Foreign Affairs, treatment of the issue as part of the human security agenda ensured it would benefit from sustained attention. As well, within the UN system, the office of SRSG Otunnu and the UN Working Group for the Optional Protocol dealing with child soldiers justified increased time and effort to the issue. Within CIDA, child health, education, and the rehabilitation/reintegration of war-affected children was increasingly becoming part of postconflict programming. For DND, the Optional

Protocol impacted directly on the National Defence Act and recruiting practices. But beyond this obvious connection, military personnel are among the first to have immediate contact with child soldiers (on the battleground and with war-affected children in the delivery of humanitarian assistance). The three departments formed into an Interdepartmental Working Group to combine efforts and expertise and to develop practical and effective policy options. Policy coherence within the Canadian government meant that Canada could lead and often set the agenda in multilateral forums.

Canadian action on war-affected children followed three tracks: (i) political advocacy; (ii) humanitarian and development programming; and (iii) defence in action. Political advocacy described Canada's proactive strategy to raise awareness and to mainstream child protection: within the UN system (alongside SRSG Otunnu, Canada pushed for child protection in Security Council mandated peace support operations); within regional organizations (such as the Organization for Security and Cooperation in Europe (OSCE), the Organization of American States (OAS), and the Economic Community of West African States (ECOWAS); and in our bilateral relationships with other states and NGOs. Humanitarian and development programming focused on the more than $25 million (Cdn) which CIDA had provided to activities dealing with war-affected children in such countries as Angola, Liberia, Sierra Leone, Rwanda, and Uganda. Finally, defence in action centred on the role of the Canadian armed forces in promoting human security for children through peacekeeper training in child protection and constructive engagement with other militaries (such as the US and UK) on the issue of child soldiers.

An important aspect of Canadian policy development on this issue was the government's effective partnership with NGOs. Initially, Canada worked most closely with the Coalition to Stop the Use of Child Soldiers, but the coalition's narrow focus was in some ways an impediment to progress on the broader agenda. The issue of age of recruitment had not yet captured the imaginations of Canadian NGOs. Instead, the attention of the NGO Working Group on Children and Armed Conflict was on youth networks which brought Canadian and refugee children together to support those living in war. This emphasis on voices of youth was matched by efforts to ensure better protection for children on the ground. To formalize the collaboration between government and NGOs, Senator Landon Pearson (Minister Axworthy's Adviser on Children) was named chair of an NGO-Government Committee on War-Affected Children. This working structure resulted in greater policy coherence at three levels: the political, the bureaucratic, and within civil society. With the partnership between NGOs and the Canadian government already well advanced, we were ready to begin influencing the international agenda on war-affected children.

An important element in developing this agenda and familiarizing the Canadian public with its many aspects was the appointment of United Nations Children's Fund (UNICEF's) Nigel Fisher as a Special UN fellow in the Department of Foreign Affairs. Mr Fisher was given the task of working with government and civil society to develop Canada's strategy on war-affected children. He consulted with officials in the department and with the minister's advisers, and travelled the country speaking to Canadians on this critical issue – informing them of the reality for so many young people caught up in conflict situations and challenging them to take action.

(ii) the international agenda

When Canada began to seriously examine the plight of war-affected children, our international standing on this issue was strong as a result of the success of the Ottawa Convention banning landmines. Many of the NGOs who had been part of the landmines campaign were now also engaged in a new campaign to end the use of child soldiers. It seemed that the injustice behind the cynical use of children as soldiers had captured the world's attention.

I was abducted while my mother and I were going to the field ... One of the other abducted girls tried to escape but she was caught. The rebels told us that she had tried to escape and must be killed. They made the new children kill her. They told us that if we escaped, they would kill our families. They made us walk for a week ... Some of the smaller children could not keep up, as we were walking so far without resting, and they were killed ... Some of the children died of hunger. I felt lifeless seeing so many children dying and being killed. I thought I would be killed.[3]

Sharon, 13

Using testimonies such as these, the NGO Coalition to Stop the Use of Child Soldiers mobilized global public opinion around raising the minimum standard (Article 38 of the Convention on the Rights of the Child) for recruitment and participation in fighting factions, from fifteen years to eighteen years. The coalition held a series of regional meetings with governments and local NGOs to build momentum around the highest possible standard (eighteen years).

As a result of this movement, the issue of war-affected children became a highly politicized one, with governments breaking off into alliances based on age preference and the broader issue of war-affected children being swiftly swept aside. The Optional Protocol became a lightning rod, attracting attention away from the equally important issues of protection of children during conflict, programming for the welfare of children in armed conflict, and important preventive measures such as education for peace. It had divided the international community to such an extent that officials could not meet to discuss child protection measures without ending in an acrimonious debate about the minimum age of recruitment. (See the following case study, "The Optional Protocol on the Involvement of Children in Armed Conflict.")

On child soldiers, Canada's strategy comprised two objectives: to significantly raise the age standard; and to end the impasse over the Optional Protocol which had inadvertently prevented progress on the broader issue of protection of war-affected children. Canada was the first country to support the NGO coalition, and remained a close partner throughout the process leading up to the final UN session of the Working Group on the Optional Protocol. However, from the outset, Canada viewed child soldiers as numbering 300,000 within the millions of war-affected children, and never lost sight of the broader picture.

WITHIN THE UN SYSTEM

In the meantime, SRSG Otunnu had set up his office and had made a number of visits to countries to advocate on behalf of children. Initially, his efforts concentrated on obtaining commitments from warring factions not to recruit children under the age of eighteen. Fairly quickly however, Otunnu also turned his advocacy talents to the issue of mainstreaming child protection within the UN system. Canada actively supported him in this endeavour.

In August 1999, with Namibia in the presidency of the Security Council, Otunnu drafted a forward looking Resolution 1261 on the protection of children in armed conflict. In its operative paragraphs, the resolution called for the following: the appointment of child protection advisers to council-mandated peace support operations; child rights training for peacekeeping personnel; steps to ensure that the protection and welfare of children are taken into account during peace processes and negotiations; recognition of the deleterious impact of small arms on the security of civilians, particularly children; facilitation of the disarmament, demobilization and rehabilitation of child soldiers; and the rehabilitation and restoration of educational and health facilities for all war-affected children.

Canada was among the council members to cosponsor Namibia's groundbreaking resolution for child protection. During Canada's first presidency of the Security Council, under the theme of "Protection of Civilians," we invited SRSG Otunnu to address the council on the issue of war-affected children. In the ensuing *Report of the Secretary-General to the Security Council on the Protection of Civilians in Armed Conflict,* child protection was highlighted throughout and many of the recommendations built on the gains of Resolution 1261. Indeed, the protection and well-being of war-affected children featured prominently in many of Canada's Security Council activities, as we called for child protection advisors in mandated-missions to Kosovo, Sierra Leone, and the Democratic Republic of Congo.

Canada cultivated support for war-affected children in other fora as well. For instance, in preparation for the 27th Conference of the International Committee for the Red Cross (ICRC) in October, 1999, Canada sought to further highlight the issue of war-affected children. The Canadian government, in partnership with the Canadian Red Cross, put forward a pledge on war-affected children and convened a workshop on the same theme with the Colombian and Sierra Leonean National Societies. The objective was to begin to shift the global focus from the divisiveness of the Optional Protocol towards child protection. The pledge was purposefully noncontroversial in order to attract the widest support from both countries and the Red Cross/Red Crescent movement. In the end, the pledge attracted more than sixty signatures – close to forty of which were from governments (including Germany, Japan, Brazil, Mexico, Colombia, Sierra Leone, Ghana, South Africa, Norway, Sweden). Significantly, the United States delivered a statement in support of the Canadian pledge.

In the G-8, Canada and the United Kingdom developed an initiative on Children and Armed Conflict dealing with the political dimensions of the broad agenda. This included the need for military training; special attention to children during peace processes; explicit incorporation of child rights provisions into negotiated peace agreements; and full implementation of existing norms and standards. The United Kingdom and Canada took widely divergent positions on the Optional Protocol when it came to age of recruitment, but the two countries worked well together on other, equally pressing aspects of the agenda. The G-8 also seems poised to take forward the issue of war-affected children.

PLEDGE ON WAR-AFFECTED CHILDREN
1 To protect and assist children affected by armed conflict and to prevent the targeting of such children, inter alia:
– by respecting and promoting the rights and welfare of all children affected by armed conflict, including the right to education, birth registration, family reintegration, and protection from violence and exploitation;
– by addressing psycho-social as well as physical needs of war-affected children;
– by adopting a child-centered approach to humanitarian assistance.
2 To work to ensure the successful completion of a strong Optional Protocol on the Involvement of Children in Armed Conflict for the tenth Anniversary of the coming into force of the Convention on the Rights of the Child.
In so doing, we invite all governments, the Red Cross/Red Crescent Movement, civil society, and other relevant actors to work in partnership to realize these goals.

****

Signed by:
Governments:
Argentina, Brazil, Bulgaria, Canada, Chile, Colombia, Costa Rica, Czech Republic, Hungary, Ireland, Jamaica, Japan, Germany, Ghana, Guatemala, Lithuania, Luxembourg, Madagascar, Mexico, Morocco, Mozambique, Niger, Norway, Poland, Portugal, Slovakia, South Africa, Spain, Sweden, Switzerland, Thailand, Uruguay, and Venezuela
National Societies:
Barbados, Brazil, Canada, Croatia, Czech Republic, Equatorial Guinea, Gambia, Ghana, Guyana, Haiti, Hungary, Kenya, Lesotho, Liberia, Lithuania, Madagascar, Malawi, Mali, Morocco, Mozambique, Namibia, Niger, Poland, Sierra Leone, Slovakia, South Africa, Suriname, Togo, and Tunisia
International Conference of the Red Cross and Red Crescent Movement, Geneva, November 1999.

WEST AFRICAN CONFERENCE ON WAR-AFFECTED CHILDREN

In April 2000, Canada cohosted with Ghana a West African Conference on War-Affected Children. The conference brought together West African ministers, representatives from West African militaries, NGOs, and young people. The central aim of the conference was to launch regional initiatives for child protection. The conference succeeded as a regional initiative because it catalyzed political interest and commitment among other West African states. Two states in the subregion, Sierra Leone and Liberia, have been profoundly disturbed by conflict, and children have been the most prominent victims in both cases. More than 10 percent of the population of a third country, Guinea, is comprised of refugees from its two neighbours. Beyond these three states, virtually every country in the subregion has been affected in some way by smaller internal conflicts (e.g. currently in Senegal, Guinea-Bissau, and Nigeria) or by refugee flows. Equally important in securing a regional stake in the issue was the fact that West African governments have a track record, through the Military Observer Group of the Economic Community of West African States (ECOMOG) under Nigerian leadership, of paying the price in terms of lives, money, and political effort to intervene to deal with crises in their own region. Finally, the vicious attacks on children in West African conflicts seem to have highlighted the importance of strengthening implementation of traditional societal values and norms for child protection.

"One of the most basic human instincts is to protect one's child from harm and suffering. Children represent our global future and the desire to guard them from the many forces that can destroy their hope and innocence is universal. Doing so is an essential part of our broader aspiration to promote human security and to create stable, peaceful societies."

Address by Lloyd Axworthy, West African Conference on War-Affected Children, Accra, Ghana, 27 April 2000

What emerged from Accra was a substantive Declaration and Plan of Action for War-Affected Children within the subregion. For the first time, governments supported a full agenda on war-affected children, which included such elements as: a call to release all captive children, an agreement to honour a week of truce each year in solidarity with war-affected children to permit negotiations and humanitarian activities; training of military units in child rights; an end to impunity; the need for effective youth engagement in public meetings on issues which concern them (such as peace processes); and finally, the creation of a child protection unit within ECOWAS. Canada helped catalyze this made-in-Africa response to a crisis that has shaken the foundations of many West African communities. The resolve and commitment of African leaders to effectively address the issue of war-affected children, and to demonstrate this leadership to the rest of the world, was both moving and impressive.

These examples are meant to demonstrate Canada's commitment to the issue, and our willingness to promote it in both the human rights and the peace and security agendas. Canada will continue to advance the issue through the OSCE, the Francophonie, the Commonwealth, the OAS, and the G-8, among others, to build support for concrete initiatives for child protection.

CONCLUSION: THE CHALLENGE AHEAD

Whatever the causes of modern-day brutality towards children, the time has come to call a halt ... Its most fundamental demand is that children simply have no part in warfare. The international community must denounce this attack on children for what it is – intolerable and unacceptable.[4]

Despite the many advances in the area of child protection since Graça Machel first expressed moral outrage at the tragedy affecting children in situations of armed conflict, children continue to suffer the direct and indirect impact of extreme violence. The international community has not been successful in preventing the targeting, abduction, and suffering of war-affected children.

There are a few hopeful signs. First, the issue of war-affected children is being increasingly mainstreamed into the UN peace and security agenda. It is no longer viewed as purely a human rights issue, and now sits comfortably in the Security Council, in the Department of Political Affairs, and even in the Department for Peacekeeping Operations of the UN. With child protection advisers in relevant peace support operations, the needs of war-affected children will be taken into account.

Second, regional organizations are beginning to take account of those measures at their disposal to deal with the protection and needs of children in situations of armed conflict. Within ECOWAS, for example, the creation of a Child Protection Unit will ensure closer monitoring of children's rights, and will apply pressure on regional neighbours who are abusing the rights of children.

Third, the evolving international dialogue on dealing with nonstate actors will optimally lead to an internationally agreed upon code of conduct for rebel groups and their treatment of children. At the same time, there should be urgent consideration of those incentives and disincentives which may have effect in influencing the behaviour of nonstate actors.

Fourth, in every society, there exist fundamental norms for the care and protection of children. Increasingly, moral authorities, such as Graça Machel and Nelson Mandela, and leaders such as Ghanaian President J.J. Rawlings, and SRSG Olara Otunnu, are calling for a return to positive local values and norms for child protection. Local solutions to local problems will continue to be a critical part of preventing the targeting of children trapped in the midst of conflict. Local engagement is also critical for welcoming war-affected children back into their local communities and families.

Finally, the voices of young people on issues which affect them are being heard in fora which were previously reserved for the voices of the very few. For example, in May 2000, in New York at the PrepCom for the Special Session on Children, sitting alongside United Nations Children's Fund (UNICEF) Executive Director, Carol Bellamy, and Prof. Peter Piot, executive director, UN AIDS, was a young woman from Cote d'Ivoire, Mlle Hortense Me, speaking about the impact of AIDS on her community. In Canada's peacebuilding consultations, and as part of our working groups on issues which concern young people, we now have young voices assuming their rightful seat at the table. Effective youth engagement in the issue of war-affected children is perhaps the most encouraging sign, as young people have the energy, determination, and hope to change the future. And we, as adults, can work with them to realize their global goals.

Over the past two years, Canada has worked closely with other governments, the UN, and the NGO community to help build a legitimate and meaningful place for the needs and protection of children in peace, security, humanitarian, and development fora. These partnerships culminated in September 2000, when Minister Axworthy and the Canadian Minister for International Cooperation, Maria Minna, hosted the first Global Conference on War-Affected Children in Winnipeg. Mme Machel was the honorary chair of the conference.

AGENDA FOR WAR-AFFECTED CHILDREN

Societies have a moral obligation to put their children first, in times of peace and especially in times of war. Each child has the right to support and protection without distinction.

Conflict has the potential to forever change a child's aspirations and capabilities by subjecting him or her to horrific physical, psychological, sexual, and societal violence. While children have widely differing needs, experiences, and challenges during and postconflict situations, no child emerges unscarred and unaffected from conditions where killings, indiscriminate bombings, recruitment, torture, rape, sexual exploitation, forced labour, abductions, sickness, and malnutrition are a constant threat, and where education and nurture rarely exist. The international community must address this issue decisively, in accordance with the purposes and principles enshrined in the United Nations Charter. There is no circumstance in which it is justifiable to deliberately target children in situations of armed conflict.

The Convention on the Rights of the Child and other powerful regional and international legal instruments, including the 1951 Convention Relating to the Status of Refugees and its 1967 Protocol and the Geneva Conventions of 1949 and the Additional Protocols thereto of 1977 have been put in place to protect the rights and welfare of all war-affected children.   Notable recent advances include the Optional Protocol on Involvement of Children in Armed Conflict, the Optional Protocol on the Sale of Children, Child Prostitution and Child Pornography, and ILO Convention No. 182 on the Worst Forms of Child Labour.

What is needed now are concerted efforts to breathe life into the principles and obligations enshrined in these instruments through widespread ratification, effective implementation, and international cooperation. The results of this conference should provide building blocks for concrete initiatives for consideration at the United Nations General Assembly Special Session on Children in 2001.

It is time for states, institutions, and individuals around the world to show leadership in word and in deed. The depth of our commitment *today* to immediate action with and on behalf of war-affected girls and boys will determine their *future* commitment to peace.

Our commitment to this agenda at local, national, regional, and international levels is a commitment to children. Let us make this century a peaceful one, in which the rights of the child are respected, protected, and promoted everywhere.

1 Call for Leadership: Safeguarding children and protecting their rights in situations of armed conflict requires political, moral, economic, and social leadership.   It also demands the courage to shape a new consensus regarding the treatment of war-affected children. Leaders at all levels and in every sector of society – government, the private sector, civil society, international and regional organizations – must rise to the challenge to fulfill their responsibilities to protect children. Leadership must also be fostered directly within girls and boys, their families and their communities, to build their will and capacity to resolve and prevent conflict.

2 Fulfill Obligations: All states and other parties to armed conflict must respect fully their obligations to children affected by conflict under international human rights and humanitarian law. States are invited to sign, ratify, and subsequently implement the Optional Protocols to the Convention on the Rights of the Child on Involvement of Children in Armed Conflict and Sale of Children, Child Prostitution, and Child Pornography, and to consider or reconsider becoming parties to conventions and agreements related to the protection of children in armed conflict. Armed groups must also respect the child protection standards within international law regarding the rights and protection of children in armed conflict.

3 Increase Accountability and End Impunity: States should implement their international obligations to end impunity and to hold accountable perpetrators of violations of international human rights and humanitarian law.   States should ensure that effective accountability mechanisms are in place at the national, regional, and international levels.   In particular, we recognize the historical significance of the establishment of the International Criminal Court (ICC) to ending impunity for perpetrators of certain crimes committed against children, as defined in the Rome Statute of the International Criminal Court (art. 8), inter alia those involving sexual violence or child soldiers, and thus to the prevention of such crimes, and we encourage states to consider signing and ratifying the Rome Statute.

The international community, through the media and other appropriate mechanisms, must mobilize international opinion and action against the abuses of children's rights during armed conflicts, and, bearing in mind states' primary responsibility, must ensure that those who violate children's rights in situations of armed conflict, or collude in such violations, are identified and brought to justice for their actions. An environment of accountability also demands a commitment to the monitoring, reporting, and prosecution of genocide, war crimes, crimes against humanity, and other egregious crimes perpetrated against children.

4 End Targeting of Children: The international community condemns the killing, maiming, torture, rape, sexual exploitation, abduction, forced labour, and other violations of the rights of the child in preconflict, conflict, and postconflict situations, taking into account the particular vulnerabilities of girls.   We also condemn the recruitment and use of children in armed conflict in violation of international law, attacks on and the military use of protected places that usually have a significant presence of children, such as schools, hospitals, and homes. We must strengthen efforts to end all these practices. All peacekeeping missions should receive child-sensitive training and include child protection advisers or units to safeguard the rights of children. Whenever sanctions are imposed in the context of armed conflict, their impact on children should be assessed and monitored and, to the extent that there are humanitarian exemptions, they should be child-focused and formulated with clear guidelines for their application.

5 Release Abducted Children: States, international and regional organizations, nongovernmental organizations (NGOs), community leaders, the private sector, families, and youth must pressure parties to armed conflict, and those who fund and support them, to unconditionally release all abducted children into safe custody. We demand and are committed to ensuring that these girls and boys are

returned, rehabilitated, (re)integrated, and reunited with their families. We demand that those abducted children who have been involved in armed conflicts are also disarmed and demobilized.

6 Strengthen Humanitarian Assistance and Guarantee Access: Full, safe, and unhindered humanitarian access and the delivery of humanitarian assistance in conformity with international humanitarian law to all children affected by armed conflict in all regions must be ensured regardless of sex, race, religion, ethnicity, nationality, or political affiliation. Such humanitarian assistance must include the provision of basic social services, in particular, food, nutrition, health, and education, during and postconflict.

7 Focus on Prevention: States, international and regional organizations, NGOs, community leaders, the private sector, families, and youth must address, in concrete terms, the root causes of conflict, including inequity, poverty, racism, ineffective governance, and impunity, which lead to the denial of children's economic, social, cultural, civil, and political rights. We commit to practical and comprehensive conflict prevention measures, including conflict prevention initiatives, mediation, child protection networks, early warning and response systems, alternatives for adolescents at risk, and the promotion of conflict resolution skills and education.

8 Suffocate the Supply of Arms: States commit to addressing the impact of small arms and light weapons on war-affected children. We recognize that the illicit trade in natural resources and illegal drugs, and the illicit production and trafficking of small arms and light weapons have devastating effects on children. States and the private sector must also ensure that funds and facilities are not used by armed groups which target children for participation in armed conflict.

9 Promote Health and Well-being: Initiatives designed to help war-affected children must be developed to address all the needs of the child – mind, body, and spirit. These initiatives must take into account the widely differing needs, experiences, and challenges faced by girls and boys, adolescents and younger children, refugee and internally displaced children, child soldiers and orphans, children from different religious and ethnic backgrounds, and children with disabilities. All children, particularly girls, must be protected from rape and other forms of sexual and gender-based violence in situations of armed conflict. The international community must work with families, local communities, governments, civil society, including NGOs, and relevant international organizations to improve access to basic health and psycho-social rehabilitative services for girls and boys during conflict and postconflict situations. Health risks to children must also be reduced and eliminated, including malnutrition and preventable diseases.

10 Protect Children from HIV/AIDS: The international community must pay particular attention to the impact of the HIV/AIDS pandemic on war-affected children and intensify efforts against its spread. This includes awareness and training.

11 Educate and Equip for Peace: States, international and regional organizations, NGOs, and community leaders must ensure that access to education is rapidly restored, supported, and strengthened during conflict and postconflict situations. Specific educational initiatives should be taken in order to empower young people to relate peaceably with one another and end violence in families and communities. Additional opportunities, such as vocational training and recreation, should also be supported to promote children's healing and well-being.

   The provisions of human rights and humanitarian law protecting children must be made widely known, in particular, through training programs for military personnel, humanitarian aid workers, peacekeepers, and young people.

12 Concerted Action over the Long-term: The physical and psychological effects of war can debilitate the growing minds and bodies of children for many years. The international community, especially states, must coordinate long-term efforts, for war-affected girls and boys, their families, and their communities, to ensure their support and protection during conflict and post-conflict situations. In particular, the international community should actively support endeavours to address the devastating impact of landmines on children, through demining, rehabilitation of mine-affected children, and landmine awareness programs. Development cooperation must be sustained, consistent, and effective to support children's long-term needs for rehabilitation and (re)integration.

13 Engage Youth: War-affected children, particularly adolescents, should be involved in peace processes and in developing policy and programming for their own rehabilitation, (re)integration, and education, as well as in the development of their communities. We must also support the creation of networks between these war-affected children and other concerned youth.

14 Promote Better Research to Inform Our Action: We commit to improving the quality of our research, monitoring, and evaluation, giving greater emphasis to data disaggregated based on sex, age, ethnicity, and region, and to disseminating the results of this work more widely.

Agreed by 132 governments in
Winnipeg, Canada, 17 September 2000

The conference had two basic aims: to take stock of international progress since 1996, when Graça Machel presented her report, *The Impact of Armed Conflict on Children*; and to consolidate concrete goals and practical actions for child protection. The objectives of the conference have been captured in a "Twelve Point Plan of Action on War-Affected Children" (see text box). In preparation for the conference, the governments of Canada and Norway commissioned a review of the original Machel study which, on a chapter-by-chapter basis, examines progress in implementing Mme Machel's recommendations nationally, regionally, and internationally. The Graça Machel + 5 Review will include new chapters which take into account emerging issues which have a direct impact on war-affected children; namely, small arms, HIV/AIDS, media and communications; peace and security; and gender. The review also will make new recommendations for global action into the next decade.

Our hope is that this conference will help galvanize global public opinion against those who choose to harm children through armed conflict. The international community must demonstrate the requisite political will to act definitively in tangible and unified support of the world's most vulnerable citizens. The challenge ahead is to strengthen the capacity of both governments and civil society so that the non-violent resolution of conflict will replace the resort to violence, and that children will no longer be the victims of such conflict.

NOTES

1 United Nations, Graça Machel, *Impact of Armed Conflict on Children* (A/51/306), 26 August 1996.
2 The term "war-affected children" refers to all children under eighteen years who are directly or indirectly affected by war. Unlike current UN terminology of "children and armed conflict," the term "war-affected children" is not context-specific. It allows for a broader conception of the impact of armed violence on children as it also applies to children living in countries which are no longer in the midst of armed conflict but are recovering from a period of violence.
3 Human Rights Watch, *The Scars of Death: Children Abducted by the Lord's Resistance Army in Uganda* (New York: Human Rights Watch, 1997), 18.
4 United Nations, Graça Machel, *Study on the Impact of Armed Conflict*, 9.

REFERENCES

Bennett, Elizabeth, Virginia Gamba, with the assistance of Sarah Meek. *ACT Against Child Soldiers in Africa: A Reader*. South Africa: Institue for Security Studies, 2000.

Brett, Rachel and Margaret McCallin. *Children: The Invisible Soldiers.* Stockholm: Rädda Barnen, 1998.

Guiding Principles on Internal Displacement. Office for the Coordination of Humanitarian Affairs, 1998.

Hampton, Janie, ed. *Internally Displaced People: A Global Survey.* London: Earthscan, 1998.   <http://www.nrc.no/global_idp_survey/internally_displaced_people.htm>

Human Rights Watch. *The Scars of Death: Children Abducted by the Lord's Resistance Army in Uganda.* New York: Human Rights Watch, 1997.

In the Firing Line: War and Children's Rights. London: Amnesty International, 1999.

Plan of Action Concerning Children in Armed Conflict. Geneva: Red Cross and Red Crescent Movement, 1995.

The State of the World's Children 1996. Geneva/New York: UNICEF, 1996.

United Nations. Machel, Graça. *The Impact of Armed Conflict on Children.* (A/51/306), 26 August 1996.

CASE STUDY

The Optional Protocol
on the Involvement of Children
in Armed Conflict

ROSS SNYDER

The plight of war-affected children is one of the most devastating tragedies of our time. The pictures are haunting: children who have suffered physical and psychological injury, with fear and desperation on their faces. By now, the statistics are well known: millions of children caught up and scarred by the emotional, physical, sexual, psychological brutality of war and conflict. This includes children who have lost their parents, their homes, their schools, and the ability to play. It also comprises an estimated 300,000 who have served fighting factions – whether as soldiers, sexual slaves, or water carriers. Still others have witnessed inhuman acts against their families and carry the memories with them. The human security agenda challenges us to examine the issue of war-affected children from the perspective of those children. The problem is multifaceted, and the solutions must also be multifaceted.

Among the strategies to address the problem of war-affected children, the strengthening of international norms and standards has been one of the more high-profile efforts in the past several years. A broad range of countries and organizations have argued that work in this area, indeed, can make a significant contribution by putting into place a set of standards that, if enforced, will lead to the elimination of the use of soldiers under the age of eighteen.

New international norms work at several levels. Governments that ratify the norms can change national laws in a way that allows for taking action against rebel groups that employ child soldiers. International organizations that work with children can use the new norms to negotiate, using moral and political suasion with national governments or nonstate actors on behalf of the affected children. Of course, the impact can only be relatively limited without effective enforcement, and some have questioned the development of new norms when existing standards are routinely violated. The response must be that the strengthening of norms and improved enforcement of existing standards need to proceed in parallel. By the same token, strengthening norms and enforcing existing norms have only limited impact without efforts in other related fields, such as the political engagement of the parties involved in conflict, along with humanitarian action and appropriate development assistance.

In January 2000, the international community completed six years of often difficult negotiations on an Optional Protocol to the Convention on the Rights of the Child on Involvement of Children in Armed Conflict. The final negotiating session attracted considerable attention, and had its own share of drama. Indeed, the agreement on a final text was not certain until almost the last minute. That an agreement was achieved against some considerable odds underlines the degree to which the issue of war-affected children in the past several years has captured the conscience of the public, of civil society, and of governments. The result was a text that substantially advances international standards in regard to the use of child soldiers. The Optional Protocol was opened for signature on 5 June 2000, and Canada was the first country to sign and ratify the instrument. It will come into force three months after the deposit of the tenth instrument of ratification or accession.

THE ORIGINS OF THE OPTIONAL PROTOCOL

The reasons that governments felt compelled to develop an Optional Protocol go back to the negotiations on the Convention on the Rights of the Child in the 1980s. Before then, international law relating to the minimum age for recruitment and participation in hostilities was largely contained in Additional Protocols I and II to the four Geneva Conventions of 1949, which set the age for involvement in armed conflict at fifteen years. This tended to mirror international practice shortly after World War Two in which the school leaving age in many countries was fifteen. The Convention on the Rights of the Child, which was adopted by the UN General Assembly in 1989 and came into force in 1990, defined a child as "every human being below the age of 18 years unless, under the law applicable to the child, majority is attained earlier."[1] A number of governments sought to have this age also apply to military recruitment and participation in hostilities, but were unable to get broad agreement on such a standard. In fact, there was considerable divisiveness on this issue. As a result, negotiators decided essentially to reiterate existing international law by including Article 38, which contains the following three provisions:

- States parties undertake to respect and ensure respect for rules of international humanitarian law applicable to them in armed conflicts which are relevant to the child.
- States parties shall take all feasible measures to ensure that persons who have not attained the age of fifteen years do not take a direct part in hostilities.
- States parties shall refrain from recruiting any person who has not attained the age of fifteen years into their armed forces. In recruiting among those persons who have attained the age of fifteen years but who have not attained the age of eighteen years, states parties shall endeavour to give priority to those who are oldest.

Within three years of the adoption of the Convention on the Rights of the Child, there were renewed efforts to address the issue of age of recruitment and participation. Initially, the Committee on the Rights of the Child, set up to monitor implementation of the Convention on the Rights of the Child, recommended in 1993 the adoption of an Optional Protocol to raise the age to eighteen. The World Conference on Human Rights in 1993 also called for action in this area. In turn, the Commission on Human Rights in 1994 established an open-ended working group (i.e. open to all countries) to develop a draft Optional Protocol. The working group first met in 1994, and continued its work until January 2000.

Old divisions did not disappear, and by early 1998, the working group had reached an impasse, not surprisingly on the key issues of age of recruitment and participation. Indeed, the February 1998 session proved to be quite contentious and ended early because of the very strong disagreements on these questions. Some countries also wished to address a number of related issues such as the applicability of age limits to military schools and the extent to which the Optional Protocol should apply to so-called nonstate actors.

KEY ISSUES AND KEY ACTORS

There were several main camps on the complex issue of age. One group held that the Optional Protocol should set the age at eighteen for both recruitment and participation (the "straight-18" position), even if it meant that a few influential governments were unlikely to ratify. This group argued that it was especially important for developed countries to set this high standard to show they were part of a coalition demonstrating moral leadership. They also noted that since the Optional Protocol was "optional" in any event, the aim should be to achieve the highest standard, that would not be diluted or compromised. Over time, others would become parties as they became convinced of its value. Another group saw the main objective as preventing the use of those under eighteen in conflict, and that the focus, therefore, should be on age of participation. A third group argued that the emphasis should be on enforcing existing standards for governments, while exacting the highest possible standards from nonstate actors. The result of the 1998 session was the tabling of a chairman's report that contained a "rolling text" of the negotiated draft text with numerous "square bracketed" sections showing areas of disagreement, and a "chair's perception text" outlining what the chairman thought could be an agreed text based on his informal discussions and sense of the negotiations. It was also agreed that rather than having a formal session in 1999, the chair should pursue informal consultations to determine if agreement was possible on an Optional Protocol. As it turned out, this "recess" proved to be important in building international pressure to complete the negotiations.

During the course of 1998 and 1999, the problem of war-affected children increasingly came into the limelight. Disturbing images of child soldiers involved in conflicts in such countries as Uganda, Sierra Leone, Burma, and Colombia haunted television screens. Following on the landmark Graça Machel report on the impact of conflict on children, the UN secretary-general appointed a new Special Representative for Children and Armed Conflict, Olara Otunnu. A number of nongovernmental organizations (NGOs) formed a new "Coalition to Stop the Use of Child Soldiers" that actively lobbied governments and international organizations. The coalition, based in Geneva, initially focused its energies in northern countries, and its core leadership and membership were largely European and North American. In time, its membership base broadened. In turn, the issue of war-affected children came increasingly onto the agendas of such international and regional organizations as the United Nations (UN), the Organization of American States (OAS), the Organization for Security and Cooperation in Europe (OSCE), and the Organization for African Unity (OAU), thanks to the work of the coalition and a number of like-minded governments, including Canada.

In virtually all cases, the problem of international norms and the un-finished business around the Optional Protocol remained at centre stage. The coalition, with a small budget, but with a significant and active network, played a particularly important role in keeping the issue of child soldiers on the international agenda. It organized high-profile regional conferences in Mozambique, Uruguay, and Germany to highlight its agenda.

The result was to lend a sense of urgency to the negotiating session of the working group set for January 2000. A number of governments met several times informally, often with NGOs, to try to develop common approaches. Canada, for example, hosted a workshop for representatives from foreign and defence ministries in May 1999 to compare legislative practices. In November and December, 1999, there was an informal consultation in Ottawa of experts aimed at strengthening the draft text in a number of areas and adding new elements. The paper coming out of that latter meeting became the basis for much of the discussion in Geneva, and resulted in a number of additional strengthening provisions in the final text. All the while, the new chair of the Working Group, Ambassador Catherine von Heidenstam of Sweden, quietly met with governments and NGOs in Geneva and in capitals, also with the aim of determining possible outcomes. Behind the scenes political negotiations conducted some times at the highest level of government were also instrumental in reaching an agreement.

THE FINAL NEGOTIATIONS

By January 2000, the key divisive issues remained the following:

- age of voluntary recruitment
- age of participation in hostilities;
- whether there should be an exception for military schools;
- applicability to nonstate actors.

At the same time, it became clear shortly after delegates arrived in Geneva for the negotiations that there was strong political will to produce a result. The increased awareness manifested since the last round was having its effect. Governments also were conscious that in the period leading to the 2001 UN Special Session on Children, it would be politically costly to leave unfinished an important piece of legal infrastructure. The Canadian view and that of a number of others was that not having an agreement was getting in the way of focusing on other elements of the war-affected children agenda. At the outset, it was clear to delegations that agreement on the age of eighteen for recruitment was not feasible, and other ways of addressing recruitment were needed. However, there were real prospects of reaching closure on other issues, although the age for participation had the potential to be very difficult.

The spirit of compromise brought to Switzerland was initiated in a Canada–US summit between Prime Minister Chrétien and President Clinton in October 1999. Prospects for agreement on language for the optional protocol had been stalled in large part due to reluctance on the part of the United States to accept higher minimum ages for recruitment and deployment than were currently in place. At the summit, the two leaders recognized the importance of a compromise, and they focused on the age of deployment rather than the age of recruitment as the decisive issue. Without this personal engagement in the issue by politicians in both governments, the Optional Protocol might not have been agreed.

The success of this effort would also not have been possible without major efforts at coalition building within cabinet and between departments in the government of Canada. The help and cooperation of the Canadian Department of National Defence and Defence Minister Art Eggleton was essential in allowing Canada to take the active stance it did on the protocol. Minister Eggleton worked hard with Minister Axworthy to find an agreeable way forward that preserved the integrity of the protocol, while respecting certain traditions of recruitment in the Canadian Armed Forces. In the end that interaction proved decisive.

Back in Geneva, the two-week session became in large measure a classic multilateral negotiation. The use of "informals" proved to be a particularly efficient way of moving the discussions along. For each of the major issues, individual country representatives agreed to act as co-ordinators and met with other interested delegations to hammer out agreed texts. The chair became directly involved if there was a genuine impasse in one of the informals. This flexibility of approach allowed for considerable negotiating out of the limelight. Several countries, including Canada, played a key role in the background, including through the drafting of alternative texts. This was especially important in the contentious areas of age of recruitment and participation. In the end, many delegations demonstrated considerable flexibility. For example:

- Age of voluntary recruitment was raised to sixteen, short of what many had hoped for, but there were provisions for safeguards designed to ensure that those under eighteen are not sent into hostilities.

- Age of participation was raised to eighteen, a move that will require some countries, notably the US, to change operational practices. However, some of the language was not as strong as many delegations would have preferred.
- Those countries not parties to the Convention on the Rights of the Child, in particular the US (Somalia being the only other nonparty), will be allowed to become parties to the Optional Protocol, but in doing so agree to abide by those parts of the Convention on the Rights of the Child relevant to the Optional Protocol. Debate on this issue went down to the last half hour of the time allotted for the session.
- There are references to the importance of international assistance and cooperation, which some would have wished to contain a stronger undertaking by developed countries to provide financial assistance.

In the end, the new Optional Protocol can claim a number of significant advances in requiring states parties to:

- set eighteen years as the minimum age for compulsory recruitment, and for recruitment and participation by nonstate actors;
- take all feasible measures to ensure that members of their armed forces who are under the age of eighteen years do not take a direct part in hostilities; and
- raise the minimum age for voluntary recruitment to at least sixteen years while obliging states parties to deposit a binding declaration describing safeguards undertaken to ensure that recruitment is genuinely voluntary, is done with parental consent and reliable proof of age, and that recruits are fully informed of the duties involved in military service.

Although the Optional Protocol may not fully meet the objectives of all those involved in the negotiations, the text marks significant progress in setting standards on the issue of war-affected children. It reflects the determination of many in the international community, the importance of political negotiations, and should be considered an important contribution in the effort to eliminate the use of children as combatants.

LESSONS LEARNED

As noted, the form and process of the negotiation was relatively traditional; states engaged in a working group that developed a text by consensus, with good use of informals and "informal informals" (the latter involving a small number of countries drafting texts that were then presented to the larger informal groups). The forum was also open, with the coalition and representatives from the UN system effectively full partners in many of the negotiations and development of texts. An interesting element, referred to earlier, was the extensive work by governments and the coalition that took place during the period when the formal talks were suspended. This is perhaps one of the more important lessons from the negotiations – that thorough, patient, and low-key preparation can, indeed, be central to achieving a result in difficult, divisive negotiations.

Would a different form of negotiation have produced a stronger Optional Protocol? A few governments contemplated abandoning the working group process and the Optional Protocol altogether in the absence of a straight-eighteen result, and moving to a process akin to that used for the Landmines Treaty outside the UN. This would have resulted in a new legal instrument that would have involved only governments committed to the straight-eighteen approach. Many others, however, thought that the priority should be an improved standard that gained wide acceptance. At least in theory such an approach would benefit a larger number of children, even at the cost of a straight-eighteen outcome. In the end, the purist approach did not gain broad support. In part, this may have been because many of those involved in the issue of war-affected children believed that the Optional Protocol was one in a series of political, humanitarian, and developmental measures aiming to address the problem of war-affected children. The general view was that the Optional Protocol, as finally agreed, represented an advance in standards and did not close out options for future improvements.

The Optional Protocol will assist the work of UNICEF, the Secretary-General's Special Representative for Children and Armed Conflict, and the Red Cross by establishing a clear international norm. A number of governments proposing to ratify the Optional Protocol will need to change existing practices on recruitment and deployment, while others, like Canada, are taking or have taken steps to entrench into law existing procedures that already comply with the Optional Protocol. Even before the instrument comes into force, there are indications that some armed groups are prepared to consider the Optional Protocol as "guidance" and to make some effort to abide by its spirit. While these are promising developments, Canada and many other governments and organizations remain committed to carrying on with work across the full range of issues related to war-affected children.

NOTES

1 *The Convention on the Rights of the Child,* November 1989.

REFERENCES

Convention on the Rights of the Child. New York, November 1989.
Optional Protocol to the Convention on the Rights of the Child on the Involvement of Children in Armed Conflict. Geneva, May 2000.

Tun Channareth, corecipient of the 1997 Nobel Peace Prize, distributing literature for the International Campaign to Ban Landmines. Photograph by John Rodstead

Lloyd Axworthy at the signing of the Ottawa Convention banning landmines in the presence of Prime Minister Jean Chrétien, UN Secretary-General Kofi Annan, ICRC President Cornelio Sommaruga, and ICBL Coordinator Jody Williams (5 December 1997). Photograph by Tom Hanson, CP Picture Archive

Revolutionary United Front (RUF) soldiers at their base in the outskirts of Freetown, Sierra Leone (10 June 1997). Photograph by Enric Marti, CP Picture Archive

Mozambican woman voting in first postconflict election with Canadian election monitors observing. Photograph by Bruce Paton, CIDA/ACDI

RCMP sergeant assisting a Haitian police officer in Port-au-Prince, Haiti (1996).
Photograph by Paul Chiasson, CP Picture Archive

Canadian forensics expert investigating a mass grave site outside Pristina, Kosovo (30 June 1999). Photograph by David Brauchli, CP Picture Archive

Australian soldier patrolling the streets in Dili, East Timor following the arrival of the multinational peacekeeping force (22 September 1999). Photograph by Maya Vidon, CP Picture Archive

A young double amputee running as part of his rehabilitation program at an orthopedic centre in central Angola (15 January 1997). Photograph by Giovanni Diffidenti, CP Picture Archive

6 The Evolution of International Humanitarian Law

DARRYL ROBINSON
AND VALERIE OOSTERVELD

International humanitarian law (IHL) is primarily directed at promoting humane standards of behaviour in situations of armed conflict, a time when human security is most at risk. IHL consists of numerous rules and principles governing parties to armed conflict, requiring, for example, that combatants distinguish between military and civilian targets; that civilians not be the deliberate target of operations; and that methods of warfare causing unnecessary suffering be avoided. It also contains detailed rules requiring that civilians, prisoners of war, and the sick and wounded within a party's power be treated humanely.

The context in which IHL must be applied is changing dramatically. There has been a marked rise in violent internal armed conflicts – wars fought between factions entirely within a state's borders. In these new conflicts, civilians are increasingly in the line of fire or even deliberately targeted for appalling violence. IHL has correspondingly evolved and adapted to a changing world, both in response to the altered nature of conflict, and also due to the emergence of a people-centred approach to security.

While this area of international law has traditionally developed slowly and incrementally, in the last decade it has undergone revolutionary change. IHL has been invigorated by a synergy between the ground-breaking jurisprudence of the ad hoc tribunals, the development of the International Criminal Court (ICC) Statute, and national initatives. IHL has entered into an unprecedented period in which texts from only a few years ago have already been overtaken by developments. Thus, it has been observed that IHL as a body of law has recently "come of age."[1]

Nevertheless, while important gains have clearly been made, there still remains considerable resistance to developments in this area, as many states remain very hesitant about IHL. The traditional concern is that IHL should not become a means of interfering with national sovereignty, a concern that has increased because so many conflicts are now internal. This concern has been manifested in resistance not only to the development of new principles or rules, but even to modest commitments to promote compliance, such as providing access to monitors or providing information on national IHL activities. In addition, military powers and states engaged in conflict have sought to preserve a great deal of flexibility in their military practices.

Even more problematically, actual compliance with IHL in many of today's conflicts is abysmal, with massive violations of even the most basic rules being commonplace. The problems of enforcement and the means of promoting compliance will, therefore, also be discussed below.

EXPANDING THE REACH OF HUMANITARIAN LAW

IHL has been around for quite some time, reflected both in customary law and in important treaties such as the Hague Conventions of 1899 and 1907, the Geneva Conventions of 1949, and the Additional Protocols thereto of 1977. The resulting body of law has been valuable in promoting humane standards of behaviour, but it focuses on a classical concept of international armed conflict, namely conflict between regular armed forces of different states. The greatest challenge for human security today is the regulation of *noninternational*, or internal, armed conflicts.

In contrast to international armed conflicts, where states have perceived a reciprocity of interest in establishing basic rules, internal armed conflicts have often been regarded as a matter for domestic discretion, providing governments with the maximum latitude in fighting rebels. Many states have been more inclined to look after their own interests than community concerns or humanitarian demands. Obtaining any acknowledgement at all of rules applicable in internal armed conflict has, therefore, been a slow and difficult struggle. Even where treaty provisions provided some grudging recognition of the most elementary rules applicable in internal armed conflict, these provisions did not provide for individual criminal responsibility for serious violations.[2] At the start of the 1990s, it was still received wisdom that violations in internal armed conflicts were not "war crimes," i.e. that they did not give rise to criminal liability.

The recent recognition of the concept of war crimes in internal armed conflicts is one of the most profound but least heralded results of the ascendency of human security as an international priority. Over the last few years, several developments have prompted the international community to insist that vital humanitarian concerns not be overshadowed by narrow sovereignty concerns. The increasing prevalence, scale, and cruelty of internal armed conflicts effectively demanded a response if IHL is to remain relevant in today's world. Internal armed conflicts have not only eclipsed international conflicts in number, but they have also given rise to the most shocking atrocities, with civilians being terrorized and persecuted by reason of their race or ethnicity. At the same time, many states have become more willing to focus on the security of individual human beings, and to take firmer steps to promote basic standards of decency. The work of the ad hoc tribunals has also accelerated developments, by interpreting and applying IHL and breathing life into these doctrines.

The adoption by the Security Council of the Statute of the International Criminal Tribunal for Rwanda (ICTR), which recognized jurisdiction over war crimes in internal armed conflicts, was a major step forward. The jurisprudence subsequent to the creation of the International Criminal Tribunal for the former Yugoslavia (ICTY) continued this momentum, holding that the most well-established prohibitions from international armed conflicts might now be regarded as applicable in internal conflicts. This process of extension was continued with the adoption of the ICC Statute. Despite initial opposition from a determined minority of states, Canada and other like-minded states insisted on recognition of war crimes in internal armed conflicts.[3] In the result, the ICC Statute recognizes a significant list of well-established prohibitions from international armed conflict as also being applicable in noninternational armed conflicts.

This process of "blurring" the legal differences between international and internal armed conflict must continue, as there is still a gap in the extent of regulation of the two types of conflict. The different treatment is the product of the historical development of this area of law, but there is no compelling moral reason for the distinction to remain as extensive as it is. Future efforts of the international community will likely be aimed at further narrowing these differences, and a study of customary international law by the International Committee of the Red Cross, expected to be completed in the near future, may help advance this process. At present, however, resistance from cautious states remains strong.

Another important development in recent years is the clear affirmation that crimes against humanity are punishable not only when committed in armed conflict, but also during internal disturbances or peacetime. This issue was still being debated only a few years ago, and indeed the ICTY Statute adopted in 1993 restricted its jurisdiction over crimes against humanity to those committed during an armed conflict. Only one year later, however, the ICTR Statute was adopted, recognizing crimes against humanity without any such restriction. Jurisprudence of the ICTY has affirmed that crimes against humanity can occur even in the absence of armed conflict. This issue was hotly contested during the ICC negotiations, but eventually agreement was reached on a Canadian-proposed definition of crimes against humanity, affirming that there is no requirement of armed conflict.

Other steps are being taken to expand the scope of IHL to apply to more people in more situations. In 1999, on the fiftieth anniversary of the Geneva Conventions, the UN secretary-general announced that United Nation's (UN) forces engaged as combatants would be bound by fundamental rules of international humanitarian law,[4] removing any ambiguity over the legal nature and status of UN forces under UN command. The ICC Statute, adopted in 1998, affirmed that the principle of command responsibility includes not only military commanders but also civilian leaders and other persons in authority. The definitions of crimes in the ICC Statute, and in particular the definition of crimes against humanity, clearly encompass nonstate actors. Moreover, discussions are underway to identify any possible remaining gaps in human rights and humanitarian law protection and to identify "fundamental standards of humanity" applicable in all situations – including internal violence, disturbances, tensions, and public emergency – from which no derogation is permitted. These discussions have highlighted the interplay between IHL and international human rights law and the gradual process of cross-fertilization and convergence between these bodies of law.

BUILDING NEW NORMS: PROTECTING THE VULNERABLE

As has been graphically demonstrated in recent conflicts, civilians are not only suffering as a result of armed conflict, but they also have become the deliberate targets of war. The last decade has seen considerable advances in responding to the specific problems of vulnerable groups, which had not been adequately addressed under previously existing general rules.

For example, women have been particularly targeted for rape and other forms of sexual violence by combatants as a form of intimidation and torture, and as a means of terrorizing a population. In the last decade, important strides have been taken to overcome the traditional hesitance to recognize and deal with such atrocities. A 1992 report by a commission of experts appointed to investigate war crimes in the former Yugoslavia was precedent-setting. It not only investigated and documented accounts of rape and other forms of sexual violence, but it analyzed evidence pointing to a policy of rape. Rape was recognized as a crime against humanity in the ICTY Statute and then identified both as a crime against humanity and as a war crime in the ICTR Statute. In 1998, Canada was instrumental in ensuring the inclusion of a detailed list of sexual and gender-based crimes in the ICC Statute, including not only rape but also sexual slavery, enforced prostitution, forced pregnancy, enforced sterilization, and persecution on the basis of gender.

Children are especially vulnerable during armed conflict. They are recruited as under-age soldiers, or are murdered because they might be so recruited. Children are forced into sexual and domestic slavery, and are used as human shields. Increasing recognition of the effects of war on children has led to several important initiatives. In 1998, the ICC Statute was adopted, recognizing as a war crime the conscription or enlistment of children under the age of fifteen years into armed forces or using them to participate actively in hostilities. On 21 January 2000, a draft Optional Protocol to the Convention on the Rights of the Child on Involvement of Children in Armed Conflict was concluded, raising the minimum age levels – the age of conscription at eighteen, voluntary recruitment above fifteen, and the use of children in conflict situations at eighteen.

UN personnel and humanitarian aid workers are another group that is frequently-targeted, often as part of a deliberate effort to undermine peacebuilding efforts. The international community has taken some steps to respond to this problem, for example, by adopting the Convention on the Safety of UN and Associated Personnel, which provides protection in certain operations for UN personnel and persons deployed by humanitarian nongovernmental organizations under agreement with the UN. Further measures to protect humanitarian aid workers are necessary, in order to broaden the protective coverage for both UN and non-UN humanitarian personnel, including locally-engaged staff.

Recent initiatives to ban or otherwise limit certain weapons are another essential means to protect civilians and promote human security. The Ottawa Convention prohibiting antipersonnel mines is an obvious example. A new challenge is to address the proliferation of small arms and light weapons, especially because of the clear link with child soldiers: as weapons become smaller and lighter, ever younger children are being recruited and conscripted to fight. The UN is currently holding a series of preparatory meetings on small arms and light weapons, culminating in an international conference in 2001.

Not only are civilians extremely vulnerable in armed conflict situations, but civilian property is as well. In 1999, a Second Protocol to the Hague Convention of 1954 for the Protection of Cultural Property in the Event of Armed Conflict was adopted. Building on the ICC Statute, the Second Protocol specifically defines serious violations which result in individual criminal responsibility, such as theft, pillage or misappropriation of protected cultural property, whether occurring in international or internal armed conflict.

PROMOTING COMPLIANCE

As the previous sections have indicated, the building of new norms in IHL – both to enhance protection of vulnerable groups and to expand the reach of IHL – has been and continues to be a vital endeavour. But the critical failure, and therefore the critical front for progress, has been the *implementation* of those norms.

Several factors, flowing from the changed nature of armed conflict, have exacerbated this breakdown in compliance. In traditional state-to-state conflict, which involved professional armies under military discipline, adherence to IHL (and particularly the distinction between military and civilian targets) was consistent with the prevailing military logic. However, the new circumstances of today's conflicts commonly feature failed or failing states and bitter internecine struggles. Fighting is carried out by insurgent groups with weak chains of command, ineffective military discipline, and minimal awareness of or interest in IHL. Moreover, civilians are commonly perceived as primary targets, whether for reasons of ethnic hatred or in order to spread terror. In such circumstances, the application of IHL is under even greater strain than in traditional interstate conflict situations. Thus, even as the norms have grown stronger, actual compliance has become weaker. Media reports on any particular day attest to persistent and massive violations of even the most basic rules. Promoting compliance is literally a matter of life and death.

One method of promoting compliance, in which there has been some progress, is the effort to ensure that violators will be held accountable for their actions. The ad hoc tribunals created by the Security Council for the former Yugoslavia (1993) and Rwanda (1994) were an important innovation in dealing with those who commit the most serious violations of IHL.

The creation of these tribunals initially met with considerable pessimism and cynicism about their potential impact. Some feared that the pursuit of war criminals could hamper peace efforts; others were confident that the tribunals would never get the support necessary to apprehend and prosecute perpetrators. Even the strongest supporters had cautious expectations. However, the tribunals have garnered the international support necessary to ensure the arrest and surrender of many suspects. They have completed important cases and have issued groundbreaking decisions on IHL and international criminal law issues not addressed since Nuremberg. The tribunals also have demonstrated that international criminal justice can be a reality, and that it will not interfere with peace efforts. In fact, the work of the tribunals has been helpful in isolating extremists and preventing historic revisionism, thus facilitating real and lasting peace.

WAR CRIMES TRIBUNALS

The International Criminal Tribunal for the Former Yugoslavia (ICTY) and the International Criminal Tribunal for Rwanda (ICTR) have had very different experiences in gaining custody of indictees. When Louise Arbour assumed the post of chief prosecutor in 1996, there were few accused in the ICTY's detention unit, and few prospects for more. Arbour successfully pressed the international community, including the United Nations (UN) Stabilization Force (SFOR), to arrest accused individuals. Arrests by SFOR in 1997 triggered voluntary surrenders, and since that time a steady stream of indictees has been transferred to the ICTY. While the most senior leaders (such as Milosevic, Karadzic, and Mladic) are still at large due to lack of cooperation from certain countries such as the Federal Republic of Yugoslavia, the number of senior officials in custody has risen dramatically.

Since its creation, the ICTR has enjoyed greater success in obtaining custody over high-ranking leaders indicted for the most serious crimes. Many of the top officials involved in the genocide fled to other African countries, as well as elsewhere. These accused have been transferred to the ICTR from states such as Cameroon, Kenya, England, France, Denmark, Belgium, and the United States. The tribunal now has the vast majority of its publicly-indicted accused in custody.

It is very important that both the ICTY and the ICTR prosecute high-placed individuals to demonstrate that the murders, rapes, and other serious crimes could not have taken place on the scale and with the ferocity that they did without support and guidance from the very top of the command structure.

Valerie Oosterveld

The success of the tribunals has given impetus to the creation of a permanent ICC, which will serve a similar function but on a standing basis. The statute of the ICC was adopted in July 1998 and will enter into force once sixty states ratify it. The work of the tribunals and the efforts to create an ICC have already helped generate a global "expectation of justice." The willingness of the international community to establish international proceedings in response to serious violations of humanitarian law has prompted national systems to take more seriously their primary obligation to deal with these crimes within their jurisdiction. This expectation of justice has also led to concrete steps to establish accountability in situations as diverse as Cambodia, Sierra Leone, and East Timor.

Although it is hoped that criminal investigation and prosecution of the most serious violations will ultimately have a significant deterrent effect, this will only occur once there is greater consistency and immediacy in the application of criminal justice. Moreover, it cannot be a complete solution, as respect for IHL will ultimately depend on its acceptance by combatants. Thus, many other means must be employed to promote compliance with IHL. These include ratification, implementation, and dissemination of IHL instruments; training and education of military personnel and other potential combatants and fostering of cultures of military discipline; enhanced humanitarian access to populations in need; and greater scrutiny and monitoring of conduct, including thorough fact-finding missions. Political and public vigilance is also indispensible to ensure that violations are denounced and that pressure is brought to promote compliance. It is only through a variety of such means that greater compliance with IHL will be reached.

Great strides have been made in expanding the reach of IHL, building new norms to protect the vulnerable, and enforcing the norms of IHL, but much work remains to be done. The evolution of IHL is of pivotal importance in protecting human security, since that security is so often torn away in times of conflict. At the same time, however, efforts to advance IHL cannot take place in a vacuum. They must complement a variety of other measures to protect human security, such as preventative action, conflict management, and measures addressing the root causes of conflict. Indeed, we must recognize that creating conditions where IHL is respected is a distant second choice to creating conditions where IHL is not needed at all. Wherever conflicts erupt, however, the application of IHL will remain a critical humanitarian imperative. We must, therefore, work to bolster compliance with IHL and to ensure its continued relevance in today's armed conflicts.

NOTES

1 Theodor Meron, *War Crimes Law Comes of Age* (Clarendon Press: Oxford, 1998), esp. 296–304.

2 A short list of elementary rules applicable in internal conflicts was recognized in common article 3 of the *Geneva Conventions* of 1949 and modestly expanded by *Additional Protocol II* of 1977. However, *Additional Protocol II* was still far more rudimentary than *Additional Protocol I*, which applied to international armed conflicts. Moreover, the provisions applicable to internal armed conflict did not contain any concept of punishable crimes, unlike the provisions governing international armed conflict.

3 For example, Lloyd Axworthy, minister of Foreign Affairs, noting that civilians are bearing the brunt of the increasing brutality of internal armed conflicts, argued that "it would be short-sighted to create a Court that does not reflect this reality." Statement of Lloyd Axworthy, Minister of Foreign Affairs, to the Diplomatic Conference, 15 June 1998.

4 United Nations, Kofi Annan, *Observance by United Nations Forces of International Humanitarian Law* (ST/SGB/1993/13), 6 August 1999.

REFERENCES

Convention on the Prohibition of the Use, Stockpiling, Production and Transfer of Anti-Personnel Mines and on their Destruction. Oslo, 18 September 1997.

Geneva Conventions of 1949 and *The Additional Protocols of 1977.* 12 August 1949 and 8 June 1977.

Meron, Theodor. "International Criminalization of Internal Atrocities." *American Journal of International Law* 89, no. 1 (January 1995).

Meron, Theodor. *War Crimes Law Comes of Age.* Oxford: Clarendon Press, 1998.

Robinson, Darryl and Herman von Hebel. "War Crimes in Internal Armed Conflict." *Yearbook of International Humanitarian Law* vol. 2 (1999).

Statute of the International Criminal Court. Rome, 17 July 1998.

United Nations. Annan, Kofi. *Observance by United Nations Forces of International Humanitarian Law.* Secretary General's Bulletin (ST/SGB/1999/13), 6 August 1999.

The International Criminal Court

DARRYL ROBINSON

The movement to establish a permanent International Criminal Court (ICC) is a powerful illustration of the ability and willingness of the international community to work collectively to address a pressing human security need. Human security has long been threatened by shocking violations of humanitarian law and the pervasive culture of impunity which encourages such crimes. History has repeatedly demonstrated how the seeming security of law and civilization can be torn away and replaced by an eruption of the most barbarous cruelties and atrocities. Instead of diminishing over time, the scale of such violence only worsened in the twentieth century. Sadly, the international community has reacted to such crimes with indifference or inaction, or words of condemnation backed only by hollow threats. The resulting climate of impunity has encouraged other extremists to commit greater violations.

If human security is to be safeguarded, this culture of impunity must be replaced by a culture of accountability.[1] This is the aim of the ICC. Supporters of the ICC believe that where national judicial systems fail to investigate or prosecute persons responsible for genocide, crimes against humanity, or war crimes, then an independent ICC should stand ready to bring those persons to justice. As Lloyd Axworthy, minister of Foreign Affairs, has noted: "The reverse side of human security is human responsibility. Those who commit the most heinous crimes in times of conflict must be held accountable for their actions. This is crucial to rebuilding peace in societies shattered by war. Without justice there is no reconciliation, and without reconciliation there is no lasting peace."[2]

Experience indicates that when justice is denied, aggrieved groups often take "justice into their own hands." This leads to cycles of vengeance and precludes real peace and reconciliation. International justice can also contribute to national reconciliation by stigmatizing violent extremists and removing them from the community, and by establishing an impartial record of the crimes committed, thereby hindering historic revisionism. An ICC would help affirm the rule of law even in situations of conflict and chaos, and would help restore a sense of justice for victims.

Even more urgently needed is the deterrent effect on future violators who would otherwise be encouraged by impunity. Justice today can help to protect the potential victims of tomorrow. A sobering lesson may be gleaned from the failure of the international community to follow through on promises to prosecute the authors of crimes against humanity against the Armenians in 1915. Decades later, when Nazi leaders were planning their campaign of unprecedented cruelty, Hitler dismissed concerns about possible accountability with the rhetorical question, "Who speaks for the Armenians?" In the end, millions more died.

This is why the world needs to move beyond rhetoric and to establish the necessary mechanisms for accountability. The setting up of a permanent international criminal court was on the international agenda even before the creation of the Nuremberg and Tokyo Tribunals fifty years ago, but real negotiations were postponed and delayed for decades. The creation by the Security Council of ad hoc tribunals for the former Yugoslavia (1993) and Rwanda (1994) was a major step forward, but this ad hoc approach suffered from major weaknesses. These weaknesses included the substantial delays in getting a tribunal running, and the need for Security Council agreement to create a tribunal, leading to selective justice. A permanent independent institution was still required to overcome these deficiences and to serve as a more constant and reliable deterrent.

MAKING AN EFFECTIVE ICC: SOFT POWER IN ACTION

There were many challenges confronting the creation of an ICC. On a technical level, it would be an extraordinarily difficult exercise to develop procedures of international criminal justice acceptable to the diverse legal systems of the world. Even more daunting were the profound political differences concerning the appropriate scope, powers, and independence of such a body. For many states, the desire for justice was outweighed by a fear of scrutiny of their own deeds. Many states adhered to a narrow, traditional concept of national security which did not take into account the real benefits of human security in fostering regional and international stability. Indeed, there was a pervasive atmosphere of skepticism that states could ever agree on an effective ICC, particularly among the many observers whose worldview was firmly rooted in traditional approaches of expediency and realpolitik.

The building of support for a strong ICC was a cardinal example of the effectiveness of "soft power." A coalition of supportive states, in tandem with interested nongovernmental organizations (NGOs), worked assiduously to promote an "idea whose time had come." Preparatory negotiations to discuss the feasibility of an ICC, and then to work on a draft statute, commenced in 1994. Despite efforts by some states to prolong negotiations, a coalition of supportive states, called "the Like-Minded Group," was formed to push for a diplomatic conference in 1998 to finalize and adopt an ICC Statute. Under Canadian chairmanship, the Like-Minded Group grew to include over sixty states from all regions of the world. Canada urged the group not only to move beyond its original focus on process and to identify shared "cornerstone" positions on issues of substance, but also to coordinate on substance and strategy, making it a more effective force in the negotiations.

At the same time, NGOs played a significant role in raising public and political awareness and support for the ICC. NGOs influenced the negotiations through well-written research papers and through lobbying efforts, urging states to adhere to the "benchmarks" necessary for an effective court. Hundreds of organizations were involved in the effort to promote the ICC. The NGO Coalition for an International Criminal Court, skillfully led by William Pace, played an exceptionally valuable role in coordinating these efforts.

High-level political support was also essential in building momentum. For example, William Pace and other NGO leaders approached Minister Axworthy, because of his role in the landmines campaign, asking him to help galvanize support for the ICC. Minister Axworthy, already an active proponent of the ICC, intensified his efforts in the build-up to the Rome Conference, through bilateral and multilateral contacts and through statements to raise public and political awareness of the need for an ICC. Canadian officials at all levels lobbied in relevant fora and carried out demarches in capitals. Parliamentarians in Canada and in other countries worked together to urge governments to participate constructively in the final negotiations. To foster universal participation, Canada contributed to a trust fund enabling least developed countries to participate in the negotiations and also contributed to participation by NGOs of least-developed countries.

Canada's role became even more central at the outset of the Rome Diplomatic Conference in June 1998. Senior Canadian diplomat Philippe Kirsch was chosen by acclamation to chair the pivotal negotiating body of the conference. Minister Axworthy attended the Rome Conference to lobby states to hold fast on fundamental principles necessary for a "court worth having." During the final negotiations, Minister Axworthy also made calls to foreign ministers to address particular concerns at critical stages of the negotiations. In addition, the Canadian delegation played a brokering role in all areas of negotiation – the definition of crimes, jurisdiction, general principles, procedures, and the structure of the institution – by bridging gaps and finding creative ways to address legitimate concerns while maintaining a strong court.

After a gruelling five weeks of negotiations, tremendous headway had been made in finding agreement on literally hundreds of technical issues. However, with respect to the major political issues, there were intractable divides. These difficult political issues related to the scope of the jurisdiction of the court and the extent of its independence, as well as questions such as whether ratification would automatically entail recognition of the court's competence over all crimes in the statute or whether the prosecutor would be empowered to initiate an investigation without a state party referral. On these sensitive issues, states were unable to find generally acceptable compromises. It therefore fell to the bureau of coordinators to draft a final, global proposal. The proposal was a carefully balanced package, reflecting the clear majority trends in the conference (trends which favoured a strong court), while making every effort to accommodate minority views without undermining the court. On the final day of the conference, the package deal won broad support from delegations. India and the US sought to introduce additional restrictions into the statute, but these were opposed by the overwhelming majority of states. On 17 July 1998, the final night of the conference, the statute was adopted by a vote, with 120 states supporting, 7 opposed, and 21 states abstaining.

IMPLICATIONS OF THE ROME CONFERENCE

The statute was adopted amidst an extraordinary atmosphere of jubilation and celebration. Some observers have interpreted this reaction as a celebration of a "defeat" of the US, but this is not the case. The delegates assembled in Rome were celebrating the successful climax of years of painstaking effort, and a major milestone in bringing an effective ICC into being. The international community had overcome diverging and conflicting national perspectives, priorities, and legal systems, and agreed on a detailed blueprint for a new international criminal justice system. Participants recognized that they were adding to the international architecture a structure that has long been needed, to provide an international response to genocide, crimes against humanity, and war crimes. UN Secretary-General Kofi Annan described it as "a gift of hope to future generations and a giant step forward in the march towards universal human rights and the rule of law."3 Canada was frequently singled out for praise for its pivotal role.

The ICC Statute adopted in Rome provides the court with jurisdiction over the most serious crimes of concern to the international community, namely genocide, crimes against humanity, and war crimes. These crimes were carefully defined in order to accord with existing international law. The ICC Statute recognizes that interested states have the first opportunity to investigate and prosecute such crimes. However, where the ICC determines that states are failing to do so, the ICC is empowered to assume jurisdiction. A particularly sensitive but vital provision allows the ICC to assume jurisdiction where a state is purporting to exercise jurisdiction, but the exercise is, in reality, a sham designed to shield the person from genuine justice.

The ICC will be established in the Hague and will be composed of the Office of the Prosecutor, the Registry, and the Chambers (eighteen judges subdivided into a Pre-Trial Division, Trial Division, and Appeal Division). An ICC proceeding may be initiated at the request of a state party, the Security Council, or by the ICC prosecutor with the approval of a three-judge panel. The ICC Statute contains numerous safeguards to ensure that it will operate in a credible and responsible manner consistent with its grave mandate. The eighty-three-page, 128-article statute contains detailed provisions for this important new institution, describing its jurisdiction, procedures, principles, and its administrative structure.

The ICC Statute could not possibly satisfy all perspectives – NGOs and many states wished that it had gone further; some states felt that it went too far. This outcome was inevitable, given the contradictory and intractable positions that many participants held. But the balance struck provides a court with enough strength to carry out its vital mandate, and sufficient guarantees of credibility to attract broad support from states. The ICC Statute is a weaving together of idealism and pragmatism, demonstrating that human security and national security are not mutually exclusive.

The adoption of the ICC Statute is a promising sign for soft power and human security. In many intergovernmental negotiations, an initial draft text gets "watered down" by hesitant states, but in this case the statute adopted in Rome is far stronger than the draft statute initially proposed by the International Law Commission. For example, the ICC Statute features an independent prosecutor able to initiate proceedings, jurisdiction over war crimes in internal armed conflict, automatic rather than optional jurisdiction, greater independence from the Security Council, provisions responding to the needs and perspectives of women and children, and provisions on victim participation and reparations. Not only is the statute stronger than most observers expected, but it also obtained greater political support than expected. This is the product of the mutually-reinforcing efforts of committed states and activists of civil society. Thanks to perseverance and moral suasion by like-minded states and NGOs, features that were dismissed only a few years earlier as unrealistic came to be recognized as achievable, and indeed, necessary.

For those who had considered the establishment of an ICC as "unrealistic," the Rome Conference offered an insight into a new reality. The reality is that states are more prepared to overcome traditional sovereignty concerns in favour of the indirect benefits of protecting individuals and human security. The reality is that civil society is having a more direct impact on international negotiations. The reality is that, with the escalating scale of today's atrocities and their international repercussions, we simply cannot afford to repeat the mistakes of the past. This is the new realism.

Regrettably, the United States was one of the seven states voting against the statute. This is part of an unfortunate trend, in which the United States has declined to join its traditional allies on an issue of human security. Given the clear benefits of US support for the ICC, every effort was made to accommodate their legitimate concerns during the negotiations. Many important checks and balances were added which will prevent the court from carrying out frivolous investigations or acting inappropriately. Unfortunately, the USA insisted on an absolute guarantee that US soldiers would never be prosecuted. The great majority of delegations felt that any additional restrictions to give protection to one state would create unacceptable loopholes through which all war criminals could escape justice. It is to be hoped that, with the passage of time, the US and other hesitant states will be satisfied that the court will operate in a manner that is beyond reproach.

THE FUTURE OF THE ICC

Before the court can begin its essential work, a preparatory commission must develop technical instruments necessary for the court's operation. The mandate of this body requires that two important documents, the "Elements of Crimes" and the "Rules of Procedure and Evidence," be completed by 30 June 2000. These negotiations, again under the chairmanship of Ambassador Philippe Kirsch, proceeded well, with both documents finalized by the deadline. In addition, some states, previously hesitant about the ICC Statute, are now satisfied and are strongly supportive of the ICC.

The ICC will be established in the Hague once 60 states have ratified the statute. At the time of this writing, nearly 100 states have signed the statute and 15, including Canada, have ratified it. In addition to ratifying the statute, states must carry out the necessary legislative changes to implement the statute to enable cooperation with this new institution. On 29 June 2000, Canada's ICC legislation received royal assent, making Canada the first country to adopt comprehensive implementation legislation. Canadian efforts are underway to help other countries implement and ratify the statute.

This is only the beginning. Those who support the ICC – including political leaders, officials, NGO activists, intergovernmental officials – must work together to bring about the day when the ICC Statute is as widely ratified as the Geneva Conventions or the UN Charter, making these most elementary laws of humanity enforceable over most of the globe. We must work toward a day when those contemplating genocide, crimes against humanity, or war crimes will realize that the world will no longer turn a blind eye, that investigators will be dispatched, evidence will be collected, deeds will be exposed, and indictments will be issued. The ICC cannot deter all such crimes, but it can help.

In addition, the ICC will play a valuable role by changing international thinking about impunity. The ICC is expected to encourage states to diligently investigate and prosecute violations committed within their own jurisdiction. The ICC should be accompanied by other mechanisms to promote accountability, such as diligent national investigations, the exercise of universal jurisdiction, international extradition and cooperation in combating such crimes, military training, public pressure, and monitoring of wartime conduct.

The ICC has arguably already had an educational impact, helping to alert policy makers to the problems of impunity and helping to promote an expectation of justice. Since the adoption of the ICC Statute, we have witnessed the indictments of Slobodan Milosevic and General Pinochet, and the reinvigorated efforts to find justice in Cambodia and East Timor. The world has taken a step away from a history so often characterized by inaction and helplessness in the face of atrocities, and toward a consistent response affirming the rule of law.

NOTES

1 As was noted at Nuremberg, "crimes against international law are committed by men, not by abstract entities, and only by punishing individuals who commit such crimes can the provisions of international law be enforced." International Military Tribunal at Nuremberg, Judgement, 1 October 1946.

2 Notes for an address by Lloyd Axworthy, minister of Foreign Affairs, to a conference on UN Reform at the Kennedy School, Harvard University, "The New Diplomacy: The UN, the International Criminal Court and the Human Security Agenda," 25 April 1998. This was one of several statements by Minister Axworthy to raise international awareness of and support for the ICC.

3 Kofi Annan, "Statement at the Ceremony held at Campidoglio, Celebrating the Adoption of the Statute of the International Criminal Court," 18 July 1998.

REFERENCES

Axworthy, Lloyd. "Address to the Diplomatic Conference of Plenipotentiaries on the Establishment of an International Criminal Court. "Rome, 15 June 1998.

Kirsch, Philippe and John T. Holmes. "The Rome Conference on an International Criminal Court: The Negotiating Process." *American Journal of International Law* 93, no. 1 (January 1999).

Lee, Roy S., ed. *The International Criminal Court – The Making of the Rome Statute: Issues, Negotiations and Results.* The Hague: Kluwer Law International, 1999.

Robinson, Darryl. "Defining 'Crimes Against Humanity' at the Rome Conference." *American Journal of International Law* vol. 93, no. 1 (January, 1999).

Statute of the International Criminal Court. Rome, 17 July 1998.

Trifficerer, Otto, ed. *Commentary on the Rome Statute of the International Criminal Court – Observer's Notes, Article by Article.* Baden-Baden: Nomos Verlagsgesellschaft, 1999.

7 Resources, Greed, and the Persistence of Violent Conflict

DON HUBERT

To prevent and resolve violent conflict we must understand the sources and logic of war. Two schools of thought currently dominate thinking on the causes of contemporary conflict. The first sees violence as a response .to a range of grievances including systematic discrimination and human rights violations, inequalities in wealth and political power, or a scarcity of resources, particularly where these fall along existing social cleavages, such as ethnicity or religion. The second characterizes war as irrational, either originating in "ancient hatreds," causing a needless disruption along the normal path to development, or simply as "mindless violence." These schools recognize that leadership can play an important role in stoking the embers of conflict, but both nevertheless see the principal dynamics of conflict resulting from popular sentiment.

But what if the principal motive behind conflict is greed not grievance? And what if war is eminently rational for its protagonists, particularly their leaders? Profit rather than political power seems to be a growing motivation for violence in civil wars. Whether through diamonds in Sierra Leone and Angola, tropical timber in Liberia and Cambodia, narcotics in Columbia and Afghanistan, or even humanitarian aid in Somalia and the Sudan, the accumulation of wealth seems to be at the heart of many contemporary conflicts. According to one commentator, paraphrasing the famous Clausewitzian dictum, "war has increasingly become the continuation of economics by other means."[1]

If economic rationales do play a major role in the motivations of the warring factions, this represents a profound challenge to both prevailing schools of thought. For those who view conflict as irrational, a close examination of the economic agendas of belligerents may, ironically, make these conflicts appear less unsettling. If we recognize that the longevity of conflict can be the result not of anarchy but of economic gain, then there may be method to the perceived madness after all.

For those who see grievance or a fundamental conflict of interest at the root of violent conflict, the challenge is more profound. If economic gain is a prominent motivation for armed conflict, the very basis for the resolution of violent conflict through negotiation is undermined and the search for a political settlement may be futile. The authors of a recent book on conflict resolution pose the question starkly: "If modern conflicts are becoming neo-medieval struggles between warlords, drug barons, mercenaries and militias who benefit from war and have found it their only means of making a living, of what value will be efforts to resolve conflicts between them peacefully?"[2] Not only will these groups oppose a negotiated settlement, even more challenging to traditional thinking on war and peace, they may not want even want to win.

How far this type of analysis can be taken is the matter of debate. Some argue that economic motivations are critical to understanding the causes or origins of violent conflict. Paul Collier, the director of the Development Research Group at the World Bank, for example, argues that greed is a principal cause of contemporary conflict, and that warring factions have an economic interest in both initiating and sustaining war.[3] While Collier provides macroeconomic evidence in support of his position, the more widely accepted view is that economic agendas account less for the origins than the longevity or persistence of violent conflict.

WHAT'S NEW ABOUT WAR ECONOMIES?

The examples outlined above certainly suggest that economic motivations play an important role in the persistence of violent conflict. But is this really new? The differences between economic-driven warfare that seems to characterize some civil wars in the 1990s and conflicts during the cold war appear stark, at least on the surface. The difference is not, as is commonly suggested, a shift from wars between states to wars within states. Civil wars already outnumbered interstate conflicts during the cold war period. According to one authority, a full three-quarters of the conflicts between 1945 and 1995 were conflicts within states.[4] Two factors associated with the end of the cold war, however, do seem particularly significant. First, the loss of superpower patronage in the wake of the cold war has forced warring factions to seek support from new sources, including regional powers, the diaspora, multinational corporations, and criminal activity. Second, the worldwide collapse of communism undermined the ideological rationale for a number of insurgent groups. In many cases where fighting continued, such as Myanmar, Cambodia, and Colombia, economic motivations seem to have supplanted ideology.

Rather than a fundamentally new characteristic of warfare, however, the link between conflict and greed may be best understood as the resurgence of a much earlier phenomenon. For as the theorist of war Martin van Creveld has suggested, contemporary wars are medieval in character, lacking differentiation between state and society, soldier and civilian, external and internal transactions across frontiers, and war and organized crime.[5]

Ultimately, the question of novelty, however, misses the point. For regardless of whether economic motivations have played an important role in motivating armed conflict in the past, if they do so now, they deserve our attention. "While the international community stresses the need to halt the disintegration of states and stem the tide of communal violence, the effectiveness of outside powers in both regards is seriously constrained by their inability to examine the incentives and disincentives for violence from the perspective of the belligerents themselves."[6] But what are these incentives and disincentives, and how does war create economic opportunities?

RESOURCES FOR FIGHTING OR FIGHTING FOR RESOURCES?

From the outset, a distinction needs to be drawn between the search for resources in order to continue fighting and the accumulation of resources for its own sake. There is surely nothing new about armies needing food, supplies, and weapons, and restricting access to these is one way of encouraging warring factions to negotiate peace. More problematic are cases where the rationale for the continuation of armed conflict is the accumulation of wealth. Self-supporting armies are one thing; a self-sustaining economic rationale for war is quite another.

Obviously in practice these distinctions are seldom neat or clearly identifiable, and the motivation for fighting can easily change over the course of the conflict. While the origins or root causes of war may, in fact, lie in some genuine sense of grievance, over the course of the conflict greed can become a more prominent motivating factor. It is not difficult to envisage the process through which a transition from collective political objectives to elite private objectives occurs. Since all warring factions need resources in order to continue to fight, and in the absence of foreign patrons they must be secured independently, it is surely a relatively small step to use existing methods for new ends.

It is also likely that economic motivations are not evenly distributed among members of a warring faction. Top political leaders often set their sights on political as well as economic power. If Jonas Savimbi, leader of the National Union for Total Independence of Angola (UNITA) was only interested in economic gain, he would have been better off investing the hundreds of millions made from the trade in diamonds rather than using it to rearm. Similarly, while microeconomic rationales undoubtedly play a role in recruiting common soldiers, it is unlikely that they alone can constitute a "self-sustaining" logic for continued hostilities. The link between economic motivation and the persistence of violent conflict is most clearly evident with middle-level leadership including both paramilitaries and warlords. For example, the notorious paramilitary organization known as Arkan's Tigers led the Serb advance into Bosnia in exchange for the right to pillage and loot, while regional warlords in Sierra Leone and Myanmar are granted economic autonomy in exchange for a degree of political loyalty.

Having considered the nature of the economic rationale for conflict, and the implications for different members of armed factions, the key remaining question is how, in practice, are these economic agendas pursued. What are the methods used for the extraction of wealth in war economies? One option is to steal, extort, or tax. Pillage and plunder are time-honored means for soldiers to supplement wages, while extortion and the disingenuous offer of "protection" for a fee are also common tactics. Due to the severe decline in domestic productivity during war, there are limits to the wealth that can be extracted from the local population and economy. Thus, while local populations invariably suffer, most foreigners are far from immune: mining companies are taxed for access; corporate employees are kidnapped for ransom; and humanitarian relief is diverted from its intended recipients or stolen outright.

The alternative to theft of one sort or another is for warring factions to become profit-seeking enterprises in their own right. By controlling territory, particularly along border regions, they cannot only impose taxes and duties on the import and export of goods, they can monopolize business. And due to market distortions inherent in a war economy, such trade frequently yields unusually high profit margins, particularly where sanctions-busting results in flourishing black markets.

The real fuel for economically driven warfare however comes from natural resources, including tropical hardwood, gems, minerals, oil, and the illicit trade in narcotics. Examples abound. Estimates suggest that Charles Taylor managed to extract $200-250 million (US) per year in Liberia in the early 1990s. Key resources in order of importance were diamonds, timber, rubber, and iron ore, each accounting for between $20-40 million (US) annually.[7] In the wake of the peace agreement in Cambodia, the Khmer Rouge, with the assistance of the Thai army and Thai businesses, were selling timber and gems worth an estimated $20 million per month.[8] Diamonds have been a particularly lucrative commodity across several conflicts in Africa. Between 1992 and 1998, UNITA, the Angolan rebel groups, received $3.72 billion (US) from diamond sales, while rebels have controlled an estimated $250 million annual trade in diamonds in Sierra Leone since the mid-1990s.[9]

Without further research it is impossible to know the degree to which these economic dimensions account for the persistence of particular conflicts. But the evidence accumulated to date is sufficient to warrant the attention of those hoping to bring to an end long-standing wars. The challenges for policy makers are stark. For it seems that "war provides a legitimation for various criminal forms of aggrandizement while at the same time these are necessary sources of revenue to sustain the war. The warring parties need more or less permanent conflict both to reproduce their positions of power and for access to resources."[10]

TAKING THE PROFIT OUT OF WAR

The challenge is to restructure economic incentives and disincentives to encourage conflict resolution and to ensure that future conflict is managed without recourse to violence. Most attempts to date have focused on trying to increase the incentives towards peace – to "make peace pay." In some cases, this has resulted in the offer of sanctuary (with stolen treasures intact) for deposed dictators; in others, an effort to "buy off" the leadership of insurgent groups as was done most explicitly with the Mozambican National Resistance (RENAMO) in Mozambique. Making peace pay is also the dominant logic behind efforts at postconflict reconstruction though coherence between peacebuilding objectives and macroeconomic policy remains problematic. The central argument of this chapter, however, is that securing peace after years of war also requires limiting the benefits that some derive from the continuation of hostilities. In short, effective peacebuilding must make peace pay *and* take the profit out of war.

Acting on this conclusion requires a reorientation of our peace-building efforts. First, we must ensure that our external interventions do not have counter-productive consequences, however unintended. For example, negotiations with warring factions may bestow unwarranted legitimacy on warlords and war criminals, while tightening broad-based economic sanctions may strengthen those who control the black market.

Second, the international community must specifically target their interventions to address the economic dimensions of contemporary conflicts. Most peacebuilding activities are, in one way or another, an attempt to strengthen the hand of those who want peace, particularly civil society organizations. These organizations, however, may not be well placed to assist in reducing the profitability of war. Furthermore, effective interventions often require the imposition of criminal or economic sanctions, and are both difficult and controversial. Close cooperation between police and intelligence services are critical as shadowy networks and complex corporate relationships must be disentangled before any effective responses can be considered.

Ultimately, profiteering in the midst of conflict cannot be stopped entirely. As particular routes and networks are closed, new ones are sure to open. What can be done is to routinely disrupt established channels and thereby reduce profits. And it is here that globalization is of direct benefit. For while the global transfer of money and resources creates opportunities for entrepreneurial warlords, it also increases international leverage over them. The question is whether the international community will make use of this leverage and act decisively to address the potential misuse of humanitarian aid, to ensure the effectiveness and enforcement of sanctions and embargoes, and to curtail the excessive profiteering of commercial organizations operating in war zones.

Humanitarian Aid

In recent years, much has been made of the tendency for well-intentioned humanitarian relief to "fuel" conflicts. While there are certainly notorious cases where aid has likely done more harm than good – the massive diversion of food aid in Somalia, the rebel control of the refugee camps in eastern Zaire, and perhaps the ongoing humanitarian operation in the Sudan – the available evidence does not support sweeping conclusions. As Shearer claims: "Much of the evidence that aid has distorted or prolonged war has tended to rely on anecdotes from specific situations that are 'universalised' more widely to other conflicts."[11] Humanitarian relief is not easy to steal or resell and, in comparison to gems, hardwoods, and narcotics, is of relatively little value. Furthermore, while flows of aid wax and wane over the years, they do not seem to be closely correlated to the intensity of the fighting. These conclusions are certainly consistent with the more general claim that both the positive and negative influence of external aid have been significantly overestimated.

There is no doubt that addressing the potential harmful consequences of humanitarian relief should be a priority for the humanitarian community. For we must ensure that our interventions into war zones result in a net benefit to those suffering the effects of violent conflicts. But with the exception of a few specific cases, humanitarian relief is not a significant dimension of war economies.

Sanctions and Embargoes
Economic sanctions and trade embargoes are one of the principal tools at the disposal of the international community for ending conflict and maintaining peace and security. Sanctions, however, have come under attack in recent years, most notably in the case of Iraq, due to the combination of their political inefficacy and the human suffering they cause. Missing from this debate is the degree to which broad-based economic sanctions encourage the development of black markets and the strengthening of organized criminal organizations. Sanctions are a form of economic warfare and "economic warfare inevitably promotes economic crime."[12] While sanctions are designed as a strong disincentive to promote a corresponding change in political behaviour, these same sanctions create incentives for even law-abiding entrepreneurs to become involved in sanctions-busting. Worse still, the strengthening of the criminal underworld has negative repercussions long after the sanctions have been lifted.

Fortunately, three prominent trends evident in the evolution of sanctions policy will also help in addressing the criminal activity that inevitably follow: an emphasis not only on the imposition but also on the enforcement of sanctions; a shift from broad-based sanctions to specifically targeting key leaders; and finally, attention to restricting the actions of nonstate actors. Attempts to enforce the Security Council's sanctions regime against the Angolan rebel group UNITA, discussed in detail in the case study that follows, is the best current example of these three trends in practice.

SECURITY COUNCIL SANCTIONS

The 1990s truly were the sanctions decade. Over the course of those ten years, the Security Council imposed twelve sanctions regimes, far more than during the preceding forty years. Yet their effectiveness is open to question, and the humanitarian consequences can be severe.

From the outset of its two-year tenure, Canada's objective was to increase the political efficacy of UN-mandated sanctions regimes while mitigating their humanitarian impact. A two-track approach was adopted concentrating on both on country-specific sanctions regimes, and on revisiting Security Council policy towards sanctions more generally. On specific sanctions regimes, Canada has focused its attention on Angola and Iraq. Once on the council, Canada sought and became chair of the Sanctions Committee on Angola. The case study following this chapter offers a detailed account of Canada's effort to increase the efficacy of the Security Council sanctions against the National Union for the Total Independence of Angola (UNITA) rebel group in Angola.

In recent years the council has been deadlocked on the issue of the sanctions regime against Iraq. Shortly after joining the council, Canada attempted to break the impasse by proposing the establishment of a series of expert groups to assess key dimensions including the status of disarmament, the humanitarian consequences of sanctions, Kuwaiti prisoners of war, and reparations. The expert group reports ultimately provided the basis for Resolution 1284. While the resolution did not attract P-5 consensus (Russia, France, and China abstained), it did strike a balance between Iraq's obligations under previous resolutions and the return of the weapons inspectors, and an eventual relaxation of sanctions in return for Iraqi compliance.

Given their widespread use throughout the 1990s, Canada was convinced that a more thorough-going review of sanctions was necessary. As a first step, Canada sponsored a major independent study by the International Peace Academy on Security Council sanctions over the past decade. The report, entitled *The Sanctions Decade*,[1] contains a range of policy-oriented and practical recommendations for improving the instrument of sanctions. A number of key recommendations focus on mitigating the humanitarian impact of sanctions through narrower targeting, preassessments and monitoring, and streamlined humanitarian exemptions procedures. The report was launched during Canada's April 2000 presidency of the council by Foreign Minister Axworthy and Secretary-General Annan at a symposium involving council members and outside experts and nongovernmental organizations (NGOs).

In his foreword to *The Sanctions Decade*, Minister Axworthy outlined his key interest in promoting sanctions reform:

We must all be concerned by the negative humanitarian impact sanctions can have. The suffering of innocent civilians, particularly children, is too high a price to pay for enforcing the Council's will against tyrants. It is also unnecessary. Sanctions regimes can and must be crafted in ways that shield civilians from harm. When imposing sanctions, the Council must give the same weight to protecting civilians as it does to attaining political objectives. Otherwise, the very legitimacy - and efficacy - of this tool of enforcement will be cast into doubt.

In order to make an impact on council decision making, and to launch a process of sanctions reform, Canada pushed for the creation of a council working group on sanctions policy. The working group was formally established during an open council debate on sanctions in April 2000, the first-ever generic consideration of sanctions by the council involving wider UN membership. A key element of the working group's mandate is to explore ways of mitigating the humanitarian impact of sanctions. The working group was requested to report back to the council in November 2000 with across-the-board recommendations for improving the design, administration, and implementation of sanctions.

For the first time, the council will have a forum for considering key issues around sanctions in a comprehensive rather than isolated manner, and to explore proposals for reform from both within and outside the Security Council. It is expected that the working group should develop guidelines and thus promote greater rigour in the way the council devises sanctions regimes, particularly with regard to avoiding negative impacts on civilians.

Patrick Wittmann

1 Robert Cortright and George Lopez, *The Sanctions Decade: Assessing UN Strategies in the 1990s* (Boulder: Lynne Rienner, 1999).

As the distinction between war and organized crime fades, individual criminal sanctions need to supplement broader political sanctions. Other chapters in this volume attest to remarkable progress in holding accountable those who commit crimes against humanity and war crimes. But it has not been accompanied by international efforts to address economic or "white collar" crime. International efforts are required to restrict profiteering during war and to seize ill-gotten assets, and opportunities to do this exist. The recent Convention for the Suppression of the Financing of Terrorism is specifically intended to restrict the often coercive "harvesting" of diaspora communities. Interdiction software, designed to identify the assets of narcotics traffickers by filtering financial transactions, could be adapted for use against a broader range of war-related criminal activity. Prying open secretive banking practices to recover state resources stolen by the likes of Abacha and Soeharto also set a useful precedent for recovering warlord's loot squirreled away in tax havens. But much more needs to be done. More than two years ago the UN secretary-general recommended in his influential report to the Security Council on conflict in Africa that "combatants be held financially liable to their victims under international law ... and that international legal machinery be developed to facilitate efforts to find, attach and seize the assets of transgressing parties and their leaders."[13]

The Private Sector

A particular challenge for the international community is addressing the role of the international private sector in war economies. This is obviously a highly contentious area and the degree of complicity that can be laid at the feet of corporation active in war zones is a matter of much debate. Nevertheless, where international trading networks are used by warlords to launder stolen resources, multinational corporations may share some of the responsibility for prolonging civil wars.

Several remedies are currently being pursued to some degree. One is to develop voluntary codes of conduct for companies engaged in commercial activity in war zones, much as they have been developed for labour and environmental practices. While this is certainly an option worth pursuing, these codes tend to follow rather than precede growing public concern. A second option, raising the profile of corporate responsibility in zones of conflict, is likely necessary, including pressure from shareholders and, in extreme cases, consumer boycotts. The public backlash against Shell's activities in Nigeria and in the North Sea seem to have had a significant effect on corporate behaviour. Although the links between corporate activity and war are far less well known, the possibility of a consumer boycott on diamonds, for example, seems to have done the same.

One particular concern is the link between conflicts, resource companies, and private security. Jakkie Cilliers highlights the emergence of a tripartite relationship which enables "the governing elite to regain control over those areas that provide private and public resources, [and in this way] the mining company is ensured of a captive and malleable government that enables it to exploit its concessions while both benefit from the stability provided by the security companies."[14] Conducted behind a veil of secrecy, security is often purchased by mortgaging future mining profits. Yet, in spite of growing recognition of the challenges posed by private security firms and mercenaries, effective policy responses remain elusive. These difficulties again point to the need to address the role of a range of nonstate actors in contemporary civil conflicts.

CONCLUSION

Understanding the economic motivations underlying contemporary conflicts appears increasingly necessary for effective interventions to resolve conflicts and build peace. There is an urgent need to know much more about the dynamics of war economies – particularly where and how private greed inhibits negotiated settlements. We already know enough, however, to be sure that the tools at our disposal for responding effectively are sorely lacking. Slowly evolving international criminal law is only beginning to provide a genuine constraint on the activities of the individuals operating on behalf of criminal organizations. Our aging international security architecture is struggling to come to grips with the challenge of nonstate actors and commercial agendas. And in the face of failed and failing states, remedies are lacking to police criminal states that facilitate and even promote the extraction of profit from war.

NOTES

1 David Keen, *The Economic Functions of Violence in Civil Wars,* Adelphi Paper 320 (Oxford: Oxford University Press, 1998), 11.

2 Hugh Miall, Oliver Ramsbotham, and Tom Woodhouse, *Contemporary Conflict Resolution: The Prevention, Management and Transformation of Deadly Conflicts* (Cambridge: Polity Press, 1999), 3.

3 Paul Collier, "Doing Well Out of War: An Economic Perspective," in *Greed and Grievance: Economic Agendas in Civil Wars,* eds., Mats Berdal and David Malone (Boulder: Westview Press, 2000).

4 Kal Holsti, *War, the State and the State of War* (Cambridge: Cambridge University Press, 1996).

5 Martin van Creveld, *The Transformation of War* (New York: The Free Press, 1991).

6 Charles King, *Ending Civil Wars,* Adelphi Paper 308 (Oxford, Oxford University Press, 1997), 81.

7 William Reno, *Warlord Politics and African States* (Boulder: Lynne Rienner, 1999), 99.

8 David Cortright and George Lopez, *The Sanctions Decade: Assessing UN Strategies in the 1990s* (Boulder: Lynne Reinner, 2000), 137.

9 Global Witness, *A Rough Trade: The Role of Companies and Governments in the Angola Conflict* (London: Global Witness, 1998) and Reno, *Warlord Politics,* 126.

10 Mary Kaldor, *New and Old Wars: Organized Violence in a Global Era*, (Cambridge: Polity Press, 1999), 110.

11 David Shearer, "Aiding or Abetting: Humanitarian Aid and Its Economic Role in Civil War," in Berdal and Malone, eds., *Greed and Grievance.*

12 R.T. Naylor, *Patriots and Profiteers: On Economic Warfare, Embargo Busting and State-Sponsored Crime* (Toronto: McClelland & Stewart, 1999), 4.

13 Report of the Secretary-General, "The Causes of Conflict and the Promotion of Durable Peace and Sustainable Development in Africa," 16 April 1998, s/1998/318.

14 Jakkie Cilliers, "Private Security in War-Torn African States," in *Peace, Profit or Plunder: The Privatization of Security in War-torn African States*, eds. Jakkie Cilliers and Peggy Mason (Halfway House: Institute for Security Studies, 1999), 7.

REFERENCES

Cilliers, Jackie. "Private Security in War-torn African States." In *Peace, Profit or Plunder: The Privatization of Security in War-torn African States*, edited by Jakkie Cilliers and Peggy Mason. Halfway House: Institute for Security Studies, 1999.

Collier, Paul. "Doing Well Out of War: An Economic Perspective." In *Greed and Grievance: Economic Agendas in Civil Wars*, edited by Mats Berdal and David Malone. Boulder CO: Westview Press, 2000.

Cortright, David and George Lopez. *The Sanctions Decade: Assessing UN Strategies in the 1990s.* Boulder CO: Lynne Rienner, 2000.

Global Witness. *A Rough Trade: The Role of Companies and Governments in the Angolan Conflict.* London: Global Witness, 1998.

Holsti, Kal. *War, the State and the State of War.* Cambridge: Cambridge University Press, 1996.

Kaldor, Mary. *New and Old Wars: Organized Violence in a Global Era.* Cambridge: Polity Press, 1999.

Keen, David. *The Economic Functions of Violence in Civil Wars.* Adelphi Paper 320. Oxford: Oxford University Press, 1998.

Miall, Hugh, Oliver Ramsbotham, and Tom Woodhouse. *Contemporary Conflict Resolution: The Prevention, Management and Transformation of Deadly Conflicts.* Cambridge: Polity Press, 1999.

Naylor, R.T. *Patriots and Profiteers: On Economic Warfare, Embargo Busting and State-Sponsored Crime.* Toronto: McClelland & Stewart, 1999.

Reno William. *Warlord Politics and African States.* Boulder CO: Lynne Rienner, 1999.

United Nations. *The Causes of Conflict and the Promotion of Durable Peace and Sustainable Development in Africa.* Secretary-General's Report to the United Nations Security Council (s/1998/318), 16 April 1998.

CASE STUDY

Angola Sanctions

ROBERT FOWLER AND DAVID ANGELL

The Security Council is sometimes accused of according greater attention to the imposition of sanctions than to their implementation. For seven years, beginning with the adoption of resolution 864 (1993), the council's administration of its sanctions against the rebel movement in Angola appeared to corroborate the argument that imposition of sanctions had come to be seen as an end in itself – a political gesture unconnected to the issues of follow-up and implementation. Political will to enforce the sanctions was lacking, and the difficulty inherent in making some of the measures work appeared not to have been fully understood when those measures were introduced.

In January 1999, upon taking its seat on the Security Council, Canada sought and was assigned the chairmanship of the council committee responsible for the application of sanctions against the National Union for the Total Independence of Angola (UNITA). The sanctions regime was broad in scope and carefully targeted but had been limited in its impact. A culture of impunity had come to exist whereby individuals and governments apparently perceived the violation of the sanctions to be cost-free.

Canada set out to give teeth to the sanctions regime. Our objectives were twofold. First, Canada's interest reflected a desire to promote and restore the credibility of the council's authority for the preservation of human security and the peaceful resolution of conflicts. More than a million Angolans have lost their lives in a civil war that has lasted some thirty years. Each day, 200 more people die. More than a third of

Angola's population of approximately 12 million is internally displaced. It is a brutally vicious war in which the principal victims are innocent civilians. Five out of six Angolans alive today have never known peace. The United Nations Children's Fund (UNICEF) has deemed Angola to be the worst country in the world in which to grow up. Sanctions, on their own, cannot bring an end to the human catastrophe unfolding in Angola, but they can help to create conditions conducive to stopping this war once and for all.

Second, Canada viewed the assignment as an opportunity to curb a persistent source of conflict in Africa. For several decades, UNITA has been a destabilizing force in the region and beyond. The risk of further destabilization as a result of the civil war in Angola, and of UNITA's actions in particular, remains everpresent.

More generally, chairmanship of the Angola Sanctions Committee formed part of a broad package of initiatives through which we have sought to make sanctions a more effective, precise, and credible diplomatic tool. Other elements include sponsoring a comprehensive report on sanctions by the International Peace Academy and initiating detailed discussion within the Security Council on sanctions and their effective implementation, including through the establishment of an informal Security Council Working Group on the management of sanctions regimes.

THE SANCTIONS

Sanctions against UNITA had been introduced incrementally in response to successive failures by UNITA to respect the outcome of elections in 1992 deemed to be free and fair by the United Nations (UN) and to abide by commitments freely entered into under the subsequent Lusaka Peace Agreement. The objective of the sanctions is to foster a durable political settlement to the civil war in Angola by curtailing UNITA's ability to pursue its objectives through military means. The sanctions exist exclusively against UNITA, not the government of Angola. The Security Council has determined, on successive occasions, that UNITA, led by Jonas Savimbi, bears primary responsibility for the resumption of the civil war.

The sanctions contained in council resolutions 864 (1993), 1127 (1997), and 1173 (1998) comprise prohibitions on the following:

- the sale and supply of weapons and other forms of military assistance to UNITA;
- the sale or supply of petroleum and petroleum products to UNITA;

- representation abroad and travel by UNITA and the adult members and immediate families of the UNITA leadership; and,
- the sale or export of diamonds by UNITA.

The measures also provided for the seizing of bank accounts and other assets of UNITA.

THE ROLE OF NONSTATE ACTORS

The nature of the measures is such that their implementation requires careful consideration of the role of the private sector and other nonstate actors, and close cooperation with them. Nongovernmental organizations (NGOs), in particular, have emerged as important allies in our efforts to render the sanctions effective. Global Witness and Human Rights Watch were among the NGOs that have provided vital and very valuable assistance.

The need for close cooperation with nonstate actors is especially true with regard to the sanctions on diamonds. Diamonds remain the quasi-exclusive source of revenue for UNITA, accounting now for some $150-200 million (US) in revenue each year. This is down from more than half a billion dollars in annual revenue earlier in the 1990s. Still, UNITA has received a total of between $3 and 4 billion (US) in revenue through the course of this decade. Reducing that revenue, and increasing UNITA's costs in procuring weapons and petroleum, is essential if we are to succeed in significantly degrading UNITA's capacity to wage war. This somewhat exotic element of the sanctions regime has received the highest public profile. It is the diamond element that has provided the "sizzle" in the UNITA sanctions debate. The council's success or failure in making the diamond sanctions work will have a significant impact on public perceptions of the effectiveness of the overall sanctions regime. This will be the case despite the fact that progress in other areas – notably with regard to the restrictions on the sale or supply to UNITA of petroleum products and of arms and other forms of military assistance – may have greater impact in degrading UNITA's ability to wage war.

Cooperation with the diamond industry and the nongovernmental sector has been central to the Sanctions Committee's approach to breaking the nexus between the illicit diamond trade and armed conflict. From the outset, the diamond industry was supportive of the Sanctions Committee's efforts. The resolution adopted in July 1999 by the International Diamond Manufacturers' Association and the World Federation of Diamond Bourses, urging all members of the diamond industry to refrain from purchasing any diamonds originating from Angola without a certificate of origin issued by the government of Angola, gave expression to that support. So, too, did public commitments of adherence to the diamond sanctions on the part of the dominant company in the diamond sector, De Beers Consolidated Mines Limited and its Central Selling Organization, as well as practical collaboration on the part of individual companies and the Antwerp-based Diamond High Council.

Nonstate actors were also central to other elements of the sanctions regime. The prohibition on the provision of military assistance related directly to private security organizations – that is, mercenaries – and private arms dealers. Transportation of goods by air by pirate air services affected all aspects of the sanctions regimes.

TARGETING THE WAR ECONOMY

Canada sought first to increase public awareness of the sanctions regime. To this end, we (the authors) travelled to a dozen countries in Central and Southern Africa and Eastern and Western Europe in May and July 1999 to consult with government officials, industry representatives, and others to determine how the sanctions could be made effective. We also addressed key decision-making bodies including the Council of Ministers of the Organization of African Unity (OAU) meeting in Algiers in July, which subsequently adopted a resolution in support of the sanctions regime.

We submitted two reports to the Security Council on the basis of these travels (documents s/1999/644 of 4 June 1999 and s/1999/829 of 28 July 1999) – all of which are available on the website of the Permanent Mission of Canada (www.un.int/canada). These contained nineteen interim recommendations, a substantial number of which were directed at nonstate actors, especially the private sector. For example, it was recommended that Interpol be invited to collaborate with the Sanctions Committee, that diamond buyers be invited to assist the committee in devising practical measures to limit UNITA's access to legitimate diamond markets, and that industry associations involving companies active in Southern Africa be encouraged to sensitize their corporate members both to their obligation to respect council-imposed sanctions against UNITA and to the scope of such measures.

In addition, through its resolution 1237 (1999), the Council appointed an Expert Panel charged with collecting information on how the council's sanctions against UNITA were being violated, and by whom, and offering recommendations on how these sanctions might be made to work. This was the first time the council had created a body of this kind. A ten-member panel was appointed under the chairmanship of a Swedish ambassador and the vice-chairmanship of a colonel from Botswana, and with expert members from China, France, Namibia, the Russian Federation, South Africa, Switzerland, the United States, and Zimbabwe.

The panel members pursued investigations in almost thirty countries over the course of a six-month period before submitting their report to the Security Council on 15 March 2000. The report named names, including heads of government, and so caused a furore. In addition, it offered thirty-nine recommendations which, when fully acted upon, stand to have a real and substantial impact on UNITA's ability to wage war – by reducing its revenues, increasing its costs, and choking off its supply. Given the enormous attention it has focused on sanctions-busting, the Expert Panel report and the hands-on attention devoted to these long-neglected sanctions over the past years has already – according to the numerous observers, including the government of Angola – contributed enormously to reducing UNITA's ability to take through force of arms what was denied to it by Angola's voters in 1992.

The endless and utterly senseless civil conflict in Angola has only one enduring certainty: civilians desperately need protection. Previous speakers have made plain the dimensions of the threats faced by ordinary Angolans. It is a place where one million souls have perished in the violence; where a complete humanitarian collapse never looms far, with people barely surviving from day-to-day; where for rural dwellers it is literally too dangerous to step foot out of the house for fear they could be blown away by landmines; where children are in greater peril than anywhere else on earth; where one in three people have been uprooted from their homes; and where, quite simply, no one has escaped undamaged by war ...

Denying the National Union for the Total Independence of Angola (UNITA) the means to wage war would help promote peace. To be sure, this was the objective when measures to this end were adopted several years ago. But it is no secret that nonadherence to the relevant council decisions – deliberate or otherwise – has been the rule, rather than the exception. The Security Council took an unprecedented step to reverse this trend a year ago when it approved the creation of the independent Panel of Experts to collect specific information on compliance – and noncompliance – with the provisions of the sanctions regime, and to provide it with recommendations on how to make the sanctions work ...

The panel's efforts have also highlighted the reality and the impact of the new war economies – the nexus between parties to armed violence, the exploitation of people and resources and the commercial interests that profit from it. In a growing number of conflict situations, economic agendas coexist with political and military goals in the perpetuation of violence and the victimization of people. Addressing the implications of this situation for peace and security merits further reflection and will involve the development of creative responses by the Security Council.

Finally, the panel's findings underline that, while council's decisions reflect the will of the international community, implementation depends on the action of individual members. In applying targeted sanctions – financial or arms embargoes, for example – it means sharing the know-how, experience, and intelligence in dealing with other threats, like money laundering and the drug trade, where tactics for confronting the threat may be similar. For some countries, Canada included, it may also mean examining existing legal tools to determine whether they could be adapted to better influence the negative behaviour of actors operating in, or from, their jurisdictions.

After thirty years of civil conflict, the people of Angola deserve no less than lasting peace and stability. Hopefully, the work of the Angola Sanctions Committee will contribute to that goal. This groundbreaking effort also has, I believe, further and wider application for the council's activities and its efforts to promote human security.

Lloyd Axworthy, Minister of Foreign Affairs to the United Nations Security Council Concerning the Situation in Angola, New York, 18 April 2000

The thirty-nine recommendations in the Expert Panel's report are realistic and achievable, but little progress will be possible without the collaboration of the nonstate sector. The panel concluded that non-state actors – that is, the private brokers who constitute the international arms market, and the private pilots who run heavy-airlift "taxi services" – were central to UNITA's ability to procure weapons and other supplies.

A substantial number of the panel's recommendations related to nonstate actors.[1] In the areas of weapons and military assistance, for example, the panel recommended that governments register, license, and monitor the activities of arms brokers and make relevant information available to international organizations seeking to curtail illicit arms transfers (recommendation 2). The panel endorsed a proposal by the Ukraine to convene a conference of arms-export countries to determine how supply to UNITA by arms brokers might be curtailed.

With respect to petroleum and petroleum products, the panel called for the institutionalization of information-exchange mechanisms among oil companies and governments to facilitate the flow of information regarding possible illegal diversions of fuel to UNITA. The panel also recommended that a DNA-type analysis be conducted, possibly in conjunction with private companies, for the purpose of determining the origin of fuel obtained or captured from UNITA.

With reference to diamonds, the panel called upon the diamond industry to develop and implement more effective arrangements to ensure that its members worldwide abide by the relevant sanctions against UNITA. The panel also recommended that a conference of experts be convened for the purpose of determining a system of controls that would allow for increased transparency and accountability in the control of diamonds from the source of origin to the bourses – including the development of mechanisms for identifying, within the diamond market, those diamonds that may have been brought into diamond centres without a customs declaration, and the establishment of a comprehensive database on diamonds' characteristics and trends. Industry participation could be an element of such a conference.

With regard to finances and assets, the panel recommended that member states make provision for the forfeiture of UNITA-controlled assets whose provenance cannot be traced to a lawful source and specified that, while seized and forfeited assets should, in the main, be used to benefit the people of Angola (recommendation 19), as an incentive a substantial bounty be given to any institution, NGO, or individual that traces, tracks down, and identifies UNITA assets that are subject to sanction. The panel further recommended that banking procedures be developed to facilitate the identification of individuals covered by sanctions, and the freezing of assets.

STRENGTHENING COOPERATION

The panel also offered guidance on the management of sanctions more generally. This included recommending the establishment of formal links and regular collaboration between the UN and organizations involved in sanctions monitoring and enforcement activities, including Interpol. The panel recommended that a "Sanctions Information Package," including a web-site, be developed to increase awareness of the purpose and scope of the sanctions regime, including the responsibilities of nonstate actors.

The result of these various initiatives is that sanctions are finally beginning to work. Anecdotal evidence clearly indicates that UNITA is having difficulty getting its diamonds to market. They are also experiencing problems arranging the delivery of weapons and other commodities procured abroad as it becomes more difficult to locate suppliers prepared to risk exposure, and more expensive to deal with those willing to do so. In a debate in the Security Council, British Minister of State Peter Hain expressed the view that the military defeats suffered by UNITA coupled with renewed interest and attention on sanctions busters provided an opportunity unprecedented in twenty-five years to bring the Angolan civil war to an end.

The publication of the report of the Expert Panel does not mark an end-point. Continued vigilance is required if UNITA is to be deprived of its military capacity. The world's attention must remain focused on the matter of the effective application of sanctions. Otherwise, cut-rate suppliers and other sanctions busters will reemerge from under the rocks as the spotlight of public attention shifts elsewhere.

On 18 April 2000, the Security Council demonstrated its commitment to ensuring that the sanctions would continue to have impact in curtailing UNITA's ability to pursue its objectives through military means. At a meeting that day, presided over by Foreign Minister Axworthy of Canada and attended by Foreign Minister Miranda of Angola, the council adopted unanimously a substantial resolution which responded to more than three-quarters of the Expert Panel's recommendations. Resolution 1295 (2000) also put in place the monitoring mechanism called for by the panel in order to keep the spotlight of public and diplomatic attention focused on the sanctions against UNITA. The resolution expressed clearly the council's intention to consider action against those the council had determined to have violated the sanctions against UNITA, and set 18 November 2000 as the deadline for an initial decision in that regard.

What has been made clear is that targeted sanctions can work where the will to enforce them exists. Individual countries can have enormous impact in galvanizing that will and in overcoming perceptions of impunity. Ultimately, however, broad-based collaboration is required, including on the part of nonstate actors.

NOTES

1 United Nations, *Report of the Panel of Experts on Violations of Security Council Sanctions Against UNITA* (S/2000/203), 10 March 2000.

REFERENCES

Fowler, Robert R. "Address to the United Nations Security Council on the Report of the Panel of Exports." New York, 18 April 2000.

George A. Lopez and David Cortright. *The Sanctions Decade: Assessing UN Strategies in the 1990s.* Boulder, CO: Lynne Rienner, 2000.

Lusaka Protocol (Peace Agreement). Lusaka, Zambia, 15 November 1994.

United Nations. *Letter Dated 4 June 1999 from the Chairman of the Security Council Committee Established Pursuant to Resolution 864 (1993) Concerning the Situation in Angola Addressed to the President of the Security Council* (S/1999/644), 4 June 1999.

–. *Letter Dated 28 July 1999 from the Chairman of the Security Committee Established Pursuant to Resolution 864 (1993) Concerning the Situation in Angola Addressed to the President of the Security Council* (S/1999/829), 28 July 1999.

–. *Report of the Panel of Experts on Violations of Security Council Sanctions Against UNITA* (S/2000/203), 10 March 2000.

–. *Security Council Resolution 864*, 15 September 1993.

–. *Security Council Resolution 1127*, 28 August 1997.

–. *Security Council Resolution 1173*, 12 June 1998.

–. *Security Council Resolution 1237*, 7 May 1999.

–. *Security Council Resolution 1295*, 18 April 2000.

8 Transnational Crime in a Borderless World

TERRY CORMIER

Efforts to deal with threats from international crime and terrorism – keeping Canadian streets safe – represent the domestic side of the human security agenda, and bring home its reality. Technological advances and the lowering of trade barriers have created a seamless electronic environment which has been embraced not only by businesses, but also by criminals. Increasingly, criminal organizations (including those supporting paramilitaries) act as networks, pursuing the same types of joint ventures and strategic alliances as legitimate global businesses (e.g. Russian, Colombian, and Asia cartels). Advanced technologies benefit terrorist organizations by providing them with greater destructive power, greater ease of movement and concealment, and the means to spread their extremist messages and raise funds.

Canada first put international crime on the G-8 agenda at the Halifax Summit in 1995. As a result of the Canadian initiative, crime has become a regular feature of the G-8 Summit Process. Since the Halifax Summit, a group of G-8 experts – now called the Lyon Group – has been working on these threats. As the criminal threats resulting from globalization become clearer, the work of the Lyon Group has grown. Recognizing the nature of the threat, the United Nations (UN) is now working on the elaboration of a new Convention on Transnational Organized Crime. Work is underway on three protocols to this convention in the areas of smuggling of people, trafficking in women and children, and firearms.

In the high-tech environment, the list of "neighbours" with whom we must cooperate is much longer than at any time in the past. We share the problems not only with those countries with whom we share borders, significant trade links, and political and social beliefs, but also with those who are distant from us both geographically, historically, culturally, or even philosophically. Canadians should be under no illusion that a human security crisis halfway around the world can reach into their daily lives via organized crime and ethnically-motivated violence.

> "The unprecedented challenges posed by the modern, increasingly global criminal world have led to a clear recognition that no country alone can cope successfully with the growth of transnational crime. Issues that were traditionally considered the exclusive preserve of national governments must be addressed in multilateral settings where joint strategies can be agreed upon. If criminals are going global, those fighting them must also launch a global effort and create effective networks of technical, legal, and judicial cooperation, or they will always be one step behind. Fighting crime in all its forms is, of course, an end in itself, because the victims are individual human beings – men, women, and children who suffer when criminals rob them of their dignity, their basic rights, their possessions, sometimes their health, or even their life. But it is also part of a whole, of what must be a global effort to create a more peaceful and more prosperous world based on shared values of justice, democracy, and human rights for all."
>
> Address by the UN Deputy Secretary-General Louise Fréchette at the Tenth United Nations Congress on the Prevention of Crime and the Treatment of Offenders, April 1999

Global crime has a direct impact on the security of individuals, the stability of societies, and the ability of governments to govern. In its 1999 Human Development Report, the United Nations Development Program (UNDP) estimates that organized crime syndicates gross $1.5 trillion per year – greater than all but three of the world's national economies. That enormous sum is gained through the misery of its victims – the women and children forced into prostitution, the people killed by criminals wielding illegal firearms, the people who see their dreams disappear with their savings at the hands of swindlers, the young people ruined by drugs, and the innocent lives lost to terrorist acts. The people perpetrating these crimes are not constrained by political borders; increasingly they see a world of opportunity opening to them.

DRUGS

The international drug trade is one of the largest businesses in the world. Traffickers use the most sophisticated technologies to avoid detection. In many of our cities, drug dealers use mobile phones and pagers to confound law enforcement authorities. Trafficking routes are switched with the same ease as international shippers move their goods. Heroin and cocaine not only ruin lives; they can ruin states. In some regions, the profits generated by organized drug groups are funding paramilitary groups and destroying governments and their ability to provide the most basic security and safety to their citizens.

Countries cannot deal with these threats alone using traditional forms of international relations. From 1985 to 1994, the production of coca leaf more than doubled, and that of opium poppy more than tripled. As production increased, the international discourse on the problem essentially consisted of finger-pointing between those considered to be producers and those considered to be consumers. The rise in production of plant-based narcotic drugs was accompanied by two other trends. First, was the rise in the production of synthetic drugs, chemical substances that can be produced in small laboratories close to the clients. Second, has been the rise in consumption in those countries that used to produce for developed markets, or acted as transit points. The conclusion reached by the international community was that all countries now had a shared responsibility for the problem, as the line dividing producers and consumers was blurred.

Under Canadian leadership, the countries of the Organization of American States (OAS), recently negotiated the Multilateral Evaluation Mechanism (MEM), a process to allow the thirty-four members to assess each others' as well as the region's, drug control efforts. The objective of the MEM is to strengthen mutual confidence, dialogue, and hemispheric cooperation in order to deal with the drug problem with greater efficacy. Under the MEM, the range of drug control policies, including demand reduction through health and social efforts, and supply restriction through law enforcement efforts, will be considered in a balanced manner.

In 1999, Foreign Minister Axworthy initiated a Ministerial Dialogue on Drugs with his counterparts in OAS countries. The dialogue, which took place during the OAS General Assembly in Guatemala City, put the drug problem into a human security context. It helped draw out the connection between governance, small arms, development and trade, health and education, and public engagement. These discussions underlined how drugs drive much of the crime agenda. Narcotics lead to corruption, to money laundering, to trafficking in firearms. The dialogue also emphasized that there are both demand and supply factors at play. By putting the individual at the heart of the discussion of how to mitigate the negative impact of drugs, we are able to ensure that the demand side of the equation, and education and demand-reduction efforts, are discussed in tandem with the issue of production.

"The illicit drug trade poses another major challenge for the governments and peoples of the hemisphere. In many ways, it is a quintessential human security problem: it is multifaceted and transnational, threatens all of us, and affects the most vulnerable in our societies the most severely."

Statement by the Honourable David Kilgour, Secretary of State for Latin America and Africa at the 29th Annual General Assembly of the Organization of American States, June 1999

CORRUPTION

Using public position for private gain, the bribery of public officials and the use of bribery in business transactions are serious problems in many countries. When corruption takes hold, it can destroy entire societies. In societies where corruption and bribery are rife, economic decisions are not transparent and not made only in terms of economic criteria. The entire society pays a high price for this inefficiency and lack of clear rules. Corruption is not limited to countries at any particular level of development, but it is crippling to postconflict societies. Corruption can fuel arms purchases in conflict situations, and is a major contributor to instability and political uncertainty. Corruption more than any other single factor erodes the rule of law and the legitimacy of the political system. At the Cologne G-8 Summit in 1999, leaders urged that acts of corruption involving public officials be made criminal offenses. In December 1998, Canada enacted its own legislation on combatting bribery of foreign officials. This allowed us to ratify the Organization for Economic Cooperation and Development (OECD) Bribery Convention and actually triggered the entry into force of the OECD Convention.

MONEY LAUNDERING

Money laundering is any act or attempted act to conceal or disguise the identity of illegally obtained proceeds so that they appear to have originated from legitimate sources. Criminal proceeds must be laundered in order for organized criminals to convert funds for use in the legitimate economy. Attacking the proceeds of crime is central to any antiorganized crime enforcement. When international crime effectively circumvents sanctions regimes, it thwarts the political aims of the international community.

The Financial Action Task Force (FATF), of which Canada is a leading member, estimates that the amount of money laundered annually worldwide from the illicit drug trade alone is between $300 billion

(US) and $500 billion (US). The inclusion of laundered funds from economic and other nondrug crime could potentially double these figures. It is estimated that the amount of funds laundered in Canada per year is between $5 billion and $14 billion. The speed at which electronic transfers of money can be made greatly complicates the difficulty of dealing with money launderers. In some cases, the lure of large profits can entice otherwise honest professionals – accountants, lawyers, business agents, bankers – into facilitating the laundering of money. While the victims of these types of crimes might not be evident, all of society pays a price for this activity through the support it provides to illegal and often deadly businesses such as drug dealing and smuggling, and through lost government revenues which have to be made up by honest citizens. Internationally, money laundering is used to conceal the proceeds from illegal arms sales, or support for paramilitaries in war-torn societies.

"The demand for small arms is fueled by those whose ambitions perpetrate human misery. They are aided and abetted by the dubious business interests that profit from the marketplace of conflict. One of the failures of globalization is that it has permitted the creation of a new war economy where, in exchange for diamonds and other natural resources, certain corporations provide warlords with the financial resources they need to operate – money that is funneled back to yet other dubious businesses that are only too happy to make their profit through the illicit arms trade."

Address by Lloyd Axworthy, Minister of Foreign Affairs to the United Nations Security Council, September 1999

The Canadian government has introduced new antimoney laundering legislation in the House of Commons. This legislation calls for the mandatory reporting of suspicious transactions and the cross-border movement of large amounts of currency, as well as the establishment of a Financial Information Unit. Canada is also working internationally, particularly through the FATF and the G-8, to deal with this growing problem.

SMUGGLING AND TRAFFICKING IN HUMAN BEINGS

The International Organization for Migration estimates that the illegal smuggling and trafficking of people is a criminal activity that takes in up to $7 (US) billion globally. This activity has seriously tested the "absorptive capacity," both economic and social, of the target countries. High-profile boat cases should not overshadow the fact that there are daily arrivals at our borders. Each year an estimated 8,000 to 16,000 people arrive in Canada, largely through airports, and with the assistance of smugglers. It has been estimated that the economic and commercial impact of migrant trafficking on Canada is between $120 million to $400 million per year. It is organized criminal gangs who smuggle people into Canada. The damage which is done to the integrity of our immigration processes and to the fabric of Canadian society cannot be calculated. Of course, not every migrant seeks to go to the West. Most large-scale migration is prompted by conflicts and/or famine. Civilians in conflict situations are particularly vulnerable to those offering them an escape route at a price. When conflicts spin out of control, there is no shortage of those who seek to profit from human misery.

Even more tragic is the trafficking of women and children who are duped into schemes and end up either in sexual slavery or sweat shops. The UN is currently negotiating a new Convention on Transnational Organized Crime together with a number of protocols, one of which seeks to limit the trafficking in women and children.

FIREARMS

Controlling the trafficking in firearms and small arms is important for law enforcement, critical to reducing firearms-related death and injuries perpetrated by criminals, and essential to efforts to reduce the risks of conflict. The creation of international regimes to control trade in small arms and firearms will reinforce the Canadian Firearms Program (established by the Firearms Act) and bolster the integrity of the domestic gun registration system. At present, Canadian efforts are focused on the elaboration of the protocol against the illicit manufacturing of and trafficking in firearms, ammunition, and other related materials which will be supplemental to the Transnational Organized Crime Convention. The draft protocol is modelled closely on the InterAmerican Convention on the Illicit Manufacturing of and Trafficking in Firearms, Ammunition, Explosives, and Related Materials, which Canada has signed.

TERRORISM

Terrorism is a threat to the peace and stability of all states and the safety and well being of all citizens. It often springs from regional conflicts and failing states, but frequently spreads its tentacles to our immigrant-based societies. As our world gets smaller, it has become easier for terrorists to strike at the peace and tranquillity of our lives. With new technologies, any individual with the will can learn from the Internet how to build explosive devices which can cause maximum damage. New threats come in the form of biological weapons, and attacks on the information systems which support critical infrastructure, such as power and communications networks, can wreak havoc with our lives. Terrorism is a reminder that we are not immune from the instability and conflict which plague the far reaches of the globe. The potential use of weapons of mass destruction by terrorists will soon rank terrorism as a major national security threat, and lead us to tackle more diligently its human security origins.

CONCLUSION

There is a new urgency in working to protect individuals from the problems of transnational crime in all its manifestations. We work in many fora – the UN, the OAS, G-8, the OECD, and bilaterally to move the anticrime agenda forward. Until relatively recently, the cost of crime would have been seen as a purely domestic policy consideration. But in our ever-shrinking world, crime is more and more an international phenomenon, requiring international efforts to address it. However, countries cannot reach a consensus on the international search and tracing of criminal communications, unless we find ways to harmonize, at the international level, our domestic constitutional and human rights requirements in the sensitive areas of tracing, search, and seizure of communications.

Thinking about the impact of crime on human security keeps us looking forward: what are the new threats which individuals will face because of technological, economic, and societal change? It is already clear that the distinction between the domestic and international human security agendas is fast disappearing. For instance, work on money laundering may well be relevant to efforts to strengthen targeted sanctions regimes. Work on economic globalization and crime could inform consideration of the economic incentives and disincentives of conflict.

We must find a way to rationalize our notions of sovereignty with the reality that borders have little meaning for those engaged in many types of high-tech crime. If we are to successfully provide for the safety and security of our citizens in the fight against transnational crime, we will need to find ways to internationalize mechanisms that balance the protection of human rights and the demands of sovereignty as well.

REFERENCES

Inter-American Convention Against the Illicit Manufacturing of and Trafficking in Firearms, Ammunition, Explosives, and Other Related Materials. Washington DC, 14 November 1997.

OECD Convention on Combatting Bribery of Foreign Public Officials in International Business Transactions. Paris, 17 December 1997.

CASE STUDY

Terrorism

VICTOR RAKMIL

Societies have been confronted by terrorist threats to human security for centuries. Madmen, misguided idealists, failed, weakened, or disadvantaged constituencies have resorted to violence as a means to a political end for as long as there have been politics. Despite the spread of democracy, terrorism remains an ever-present threat. But, we can take steps to curb it, and to prevent, detect, and where necessary, prosecute terrorists. The key issue is finding the means to combat it, so that terrorism does not threaten our human security.

Canada has not seen the kinds of terrorism visited on other parts of the world. But we cannot ignore the fact that Canadians find themselves victims of terrorism every year around the globe. Fifty Canadians and Canadian residents hijacked in Egypt, a recent bride blown up in a Parisian subway, a mother and son killed in a hijacking, people kidnapped in Arabia and South America were all innocent and in the wrong place at the wrong time. As a nation made up in large part by immigrants proud of, and retaining close links to, their native lands, large numbers of Canadians are affected by events in their homelands. The concerns of Canadians for relatives and friends abroad are also part of why the fight against terrorism is an important fight for Canada.

In recent years, we have overcome major challenges in the fight against terrorism. Canada and its partners in the G-8 and the United Nations (UN), have moved beyond the political debate over the definition of terrorism to deal with practical measures against terrorism. We have enhanced the international legal framework, improved cooperation on intelligence, expanded international law enforcement, and, in some cases, even improved our science to find appropriate tools to deter, prevent, and prosecute terrorism. But it has been slow going. The debate on terrorism in the United Nations mostly stagnated from 1972 to 1994 in political disputes over definitions of terrorism.

Yet we all know terrorism when we see it. People who fear going to the market, taking the bus or subway, walking their children to school need no definition. For every cause and conspiracy no matter how violent, there are supporters, which is why it is said that "one man's terrorist is another man's freedom fighter," a notion that for a long period precluded countries agreeing on a definition of terrorism. Some scholars have argued, to get around this political minefield, that "one democracy's terrorist should be another democracy's terrorist." Still, the UN General Assembly adopted its 1994 Declaration against Terrorism unanimously, explicitly stating that "criminal Acts intended or calculated to provoke a state of terror in the general public, a group of persons, or particular persons for political purposes are in any circumstances unjustifiable, whatever the considerations of a political, philosophical, ideological, racial, ethnic, religious or any other nature that may be invoked to justify them."[1] Taken together with the thirteen international conventions against specific criminal acts such as hijacking and hostage-taking, we have today as strong an international agreement on what constitutes terrorism as we are likely to get. That agreement has enabled us to make real progress in dealing with the specifics of preventing, detecting, and prosecuting terrorism for the first time in history.

The sterile political debate over who is a freedom fighter or a terrorist obscured the fact that the tools the international community needs to fight the international trade in illicit drugs, trafficking in stolen motor vehicles, smuggled people etc. are very similar, if not identical to those needed to fight terrorism. You need intelligence, law enforcement, and the judicial process. Counter-narcotics and counter-terrorism have their elite military or paramilitary units in most countries. The forged documents that drug traffickers use vary little from those used by terrorists. Organized crime and terrorists need their bankers, their weapons, and increasingly their computers. The growth in transnational organized crime and a growing consensus to do something about it has mirrored the changes in countering terrorism. Some intelligence services charged with countering terrorism refused to see links between common crime and terrorism. At the end of the cold war, many intelligence services have come to recognize that terrorists are often involved in international crime, the drug trade, and gunrunning.

Today, law enforcement and intelligence services are combining forces to address stolen motor vehicles, drug trafficking, and alien smuggling that is used to fund terrorism. Conversely, sometimes terrorism is used as a smoke screen for common criminal activity (criminal gangs took advantage of the troubles in the Punjab; in Colombia it is hard to see where crime and terrorism begin and end, and many were surprised to see the top Sicilian mafia boss convicted of bombings long suspected to be the work of the Red Brigades). Hence, it does not matter if governments take action on illegal firearms, fraudulent travel documents, or extradition because of organized crime or terrorism. Canada's organized crime legislation of 1998 has as much potential to assist law enforcement in tackling the Hells Angels as it will in tackling terrorism. The UN conventions against bombing and on terrorist financing go further in obligating governments to take action against terrorism than, for example the previous conventions on hostage-taking and hijacking.

For its part, Canada can be proud that the agenda set by the G-8 Ottawa Declaration of 1996 has been adopted by the UN and is being actively implemented by the Organization of American States (OAS). It has also been taken up by groups of interested countries around the world from the Asia-Pacific to Africa and the Middle East. What the international community ought to be most proud of is that the agenda that has been advanced is consistent with human rights, fundamental freedoms, and the rule of law.

Has this international effort been effective? On the issue of deterrence and prevention, we can see a marked decrease in the numbers of incidents worldwide. As countries sign and ratify the twelve UN conventions against terrorism, there are fewer safe havens for terrorists. However, though there are fewer incidents, those incidents are more lethal and cause more casualties. More people are dying because the technology is more sophisticated. The means to make the bombs or obtain weapons is now accessible on the Internet.

But there has been no attempt to keep statistics on incidents that were prevented. Newspapers are full of stories of alleged threats and criminal cases where terrorism is suspected, but the intelligence and elite law enforcement units that tackle terrorism are rightly tight-lipped about their successes and methodologies, unless they must face a court of law. Even then, they will go to some lengths to protect sources and methods. Shortly after the first OAS Ministerial Meeting on Terrorism, a significant number of prisoners were exchanged between countries where they could be held on suspicion of terrorism without bail and trial, and countries where they could be tried before a court of law. Similarly, effective dialogue led to cooperative measures to ensure that terrorists on the loose for many years, for example, members of the Japanese Red Army, were arrested and placed before the courts for decades-old crimes.

What role can Canada play to protect its citizens against threats to human security, and where should our focus be in the coming years? Are there issues where we can add our own unique value? We have a strong reputation based on our ability to bring opponents together in concrete negotiations on highly technical detail in multilateral fora such as the G-8 and OAS. Canada can be proud of its legal experts' contributions to the development of the international legal framework. Our law enforcement and security intelligence services have a well-deserved reputation for their own special kind of diplomacy. We have special expertise within the government and in the private sector on bomb disposal and other technical tools of the counter-terrorism trade. Taken as a whole, and assuming that we can sustain our expertise and resources in these areas, we can continue to play a major part in assisting the international community to build a consensus on the means to curb terrorism consistent with human rights, fundamental freedoms, and the rule of law.

Terrorism, like the fight against illicit drugs, illegal firearms, or alien smuggling cannot be addressed by one country acting alone. It takes negotiation, law enforcement, lawyers, and technicians of all kinds to put in place measures to deny terrorists the means of their trade. Canada has excelled in building the kinds of multidisciplinary teams needed to tackle the complex terrorist threat to human security. This has been of particular value in developing action plans by the G-8 on issues as diverse as hostage-taking and major events management, and in bilateral discussions with the US, India, Israel, and Cuba.

Canada's efforts at building international multidisciplinary teams have helped remove unnecessary secrecy on generic issues devoid of politics where there is ample room for frank exchange and creative solutions. We have fashioned agendas on technical details, document forgery, vehicle identification numbers, bomb disposal, chemical and biological concerns, and eschewed the political agenda that, even among the closest allies, can lead to sterile discussions. This strategy continues to be of value, and the agenda is vast. Adherence to the principles espoused by the UN Declarations against Terrorism and the twelve conventions is difficult work. Countries cannot decry terrorism and at the same time fail to prosecute or extradite criminals involved in terrorism.

In the near term, we face new challenges brought about by the technologies of mass destruction and mass communication. We will need to work together to control mundane materials that can be harnessed to violent effect and differentiate between righteous activism and dangerous and potentially lethal mischief with our interlinked infrastructures, such as power grids and air traffic control mechanisms. We will need new legal concepts to deal with increasingly complex jurisdictional issues, to enhance our ability to extradite or prosecute. There is an agenda of issues dealing with victims of terrorism that has the potential in the coming years to help us curb further violence and close old wounds. France has special laws for victims of terrorism, for example, whereby victims are forgiven death duties. In poorer countries, third party assistance to victims can be a powerful sign of support against the violence. The international community needs to look closely at successful efforts in the Punjab, where both the families of terrorists and victims benefited from assistance. This has gone some way to reduce the gulf between various political factions.

The focus of human security on the security and welfare of individuals and their communities is a useful approach for counter-terrorism. People have a right to expect their governments to address issues of safety and security, but not at the expense of indiscriminate disregard for human rights, fundamental freedoms, and the rule of law. Terrorism cannot be fought at all costs. If individuals and communities are to be protected from terrorism and from overreaction, the international community has to set the standards for what measures are acceptable. In the near term, agendas focused on technical rather than political issues have greater potential for success. By building up a web of technical agreements, international cooperation is strengthened, and the safety and security of citizens is enhanced both within their own countries and overseas.

NOTES

1 United Nations, General Assembly, *Measures to Eliminate International Terrorism* (A/49/60), 9 December 1994.

REFERENCES

G-7 Declaration against Terrorism. Lyon, France, 27 June 1996.
Ottawa Ministerial Declaration on Countering Terrorism. Ottawa, 12 December 1995.
Patterns of Global Terrorism 1999. Washington DC: US Department of State, April 2000.

Summit of the Peacemakers Statement. Sharm-el-Sheik, Egypt, 13 March 1996.
25 *Paris Measures*. Ministerial Conference on Terrorism. Paris, 30 July 1996.
United Nations. *Measures to Eliminate International Terrorism*. United Nations
    General Assembly Resolution (A/RES/51/210), 16 January 1997.
Ibid., (A/RES/49/60), 9 December 1994.

9 The New Multilateralism

ROMAN WASCHUK

For all its undoubted accomplishments of the past half-century, the institutionalized global multilateral system is showing its age. Postwar arrangements no longer fully reflect the power balances and values-driven concerns of the early twenty-first century. Key disarmament fora seem hopelessly deadlocked, while management of crises affecting great power interests, channelled through the Security Council in the early 1990's, once more flows and eddies outside the council. Images of human suffering beamed around the world mobilize public opinion behind humanitarian action, which is, in turn, frustrated by the organizational failings of international institutions and sovereignty concerns of affected states.

Reacting to this state of global dysfunction, political-military alliances have persisted and, in the case of the North Atlantic Treaty Organization (NATO), expanded. Some states have sought strength in cooperation based on proximity and economic ties, prompting rapid growth in regional institutions, with their promise of smaller-scale manageability. The intensity of these regional arrangements ranges from the sovereignty pooling of the European Union (EU) at the high end, through free trade areas such as the North American Free Trade Agreement (NAFTA) and Mercosur, to cooperation frameworks such as Asia-Pacific Economic Cooperation (APEC) at the lower end. Others have sought solace in cooperation based on values, promoting a flexible new multilateralism which includes not only like-minded states, but also transnational nongovernmental organizations (NGOs) and, increasingly, the private sector. (Some groupings, are now evolving to combine all three aspects: security/ defence, economic ties, and political projection of values, most notably the EU).

Why has Canada, a cocreator and pillar of traditional intergovernmental mechanisms, taken a lead role in crafting a new multilateralism drawing on innovative forms of concerted global action? From inviting citizens to dissect the UN Security Council agenda at national forum consultations in towns and cities across the country to international coalition-building outside traditional regional or ideological groupings, Ottawa is testing the limits in existing institutions, and daring to circumvent them in pursuit of preferred outcomes.

This chapter argues that Canada's acknowledgement of the international proliferation of nonstate actors, as well as its increasing policy openness to the domestic voluntary sector, has made Canada an "early adopter" of many of the new instruments on offer from proponents of global governance. Increasing frustration with the rigidities of some international organizations (indeed, some scholars have gone as far as to describe them as "pathologies") has led to the unilateral launch of aggressive campaigns, "as a means of force-feeding the creation of new international law in contexts in which it was badly needed, but in which a dramatic stimulus was required to overcome the normal lethargy of the international rule-making process."[1] Confronted with continuing institutional blockage, Canadian diplomacy has been increasingly prepared to end-run entrenched opponents by building new issue-based state partnerships and pooling its sovereign standing and statecraft with the newfound legitimacy of transnational NGOs in an alternate process.

REDEFINING SOVEREIGNTY

Current Canadian practice assumes that sovereignty has become more diffuse. Drawing on the 1980s experience of mobilizing American environmentalists and opinion leaders behind Canadian policies targeting acid rain, Canada has been quite prepared to go beyond executive bodies in foreign relations and reach out to nonstate actors. If one were to accept James Rosenau's image of an inchoate Domestic-Foreign Frontier, with constantly evolving spheres of authority for both state and nonstate actors, then Canadian policy makers in areas such as human security and the environment are deep in the frontier thickets, carving out space, searching for partners, and exploring new routes.

Diffusion of sovereignty, though, by no means implies the disappearance of the state. It remains the most-desired form of large-scale political organization in today's world, and is proving remarkably adaptable. Most states still:

- share the aspiration of people for concerted policies that protect their well being and physical security;
- provide a collective means for procuring resources and legitimacy from the world beyond their borders;
- possess jurisdiction over instruments of coercion and the right to use them.

In the broader global system, states remain the sutures which hold the system of governance together as they distribute power upwards to the international level and downwards to subnational agencies.

Canada, with its constant and self-conscious redefinition of national identity, has been better placed than most to recognize the widening overlap of domestic and foreign affairs, and to acknowledge the narrowing of the traditional scope of sovereignty. Canadian diplomacy has set to work in these new parameters to mobilize the public on behalf of international aspirations and obligations. The domestic experience of the "fame garnered over the landmines convention ... in uncomfortable contrast to the flaming campaign against the Multilateral Agreement on Investment (MAI)" has anchored consultations with civil society firmly in government practice.[2] Projecting core Canadian values – respect for human rights, democracy, rule of law, and the environment – to a global public (and then seeing them reflected back for nation-building unity purposes at home) has encouraged the government to pursue traditional internationalist goals with renewed vigour. Consciously or not, Canada's partners in the multicentric world of transnational NGOs are helping to strengthen it as a state. In return, they have received unprecedented access and codecision rights to a toolkit of capabilities hitherto available only to sovereign entities.

This pattern of partnership makes Canada a prime example of a "catalytic state," "one that seeks its goals less by relying on its own resources than by acting as a dominant element in coalitions of other states, transnational institutions, and private sector groups, while retaining its distinct identity and its own goals."[3]

Nonstate actors on the world stage have been with us for centuries, exercising both economic influence (e.g. the Dutch East India Company and early modern bankers' networks such as the Fuggers and Rothschilds) and moral suasion (transnational religious denominations, and, since the mid-nineteenth century, the Red Cross). Continent-spanning networks of moral entrepreneurs also date back to the nineteenth century, with examples such as the British-led movement to

Figure 2
Growth of International Civil Society

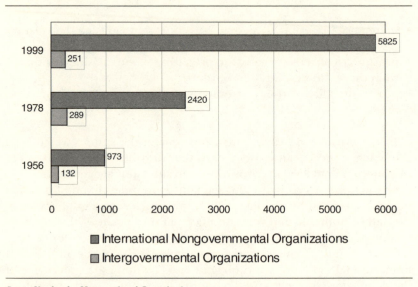

Source: Yearbook of International Organizations, 1990–2000.

abolish slavery, and the pan-European campaign to put an end to atrocities in the Congo. The early twentieth century saw a brief opening for public opinion to influence the restructuring of the international system through us President Wilson's post-World War One "open diplomacy." This period also saw the formation of the International Labour Organization, the first (and so far last) world body to be set up on a tripartite (government, business, labour) basis.

The key post-World War Two multilateral institution, the United Nations (un), combined elements of a great power "concert" with considerable opportunities for middle powers, pioneering human rights provisions, and a limited opening to ngos, initially on a strictly consultative basis, subsequently comprehensively expanded through the major un conferences of the 1990s: Rio, Copenhagen, Cairo, Beijing.

Given this rich history, what, then, is the qualitative leap that sets the new multilateralism apart from the old? Ironically, the answer is in part quantitative: in addition to 189 states (among which the number of democracies doubled from 1970 to 1990), there are now more than 250 intergovernmental organizations and over 5 800 recognized international ngos (see figure 2). This associative proliferation has, on the one hand, increased complexity, but also holds the potential for a remarkable expansion of collective power, harnessing statecraft and public engagement in common cause. The myriad interactions among these organizations are by now part and parcel of the rule system that govern the course of events. Yet another quantitative factor is the immense growth in the density of information exchange among these players due to advances in communication technology and travel. E-mail and the Web, as well as regular international conferences, are the lifeblood of a phenomenon destined to shape the twenty-first century – the transnational issue network.

THE NEW NETWORKS

Marked by diversity and overlap, such networks can include international and regional organizations, international and domestic NGOs, private agencies and foundations, church groups, and governments. Unlike traditional interest groups, their activities are not confined to any single domestic political system. (In the case of the landmines campaign, the US-based International Campaign to Ban Landmines (ICBL) activist Jody Williams enjoyed Canadian diplomatic support for advocacy in third countries.) Though many of the causes espoused by the networks have been grouped under the rubric of "global issues," their precisely targeted goals indicate a tactical move away from the sweeping aims of the old multilateralism, such as general disarmament or world peace, to pragmatic deliverables that can be achieved without raising disruptive cross-cutting societal issues.

Government involvement in such a network can be described as "catalytic diplomacy," in which a state contributes some of the resources provided to it by the sovereignty-related rules which continue to be key influences in the operation of the international system. Sovereignty-free actors, on the other hand, can draw on their moral authority to confer enhanced legitimacy upon their partners in government, whose traditional roles as protectors of domestic business, labour, and social interests have been eroded by global economic forces and an inability to meet inexorably rising public expectations. (Given the many instances in which the democratic mandate of the NGOs themselves is questioned, some of them no doubt also benefit from the respectability conferred by consorting with elected governments.) The single-issue politics of most transnational networks often addresses values on which governments appear ready to compromise. The networks are also able to undertake direct action in a manner which most governments would find difficult to countenance.

Within these transnational networks, mutual needs can create complex and troublesome relationships. Governments know well the advantages of cooperating with NGOs for domestic and policy purposes.

Yet tactical or strategic differences with NGO partners unafraid to speak out can lead to embarrassment for diplomats, as they seek to contain the domestic and international media impact. "Subcontracting" sensitive investigative or analytical efforts to determined and forthright NGOs runs the risk of offending governments whose cooperation is crucial to resolving conflicts or isolating odious regimes or warlords. There is a danger as well in neglecting the comparative advantage of traditional diplomacy: legitimate direct access to foreign government counterparts for advocacy purposes. NGOs, for their part, fret about cooption through state sponsorship, and worry about the constancy of governmental partners pursuing a necessarily broader agenda.

Despite such persistent concerns, there are signs of a growing symbiosis, as NGO specialized expertise becomes central to policymaking in areas where joint research is a common interest. Rather than trading concessions with other states or nonstate actors, many negotiations today involve processes of mutual learning, with participants exchanging best practices and identifying comparative advantages in jointly tackling seemingly intractable multidimensional problems such as complex political emergencies. In the Canadian case, these approaches are being applied primarily in the fields of human rights, conflict prevention, and peacebuilding. Canada's new hemispheric initiatives in the Americas have major built-in civil society components. Quite apart from the ministerial commitment to these issues, "the impetus for government to work with NGOs in this area lies in the belief that it offers a relatively low-cost, low-profile means for governments to engage in dispute management before it results in violence, whilst maximizing freedom of manoeuvre and avoiding the costs of disengagement where this proves necessary."[4]

The new multilateralism has so far had its greatest successes in setting new rules for international behaviour, as "the positive impact of transnational networks is most easily viewed at the level of agenda setting, framing and spread of norms, and change in government discourse."[5] Canada has sought to go further, contributing to an implementation track for the Ottawa Process that foresees roles (and funding) for state and nonstate partners in the landmine ban transnational network as work proceeds on demining and stockpile destruction.

THE NEW/OLD MULTILATERALISM

Building on the momentum of the Ottawa Process, two of its leaders, Canada and Norway, met bilaterally to call for "a new diplomacy to fashion a humane world." This would become known as the "Lysøen process." That the initiative came from these two particular states testifies not only to the humanitarian impulse in their respective foreign policies, but also to the search for new regional and global roles by post-NAFTA Canada and non-EU Norway. While paying tribute to traditional multilateral institutions, Foreign Ministers Axworthy and Vollebaek stressed the "need to work with like-minded countries inside and outside those institutions to pool resources and extend our influence ... And this partnering should not stop with states. We must cooperate with non-governmental organizations, the private sector and other nonstate actors." The reference to the "like-minded" recalls the long history of Canadian collaboration with a group of primarily northern European states "with similarly limited capacities and comparably vital stakes in the maintenance of a stable international order,"[6] as well as strikingly similar outlooks on development and humanitarian issues. A number of these traditional partners responded to the call from Ottawa and Oslo: the Netherlands, Switzerland, Austria, and Ireland. The significance of the Lysøen process was, however, in broadening the geography of like-mindedness to include South America (Chile), the Middle East (Jordan), Asia (Thailand) and Central Europe (Slovenia). South Africa has attended meetings of this network as an observer. The unwritten goal was to create an Humanitarian 8 (H-8) to rival the more traditional concerns of the G-8. That the numbers did not match did not matter. The idea was to create a new group to tackle the new human security agenda. (See case study, "The Human Security Network," p. 231.)

Uniquely among the old and new "like-minded" middle powers, Canada is itself a member of the G-8 – where it sits with the great powers. It is thus well placed to act as an interface, connecting the ideas circulating among the Lysøen states and their transnational nonstate partners with the interest-driven yet image-conscious world of the G-8. (Partners such as the Netherlands and Ireland have their own, albeit more indirect, channel of influence as EU members: the European Commission sits as an informal member of the G8.) The empathy of the current British and German governments with "like-minded" thinking also helped smooth the way for the introduction of the human security concept into G-8 discourse at the 1999 Cologne Foreign Ministers' Meeting. Indeed, the G-8 has, with Canada's encouragement, moved at the December 1999 Berlin Ministerial to adopt four of the ten Lysøen human security elements (small arms, organized crime, children in armed conflicts, and conflict prevention capacity-building) as part of its own conflict prevention agenda. The focus on prevention and remediation, rather than on tackling controversial conflict drivers head-on, has allowed these agenda elements to survive the political turbulence generated within the G-8 by the Kosovo and Chechnya conflicts. The relative informality of G-8 proceedings, as well as the presumption of shared values, has permitted the development of language and decisions that might have been still-born in the more restrictive procedural atmosphere of the UN Security Council.

COMBATTING THE PROLIFERATION OF SMALL ARMS

United Nations (UN) General Assembly Resolution 50/70 B, adopted in December 1995, called for the first in-depth governmental study of the problem of small arms and light weapons, which had "become a priority concern in efforts to rid the world of the scourge of war and the burden of armaments." The seminal report by the 1997 Panel of Governmental Experts on Small Arms, together with the follow-up report of the 1999 Group of Governmental Experts, have set the stage for concerted and comprehensive international action to counter the deleterious effects of the destabilizing accumulation and uncontrolled spread of small arms and light weapons into zones of armed conflict and tension. The experts stressed that only a truly comprehensive approach, encompassing action on legal transfers, illicit trafficking, and postconflict disarmament and demobilization, had any reasonable prospect of sustainable success at the global, regional, and national levels.

To promote this comprehensive strategy the General Assembly of the UN has decided, by resolution 54/54 V adopted in December 1999, to convene an International Conference on The Illicit Trade in Small Arms and Light Weapons In All Its Aspects during the months of June and July, 2001. A Preparatory Committee has been struck and is actively laying the foundations for the 2001 Conference. A key objective of the conference is expected to be the elaboration of an International Program of Action comprising an array of legal, political, and practical measures to tackle an issue that continues to threaten human security in virtually every region of the world.

Mark Gaillard

The UN remains hostage to a broad cross-section of member states unwilling to cede ground on one or more of the principal tenets of the new multilateralism: activism on people-centred humanitarian concerns, willingness to question the absolute interpretation of sovereignty, and openness to transnational NGOs. The current UN Secretary-General, Kofi Annan, is, however, making his mark as a firm believer in moving these issues ahead. Thanks in large part to cooperation with the secretary-general, Canada's 1999–2000 membership on the Security Council has therefore seen some progress in agenda-setting on protection of civilians in armed conflict, and in the deployment of robust peace implementation forces under UN mandate (East Timor, Sierra Leone). Canadians have also experienced considerable frustration at the UN's inability to act at the height of the Kosovo crisis. In this latter case, as in the Conference on Disarmament landmines negotiations, Canada ultimately chose to act outside the UN process, though this time as part of a war-fighting military alliance. Throughout the air campaign, the foreign ministry and the minister stayed in touch with domestic and transnational NGO partners, recognizing their key role in humanitarian relief and, over the longer term, in rebuilding a postconflict Kosovo. Reflecting its continuing preference for rules-based conflict resolution, Canada made a substantive contribution to the G-8 negotiations of a draft UN Resolution, which provided a mandate for the Kosovo Force (KFOR) and set up the UN mission in Kosovo.

Canada's championing of the new multilateralism at the turn of the millennium has thus taken the form of nontraditional coalition-building, both with states and transnational networks, and of grafting the issues driving these coalitions, notably human security, onto the agendas of more established fora such as the UN and the G-8. The challenge for the future will be to situate the lessons of the Ottawa Process, Canada's textbook example of catalytic diplomacy, in a broader context, recognizing issue-specific limitations alongside the models and techniques that can be directly applied in such new collective efforts as protection of civilians in armed conflict or preventing the spread of small arms. Pursuing these causes will require Canadian foreign policy practitioners to strike in each case a unique balance in the facilitator/mediator role, requiring "on the one hand, the capacity to identify and mobilize non-governmental resources in pursuit of government objectives, [and on the other] the ability to monitor how and when governmental diplomatic resources will be made available to other actors in pursuit of their international policy objectives."[7] The promise of success in working with recently recruited partners through new multilateral networks will need to be weighed against the costs of upsetting arrangements (or key allies) in time-tested fora such as NATO or the UN Security Council. The right balance of openness to civil society and empathy with emerging international partners, on the one hand, and diplomatic skill and political savvy, on the other, can maximize accomplishments and benefits for Canada and the world.

NOTES

1 Denis Stairs, "Global Governance as a Policy Tool, the Canadian Experience," *Globalization and Global Governance*, ed., Raimo Väyrynen (Lanham:
   Rowman & Littlefield), 76.
2 Alison van Rooy, "*Fame and Flames: Reflection on Government Engagement with
   Civil Society,*" (Ottawa: North-South Institute, November 1999).
3 M. Lind, quoted in Brian Hocking, "Catalytic Diplomacy: Beyond Newness
   and Decline," in *Innovation in Diplomatic Practice*, ed., Jan Melissen
   (London: Macmillan Press, 1999), 31.
4 Hocking, ibid., 36.
5 Susan D. Burgerman, "Mobilizing Principles: The Role of Transnational
   Activists in Promoting Human Rights Principles," *Human Rights Quarterly*,
   20 (1998): 913.
6 Stairs, "Global Governance," 68.
7 Hocking, "Catalytic Diplomacy," 36.

REFERENCES

Axworthy, Lloyd and Knut Vollebaek. "For a New Diplomacy to Fashion a
   Humane World." *International Herald Tribune* (21 October 1998).
Burgerman, Susan D. "Mobilizing Principles: The Role of Transnational
   Activists in Promoting Human Rights Principles." *Human Rights Quartely* 20
   (1998).
Canada in the World. Ottawa: Government of Canada, 1995.
Hocking, Brian. "Catalytic Diplomacy: Beyond Newness and Decline." In ed.,
   Innovation in Diplomatic Practice, edited by Jan Melissen. London: Macmillan
   Press, 1999.
Rosenau, James N. *Along the Domestic-Foreign Frontier: Exploring Governance in a
   Turbulent World*. Cambridge: Cambridge University Press, 1997.
Stairs, Denis. "Global Governance as a Policy Took, the Canadian Experience."
   In *Globalization and Global Governance*, edited by Raimo Väyrynen. Lanham:
   Rowman & Littlefield, 1999.

CASE STUDY

The Security Council
and the Protection of Civilians

ELISSA GOLBERG AND DON HUBERT

A key challenge for Canada as it joined the Security Council was to demonstrate the practical relevance of human security. Although intimately tied to contemporary armed conflicts, the discourse of human security was foreign to the conservative confines of the council where the atmosphere is risk averse, and where the principles of sovereignty and territorial integrity outweigh those of human rights. From a Canadian perspective, the most effective entry point was the protection of civilians in situations of armed conflict. This approach could most clearly be tied to the responsibilities of the council and the more holistic definition of "threats to international peace and security" evolving throughout the 1990s. This case study reviews Canadian efforts to consolidate this shift in council thinking, and describes the tools and strategies employed.

PROTECTION IN 1990S

The intensity of Security Council activity throughout the 1990s has been directly related to its engagement in humanitarian crises. Already in 1992 the council recognized that "nonmilitary sources of instability in economic, social, humanitarian, and ecological fields have become threats to peace and security"[1] and were, therefore, directly relevant to the council's core mandate. Throughout the decade, the council authorized a series of peace support operations, many with Chapter VII mandates explicitly permitting the use of force. Whether Northern Iraq, Cambodia, Somalia, Bosnia, Haiti, or Rwanda, these operations all had prominent humanitarian dimensions.

While signalling a significant transformation in international approaches to peace and security, Security Council reaction to humanitarian crises remained grossly inadequate. Not only were responses highly inconsistent, even where action was taken, insufficient emphasis was given to providing safety and security of civilians. The failures of the council in Rwanda in 1994, its unwillingness to defend the "safe havens" in Bosnia in 1995, its inaction in the face of mass insecurity in the refugee camps of eastern Zaire in 1996, and its paralysis over Kosovo, attest to the council's uneven response. Equally problematic, Security Council action in support of humanitarian imperatives was principally directed at the delivery of humanitarian assistance rather than the physical safety of people.

In recent years, the council has condemned the targeting of children in armed conflict, decried attacks against humanitarian personnel and operations, recognized the need for peacekeeping operations to better account for the needs of civilians, and taken steps to address impunity in the face of war crimes and crimes again humanity. Yet these examples reflect the piecemeal approach which characterized the council's response to the protection of civilians heading into 1999.

ADVANCING THE PROTECTION AGENDA

While the council's predominant mode of interaction is crisis-driven and country-specific, a new trend towards more thematic, cross-cutting approaches to security emerged in the 1990s, largely on the initiative of nonpermanent members. Canada thus opted for a strategy that combined a case-by-case approach with a thematic one. Under the first element of this strategy, Canada sought "operational entry points" for advancing human security in the council's day-to-day decisions on key security issues, peacekeeping mandates, and sanctions regimes. A number of examples are detailed elsewhere in this volume. The second element of the strategy, promoting a more comprehensive approach to human security, was realized through our thematic initiative on the protection of civilians in armed conflict.

Canada's first presidency of the council was in February 1999, only one month into our mandate. This provided an early opportunity to determine how best to incorporate human security into the council's program of work. The "protection of civilians in armed conflict" was an attractive theme because it provided an umbrella for a number of issues of concern to Canada, including the humanitarian impact of economic sanctions, children and armed conflict, strengthening peacekeeping mandates, and peacebuilding and conflict prevention, even while building on existing council activity.

By focusing on the protection of civilians in armed conflict, Canada's objective was to consolidate previous council work and provide a holistic framework for protection related efforts. But the approach adopted also represented an important departure from past council practice. Humanitarian action had been closely associated with meeting the material needs of victims of armed conflict, and where access to victims was possible, the distribution of relief was usually effective. What was systematically lacking, however, was safety for civilians in war zones. The fundamental challenge, in the words of one commentator, was that too often those that received assistance ultimately became the "well-fed dead." By focusing upon explicitly the safety of civilians, Canada hoped to demonstrate that legal and physical protection of people was central to the council's work. To remain relevant in the evolving international security environment, the council needed to respond to these challenges consistently and effectively.

THE FEBRUARY PRESIDENCY

A two-pronged approach was developed to ensure that the initiative would have a sustained impact beyond a single Security Council debate. In the first phase, Canada would hold a formal debate in February, and call for the secretary-general to prepare a report including concrete recommendations for Security Council action. In the second phase, the report and possible follow-up would be considered by the council during the Dutch presidency in September.[2]

Support for the thematic debate was secured through diplomatic démarches of council members to the capitals, including ministerial contact with counterparts from the permanent five. Working closely with the United Nation's (UN's) Emergency Relief Coordinator, Sergio de Mello, and other humanitarian actors including the International Committee of the Red Cross (ICRC), Canada chaired an open debate on the "Protection of Civilians in Armed Conflict" on 12 February 1999. The debate, presided over by Minister Axworthy, included briefings by the Executive Director of the United Nations Children's Fund (UNICEF), the Special Representative of the Secretary-General on Children and Armed Conflict, and for the first time the president of the ICRC. The Presidential Statement that was adopted successfully consolidated the council's commitment on a range of protection issues and established a follow-up process by calling on the secretary-general to submit a report by September. A second open meeting was held at the end of February to allow noncouncil members to make statements and offer recommendations on the scope and content of the report.

THE REPORT OF THE SECRETARY-GENERAL

On 8 September 1999, the secretary-general presented his report aimed at improving the legal and physical protection of civilians before and during situations of armed conflict. The report put forward forty recommendations providing a graduated menu of options ranging from diplomatic and political initiatives to peacekeeping and enforcement operations. While placing the onus of responsibility for protecting civilians directly on the warring parties, the report also highlighted the clear responsibilities of the wider international community.

The overarching theme of the report was the need to create a "climate of compliance" with existing norms and standards. The report was clear that the legal foundations for protecting civilians are largely in place, and what is lacking is adherence to international human rights, humanitarian, and refugee law. Only a few specific gaps in existing international law were highlighted, including the specific needs of the internally displaced persons, war-affected children, and humanitarian personnel.

Noting that the most effective form of protection was conflict prevention, the first series of recommendations focused on enhancing UN conflict prevention mechanisms. Emphasis was given to the use of preventive peacekeeping deployments, ensuring that sanctions are carefully targeted to minimize their humanitarian impact, and the importance of halting illegal trafficking in small arms.

A range of initiatives were proposed to improve the ability of peacekeepers to protect affected populations, including strengthening the UN's capacity to plan and deploy rapidly, curbing the use of hate media (building on the experience of radio "mille collines" in Rwanda), and making sure troops have appropriate training in human rights and humanitarian law. Ensuring the civilian and humanitarian character of refugee camps is identified as an underdeveloped protection strategy, while the use of safe corridors and humanitarian zones were identified as possible options in the face of mass atrocities.

The final and most controversial recommendation called for military humanitarian intervention in the face of ongoing and systematic violations of human rights. Five factors to be taken into account were highlighted: the scope of the breaches, the inability of local authorities to protect affected populations, the exhaustion of alternative dispute mechanisms, the ability of the council to monitor actions undertaken, and the need to ensure a proportionate use of force.

RESOLUTIONS 1265 AND 1296

A Canadian-led resolution was adopted following the debate of the report on 17 September. Resolution 1265 responded to several of the report's recommendations, particularly those focused on legal protection, but did so without prejudicing further careful council deliberation of the report's content. Although some of the report's recommendations were controversial, a number were reflected in the follow-up resolution negotiated. Traditional concerns over the inviolability of state sovereignty were raised. But positions of council members were converging due in part to the atrocities in Kosovo and Sierra Leone, the ongoing crisis in East Timor, and the impending publication of reports on the UN's failure to act in Rwanda and Srebrenica. In one of the most important paragraphs of resolution 1265, the Security Council expressed its commitment to respond where "civilians are being targeted or humanitarian assistance to civilians is being deliberately obstructed."

In December 1999, Canada began chairing an informal working group tasked with reviewing the report's recommendations and reporting to council on proposals for further action during Canada's next presidency in April 2000. Follow-up on the specifics of the report proved extremely contentious. Ultimately, matters pertaining to legal protection were left to the General Assembly, and Canada drafted a detailed resolution focused on physical protection. Concerns were expressed by several members that the resolution not unduly tie the hands of the council. Serious reservations were expressed by other members that several recommendations were not within the purview of the Security Council or undermined state sovereignty. This controversy was exacerbated by a Security Council debate in March 1999 on "humanitarian action," where the heated discussion of sovereignty in relation to human rights and humanitarian access nearly jeopardized the entire resolution.

Finally, on 19 April, the council agreed to resolution 1296. Taken together, resolutions 1265 and 1296 offer important tools and strategies for enhancing the protection of affected populations. Both condemned attacks on civilian populations and commit the council to act in their defense. Both underscored the importance of conflict prevention strategies, the need to ensure peacekeepers have appropriate training in human rights and humanitarian law, the effects of the excessive accumulation of small arms and impact of landmines, and reaffirmed the need to consider the humanitarian impact of sanctions. In resolution 1296, the Security Council indicated its willingness to take action in the face of crimes against humanity and serious violations of international humanitarian law. It also committed itself to respond when access by humanitarian personnel to civilians is denied, when refugees or internally displaced persons are seriously threatened, and when media broadcasts incite genocide.

Resolution 1296 called for peacekeeping mandates, "when appropriate and feasible," to be provided with adequate human and financial resources to protect civilians under imminent physical threat. It also reaffirmed the need to include special provisions for women, children, and other vulnerable groups in peacemaking, peacekeeping, and peacebuilding operations, including disarmament, demobilization, and reintegration (DDR) for child soldiers. On sanctions, the resolution called on the newly-created council working group to consider the secretary-general's recommendations aimed at mitigating the humanitarian impact of sanctions. Finally, 1296 requested the secretary-general to incorporae an explicit assessment of the situation facing civilians into the country reports he regularly submits to the Security Council, and to submit a comprehensive follow-up report in March 2001.

ACHIEVEMENTS AND CHALLENGES

Canada's Security Council initiative on the protection of civilians has yielded concrete results. By developing an overarching approach, Canada has drawn together, and advanced, previous council work on the protection of civilians. There is now general agreement among members that the safety of civilians in times of war is a central, rather than tangential, concern of the UN Security Council.

Canadian leadership has also resulted in firm commitments to the protection of civilians in Security Council Resolutions on Kosovo (1244), Sierra Leone (1260), and East Timor (1264), including specific references authorizing peacekeepers to intervene where the safety of people was at risk. During our April presidency, further progress was made with a session devoted to the council's dismal role in the 1994 genocide in Rwanda, a systematic review of the humanitarian impact of UN imposed sanctions regimes, and a discussion of the plight of civilians, especially women, in the ongoing war in Afghanistan.

The protection initiative has resulted in unprecedented exposure of council members to key humanitarian actors. The under-secretary general for Humanitarian Affairs has formally addressed the Security Council four times since January 1999. Heads of key UN agencies including the United Nations High Commissioner for Refugees, the World Food Program, UNICEF, and the secretary-general's Special

Representative on children in armed conflict have briefed the council on humanitarian matters. And the president of the ICRC addressed formal sessions of the Security council for the first time during the original council debate in February, and again in April 2000.

Following on earlier practice, thematic debates have become a routine part of the council's operations in the last year. Several debates have been convened on subjects directly relevant to the report and its recommendations. Examples include conflict prevention by Slovenia, DDR of combatants by Malaysia, small arms by the Netherlands, children and armed conflict by Namibia, refugees and internally displaced persons in Africa by the US, the protection of humanitarian personnel by Argentina, and humanitarian action by Bangladesh.

While tensions between effective humanitarian action and the principle of state sovereignty have yet to be resolved, the council now consistently calls for full compliance with both human rights and international humanitarian law. The systematic promotion of human rights in the context of humanitarian crises has been a particularly contentious issue. Nevertheless, the protection of civilians initiative provided a platform for the unprecedented appearance before the council of Mary Robinson, the UN high commissioner for Human Rights; and attention to human rights concerns has also translated into the systematic inclusion of human rights monitors in peace support operations.

Getting members of the council to take the protection of civilians seriously has been an important accomplishment. Achievements to date, however, have been more in what the council says than in what it does, and even here there have been important limitations. For example, Canadian efforts to hold council debates on the plight of civilians during conflicts in Chechnya and Sudan were unsuccessful due to opposition from other council members. The pressing task ahead, however, is to implement human security rather than simply debate it. In this respect, the challenge in enhancing protection is at the same time the greatest one facing the council more generally – the implementation and enforcement of Security Council decisions. Whether by avoiding conflicts or limiting their worst effects, the Security Council must move from words to deeds.

Effective action depends on a broad range of factors. Among the most important are: the development of a culture of prevention; the marshalling of sufficient human and material resources to ensure effective UN operations; bold leadership and the mobilization of political will; and engaging conservative states who continue to perceive sovereignty as a bulwark against interference rather than a responsibility to their people.

The role afforded Canada as a member of the council has provided a unique opportunity to lead through the value of our ideas and proposals. It has been an important step in ensuring that people under extreme threat are not left without the attention and protection of the international community.

NOTES

1 United Nations, *Statement by the President of the Security Council* (s/23500), 31 January 1992.
2 The Netherlands supported the initiative and offered to schedule a debate during their presidency. In the months leading to up to September, Canada and the Netherlands worked closely with the UN secretariat to secure a viable product for the council.

REFERENCES

Bruderlein, Claude. "Towards a New Strategic Approach to Humanitarian Protection and the Use of Protected Areas." *OCHA Working Paper.* New York: United Nations, May 1999.

Frohardt, Mark, Diane Paul, and Larry Minear. *Protecting Human Rights: The Challenge to Humanitarian Organizations.* Occasional Paper #35. Rhode Island: Watson Institute, 1999.

"Principled Aid in An Unprincipled World: Relief, War and Humanitarian Principles." *ECHO/ODI Conference Report.* London: Overseas Development Institute, 7 April 1998.

United Nations. *Report of the Secretary-General to the Security Council on the Causes of Conflict and the Promotion of Durable Peace and Sustainable Development in Africa.* (s/1998/318), 13 April 1998.

–. *Report of the Secretary-General to the Security Council on the Protection of Civilians in Armed Conflict.* (s/1999/957), 8 September 1999.

–. *Security Council Presidential Statement.* (s/PRST/1999/6), 12 February 1999.

–. *Security Council Resolution 1265,* 17 September 1999.

–. *Security Council Resolution 1296,* 19 April 2000.

CASE STUDY

The Human Security Network

MICHAEL SMALL

The Human Security Network, launched in 1998, is an attempt to institutionalize a "coalition of the willing" to motivate international action on a broad range of human security initiatives. The network had its genesis in the close partnership that developed between Canada and Norway during the negotiation of the Ottawa Convention on Antipersonnel Landmines. Following the signing of the Ottawa Treaty in December 1997, Lloyd Axworthy and his then Norwegian counterpart, Knut Vollebaek, found they shared a similar ambition: to see if the winning formula which produced that landmark treaty could be replicated again with other issues.

Vollebaek invited Axworthy to a bilateral retreat in Bergen on 10–11 May, 1998, immediately after the G-8 foreign minister's meeting that year in London. Vollebaek, according to his officials, particularly enjoyed staging diplomatic gatherings in remote, geographic and historic settings around the country – and instructed his ministry to try out new settings for different kinds of "retreats." (This technique, in fact, has become a hallmark of Norway's approach to bringing together hostile parties in third party mediation efforts.) For the bilateral with Lloyd Axworthy, the eccentric wooden home of a nineteenth century violin virtuoso, Ole Bull, was chosen on the small island of Lysøen, in a fjord near Bergen. The setting was inspirational, the chemistry between the ministers good, and what emerged the next morning was the "a Canada-Norway Partnership for Action: The Lysøen Declaration."

THE LYSØEN DECLARATION:
NORWAY-CANADA PARTNERSHIP FOR ACTION

Norway and Canada share common values and approaches to foreign policy. With the evolution of international affairs, particularly with regard to emerging human security issues, we have agreed to establish a framework for consultation and concerted action.

Shared Objectives

To enhance foreign policy consultations and cooperation on priority issues of international concern.

To strengthen Arctic and northern cooperation.

To coordinate and concert actions with a view to:

- enhancing human security;
- promoting human rights;
- strengthening humanitarian law;
- preventing conflict; and
- fostering democracy and good governance.

To develop and enhance partnerships between governments, international organizations, nongovernmental organizations, and other elements of civil society.

Framework

To achieve these foreign policy objectives, we agree to establish a flexible framework for consultation and cooperation, to include:

- ministerial meetings at least once a year to review progress, set priorities, and impart direction;
- bilateral teams to develop and implement joint ministerial initiatives;
- meetings to be held alternately in Norway and Canada or, where convenient, on the margins of international meetings.

In pursuing these goals, we will seek the advice and involvement of civil society and relevant international bodies.

Using the bilateral cooperation framework as a basis, we intend, where practicable, to involve other countries as well.

Bergen, 11 May 1998

Partnership Agenda

- Landmines
- International Criminal Court
- Human rights
- International humanitarian law
- Gender dimensions in peacebuilding
- Small arms proliferation
- Children in armed conflict, including child soldiers
- Child labour
- Arctic and northern cooperation

The Lysøen Declaration was the first time that the concept of "human security" appears in an official agreement, negotiated between Canada and another government. More importantly, it outlined a "partnership agenda" of nine human security issues for further bilateral collaboration. As one official who attended the meeting recalled: "For the first time, you could see an entire agenda emerging around the idea of human security, rather than a disparate set of issues." It was immediately recognized in diplomatic circles in Canada, Norway, and beyond as a harbinger of a new international agenda.

Both sides were keen to use the Lysøen Declaration to anchor a strong bilateral partnership. Over the balance of 1998, officials worked out specific action plans under each of the agenda items, identifying common goals in specific multilateral fora and a number of joint initiatives, particularly dealing with landmines and small arms.

However, Axworthy's broader interest was to use the Lysøen Declaration to launch an open-ended process which could engage other countries as well. His short-hand expression for this was to create an "H-8" or "Humanitarian Eight": a standing group of like-minded states which would rally around a human security agenda, just as G-8 members rally around the goals of international stability and economic growth.

In the early summer of 1998, Axworthy used other trips to the North Atlantic Treaty Organization (NATO) the Organization of African Unity (OAU) Summit, and the Association of South east Asian Nations (ASEAN) Post Ministerial Conference to sound out interest among a number of other foreign ministers. Flavio Cotti of Switzerland, Wolfgang Schussel of Austria, David Andrews of Ireland, and Surin Pitsuwan of Thailand all registered enthusiasm in joining a new human security group. In consultation with Norway, it was decided to approach the Netherlands, Slovenia, Jordan, South Africa, and Chile as well – the latter four countries in particular were invited in order to provide a cross-regional balance. To test the waters, Axworthy and Vollebaek agreed to cohost a lunch in New York on the margins of the General Assembly for Foreign Ministers from the countries listed above to determine their interest in launching such a group.

The meeting proved to be a great success. There was a clear interest among the ministers present to capitalize on the perceived momentum of both the landmines treaty and the recent Rome negotiations on the International Criminal Court (ICC) to develop the agenda which Canada and Norway had developed bilaterally. The potential influence that this cross-regional group of middle powers (Canada was the only G-8 country) could muster was appealing. Vollebaek offered to invite all the ministers to Bergen in May 1999 for a meeting to build on "the spirit of Lysøen."

The intervening months between September and May saw an intensive process of consultation between Ottawa and Oslo. At Minister Axworthy's suggestion, a retreat was held in Aylmer, Quebec in February 1999 by the two foreign ministries, which brought together a small group of officials and civil society experts from academia and the nongovernmental organization (NGO) communities in each country, covering the fields of security, development, and human rights. The two-day meeting, conducted at a very high level of debate, forged a much deeper understanding on both sides of the potential of human security as a concept which could integrate the interests of disarmament activists, human rights advocates, and development practitioners. The results of the retreat fed directly into the thinking which produced the Canadian concept paper, written for the Bergen Ministerial: "Human Security: Safety for People in a Changing World."

The Bergen meeting itself brought together leading international NGOs and governments for the first time under a broad human security banner. The meeting began with a powerful speech by Madame Ogata of UNHCR laying out her perception of human security imperatives, based on her work in protecting refugees. Her speech was followed by NGO statements dealing with landmines, small arms, children in armed conflict, and international humanitarian law. That evening, everyone returned to the island of Lysøen; and the following morning the governments met again in a closed session. A chairman's statement was issued by Minister Vollebaek at the end of the meeting, outlining a broad vision of human security and a more specific ten point agenda for action.

Behind the scenes, matters were a little more complicated. The South African delegation came with unwavering instructions that they could not agree to sign any declaration emerging from this meeting – given South Africa's procedural concerns that there had been insufficient time for them to consult with their partners in the nonaligned movement (NAM) – of which South Africa was the chair. So the planned declaration was scaled back to a chairman's summary. The interaction at this meeting between government and NGO representatives, although cordial, was a little stilted, since there were no concrete proposals for collaboration. And the discussion between the ministers proved somewhat unfocused – again, due to the breadth of the agenda. In the end, one of the more lively topics of discussion proved to be the name for the group itself. What emerged was the "Human Security Network," which emphasized the open-ended nature of both participation (governments and NGOs) and the agenda.

Viewed from a traditional institutional perspective, the network lacks clear criteria for participation, based either on geography (e.g. the Organization of American States (OAS)), on economic weight (e.g. the G-7), or on adherence to a common negotiating objective (e.g. a commitment to ban landmines). Every participating minister brings his or her own priorities to the table, and all are given equal weight. In this sense, the network resembles a "ginger group" for human security causes. Its agenda is a function of the personal interests and commitments of the participating foreign ministers.

Despite these limitations, the second ministerial meeting, hosted by Switzerland in the lake-side town of Lucerne in May 2000, demonstrated the resilience of this new approach to multilateralism. In the eighteen months since the first meeting of the group in New York, a majority of the countries represented had changed foreign ministers, including Switzerland (the host) and Norway (one of the two cofounders). Nevertheless, the political dynamics among the ministers present were excellent and encouraged innovation. Norway tabled an initiative on women and peace processes; Austria tabled one on small arms. South Africa advertised their forthcoming ministerial meeting on diamonds and conflict. Greece (attending for the first time) promoted their concept of an Olympic truce. Minister Axworthy circulated the results of the West African Conference on War Affected children and convened an "emergency session" to review the current crisis facing the UN in Sierra Leone. The nongovernmental experts present had been carefully chosen by the Swiss for their broad expertise on human security issues. Their presence helped focus the discussion, in particular, on the difficult issue of engaging nonstate actors to promote human security. Network members agreed to a caucus in the autumn to help animate the preparatory process of the 2001 UN Conference on Small Arms, and to meet in Canada before the next ministerial meeting to discuss the issues of corporate social responsibility. Jordan offered to host the 2001 Ministerial.

In sum, the Lucerne meeting validated the underlying logic of the network. Without being encumbered by fixed membership or inherited agendas, a cross-regional group of this kind can respond to new ideas, engage outside experts, and take up timely initiatives. The network has already proved its value to Canada and to other participating states, as an incubator of new partnerships to promote human security.

REFERENCES

A Perspective on Human Security: Chairman's Summary. Lysøen, Norway, 20 May 1999.

Ogata, Sadako. "Human Security: A Refugee Perspective." Speech to the Human Security Network. Bergen, Norway, 19 May 1999.

The Lysøen Declaration, Norway-Canada Partnership for Action. Bergen, Norway, 11 May 1998.

10 Human Security, Connectivity, and the New Global Civil Society

ROB MCRAE

The human security agenda faces many new and diverse challenges, as noted in the chapters above. Key to success has been the ability to put together new kinds of coalitions of the willing – task forces with variable geometry – to pursue specific initiatives. One of the principal lessons of this task-force approach is that diplomatic breakthroughs have been conditioned by our ability to:

- convey the inherent attractiveness to policy makers of a paradigm shift that places human security at the heart of the new foreign policy;
- deepen public understanding of the new threats to human security, and public support for the often innovative approaches that must be adopted to deal with them;
- engender horizontal networks linking international organizations, national and local governments, businesses, nongovernmental organizations (NGOs), and citizens, so as to enhance collective intelligence and permit coalitions of the willing where needed.

All of these conditions – and opportunities – for advancing the human security agenda are increasingly a function of the new technologies. These technologies are changing the nature and practice of diplomacy and reforming the international system. Conversely, these same technologies are "facilitating" some of the most complex threats to human security, and the international system, we now face. Ethnic conflicts are often fuelled by international criminal networks, money

Figure 3
Growth of Internet Population
Projection 1999–2005

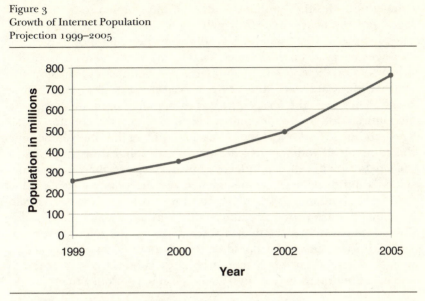

Source: Commerce Net & Nielsen Media Research.

laundering, the "harvesting" of the diaspora, and gunrunning, – all greatly assisted by the new communications architecture and the concomitant "death of distance." When the cost of communication approaches zero, geography does not matter anymore. The tentacles of terrorism or crime can stretch from the Middle East or the Balkans to the backyards of Toronto.

The coming period will be marked by both technological proliferation and convergence: the convergence of internet/voice/television technologies into a single, wireless, highly-mobile platform; and the proliferation of these media to virtually the entire Western world and increasing numbers in developing countries (see figure 3). Those who have access to these media will become the citizens of a new world, a virtual world without borders or any geographical contours at all. Indeed, this world will be relatively impervious to boundaries, controls, and hierarchies of any kind. At the same time, the risk of a "digital divide" is greater than ever. In the developing world, access to the new technologies will mean participation in the knowledge economy and escape from the traditional confines of geography, illiteracy, and economic isolation. Those without such access will be condemned, in a new meaning of that phrase, to "repeat history."

It will be impossible for governments to monopolize information or control its dissemination or impact. Indeed, governments will be competing with other multiple sources of information to get its "messages" out and heard, increasingly through interactive strategies. Ironically, people will be less and less willing to hear, let alone listen to, messages from anyone. Messages, image, and profile are relics of the broadcast era, the era of radio and television. Radio and television created the mass audience and the very concept of a passive, receptive public. They were the levers of mass tastes, public opinion, and popular culture. Modern political life has been based on the creation of images and initiatives for mass consumption, where consumerism became the common denominator of economic and political organization in the late twentieth century. Indeed, in Western society, becoming a consumer of products has become equated with becoming a civilized human being. The mass, the public, and the consumer all share certain common characteristics, as children of the broadcast age: they are defined by mass culture, the mass market, and populist politics. Freedom and individualism in the broadcast age is defined by the choice of brands, where even whole countries are "rebranded" in order to enhance their image to the investor-as-consumer ("Cool Britannia").

ELECTRONIC MEDIA
AND THE NEW CONFLICTS

The advent of broadcast media has had a huge impact on the nature of conflict, and on humanitarian intervention. Radio was the weapon of choice in Rwanda when Hutus' were incited to kill their Tutsi neighbours, ending in one of the worst genocides in the post Second World War II period. The use of radio in Rwanda was a bloody conclusion to the political career of radio dating back to the 1930s, when its potential for the dissemination of propaganda and hate was first fully exploited by the Nazis. What has never been fully understood is why radio was particularly adept at inducing mass hysteria and violence. (Even in our own societies, the radio is a tribal drum in the distance, calling adolescents everywhere "to arms.") It may be that radio's "inner voice" connects with religious or racial messianic fervour in ways that the distracted and distracting images of television do not. The disembodied voice of radio commands attention unlike any other media. In recognition of the dangerous potential of broadcast media, peacebuilding efforts in societies torn by ethnic strife have put the establishment of "free media," both television and radio, at the top of their agenda. "Free" here means both free from ethnic hatred, on the basis of international standards, and free from official control, especially where the states or factions controlling the media have been involved in recent conflict.

In Kosovo, radio channels were also used by the Serb forces to coordinate their ethnic cleansing operations. But it was television that played the key role, and the television-war proved almost as important as the military campaigns in the air and on the ground. In fact the role of television has evolved over time, and many foreign policy practitioners and military planners will look at the Kosovo experience to draw conclusions for the future. It was Vietnam that first highlighted the impact of television on the public perception of international conflict. Television brought the war in Vietnam into America's living-rooms, and the scale of the violence, relative to what was understood as the rationale for the war, turned people off. In the Gulf War, the rationale was clear, but the broadcast of film footage from precision-guided weapons gave the war an unreal aspect. It looked to many like a computer game, devoid of life and death decisions. In contrast, television coverage of the war on the ground, and the Allied casualties there, reminded our publics that this was not, in the end, a game. Indeed, television footage of US soldiers being dragged through the streets of Mogadishu effectively put an end to the United Nation's (UN) peace support operation in Somalia. Where vital national interests were not at stake, the television public was unwilling to see its soldiers either killed or humiliated. Television was instrumental in both putting new constraints on the use of US forces abroad and contributing to a sharp downturn in the number of UN-led peace support operations.

The conflict in Kosovo brought the integration of the new technologies to a new level, and changed both the conduct of humanitarian intervention and the way it was perceived. Video cameras on precision-guided munitions showed how neatly and carefully military targets could be taken out, but also how civilian targets could be hit by mistake. If anything, the *bravado* television images of how accurately military targets could be hit made the errors appear all the more upsetting. Serb television provided footage of the resultant calamity hours before the North Atlantic Treaty Organization (NATO) could confirm that, indeed, something had gone wrong. Because of television, the air campaign was conducted from altitudes that minimized the risk to Allied pilots. Though every commander is concerned about the welfare of his or her soldiers, the rationale for prudence had more to do with the impact that a downed pilot, dead, or alive in captivity, would have on public opinion. This was the Somalia syndrome. If NATO began to lose planes week by week, the media would begin the death-count as if it was a score-card, and public support for the operation would soon erode. The truth was that, even without losses, NATO could never win the media war. This was due to two facts: foreign journalists, especially television crews, were not allowed free access to either Serbia or Kosovo by the Federal Republic of Yugoslavia (FRY) government; and the photo imagery from US satellites of the "collateral damage" took a day to obtain and process.

But there was another media dimension to the intervention in Kosovo that took many by surprise. Over the past decade, foreign policy makers had become used to talking about the "CNN factor." The CNN factor was the ability of television to bring just about any conflict into the living rooms of the West. And as it did so, there was public pressure on governments to "do something." The problem for foreign policy practitioners was that many conflicts around the world did not engage the vital interests of most Western countries. But still there was pressure to take action. It was as if CNN, in the guise of a global news outlet, was a window on the world for every household that subscribed to it. Implicit in the CNN factor was the message that it gave you the news as it was happening, objectively, on your screen, and without editorial interpretation. Of course, nothing could be further from the truth. As businesses, world news networks have grasped the adage that "news sells." But it turned out that not every human calamity made it onto the news: Sierra Leone, the Sudan, and many of the events in Chechnya were recent examples. Some of the worst conflicts went unseen simply because it was too dangerous to cover them. In other cases, the calamity was not newsworthy enough to make it on air. The thousands of civilian casualties victimized by the use of landmines was one example. Here, there was no news, nor the consequent pressure to do anything, despite the admonitions of experts and NGOs on the ground. And it turned out that NGOs and governments put landmines on the map and in the public mind – not broadcast television.

There was another limit to the CNN factor that emerged with regard to Kosovo. Though at the beginning of the air campaign the ethnic Albanian refugees were front and centre on television, soon "refugee fatigue" set in, as the journalists called it. After the first week or two, the editors of both print and electronic media refused to play any more stories about the 1 million refugees pushed by Serb forces out of Kosovo. They judged that the public had enough of the plight of refugees: it was yesterday's news, whether or not the tragedy continued, and despite their stories of atrocities being committed inside Kosovo. In the meantime, there was steady news coverage about the few percent of NATO's guided munitions that went wrong.

Of equal concern is the fact that the Kosovo air campaign came closer to looking like a computer game than ever before. Unlike the Gulf War, it soon became apparent that our soldiers were not at risk. Cruise missiles and pilots did their work with impunity, often on videotape. The public could take it all in from their living-rooms, without the reality of war, the death of their soldiers, intruding. The Kosovo air campaign represented the next step in progress toward standoff war fighting, a trend that will only exacerbate the public's impression that, with the new technologies, we can engage in military operations around the world without cost in terms of Allied lives. This may not be a healthy attitude toward war, or toward humanitarian intervention and peace support operations generally. The message seems to be that war is safer than peace support operations as in the case of Somalia.

CONNECTIVITY AND CIVIL SOCIETY

What is increasingly undermining the impact of broadcast media are the interactive technologies, especially the Internet and cellphone. The Net is fragmenting the market-place, including sources of information. No single story can "crowd out" information about another, because the Net essentially empowers an increasingly connected civil society. Issues now find their constituency in virtually every corner of the globe by means of the connective reach of the Internet and the sharp decline in the cost of communication. For a long time, governments and large corporations had a stranglehold on both the sources and technologies of information and communication. This enabled governments to influence public opinion, and indeed world events, by controlling the dissemination of information to "publics" who were starved of the details. The vertical, hierarchical structure of government, inherited from Westminster, was well suited to this role. Now, that same structure ill-suits the role of government when the rapid dissemination of information is the way to have influence. It is not by withholding information, but by sharing information, by connecting and empowering people, that governments can best lead in a connected world. Governments should help us go where the private sector, and economic globalization, do not.

Interestingly, to the extent that broadcast media create publics, the interactive media are generating a new form of civil society. Civil society connotes that network of voluntary groups and organizations that occupy the middle ground between the state and the citizen. Hardly a recent phenomenon, civil society came into its own during the nineteenth century. In fact, some of the social causes of the last hundred years were not so different from the landmines campaign. But the Internet and the new interactive technologies have made two crucial differences: they both accelerate those movements in terms of the timescale for achieving their objectives; and they offer up a potentially global support base. Indeed, the landmines campaign, through the use of the new technologies, actually promoted the growth of NGOs, and civil society, in some postcommunist countries where none had previously existed. It is increasingly apparent that it is the technology itself, almost regardless of the issue, that is the lifeblood of civil society wherever it penetrates. It magnifies the power of nonstate actors by enhancing collective intelligence and facilitating collective action.

DRUGS AND CONNECTIVITY IN THE AMERICAS

Canada is taking the lead to bridge the Digital Divide through two important pilot projects. First, in collaboration with the International Development Research Centre (IDRC), the Department of Foreign Affairs and International Trade (DFAIT) has begun a pilot project that would establish two Internet access sites in South America (one in Colombia and the other in Ecuador), in collaboration with local organizations working with street children, in order to offer education and training opportunities through Internet and computer resources. The second project is championed by Foreign Affairs and the Canadian Centre on Substance Abuse (CCSA). The CCSA has developed and maintained the Virtual Clearinghouse on Alcohol, Tobacco, and Other Drugs (VC-ATOD) since 1995. It is an Internet-based library of material concerned with all aspects of the prevention and treatment of substance abuse. The information on the VC-ATOD is maintained by member organizations from around the world. Minister Axworthy approached the CCSA with an offer to assist with the augmentation of the VC-ATOD and with the expansion of its membership into Latin America and the Caribbean. The new and improved VC-ATOD will have a wider membership base in the Americas, host more material related to youth, and boast several new technological features, such as a multilingual translation program to facilitate communication. These connectivity projects are bringing people from different corners of the Americas together, and are making credible and useful information more accessible to those who need it most.

Stephen Bolton

The advantages of this development for the human security agenda are obvious: the interactive technologies make possible the creation of broadly-based coalitions of the willing in the pursuit of humanitarian objectives. But the new connectivity is also instrumental to the emergence of another trend, that would otherwise have remained hidden, if not obscured, by the broadcast mode. This is what appears to be the emergence of a global civil society based on a surprisingly strong set of shared values. These values are not necessarily exports from the West, but seem to represent a core set of principles that are cross-cultural.

They lay behind such things as the worldwide condemnation of land-mines, the universal demands for justice in the aftermath of war crimes, and the growing ecological awareness of environmental degradation. For the increasing number of citizens in this global civil society, war is becoming unacceptable as a way of resolving disputes, as "politically incorrect," as slavery became a hundred years ago. The new technologies are engendering a global consciousness-raising – and new norms – whose full extent is still unclear, but which is already having an impact through the innovative approaches to the challenges posed by human security.

FUTURE CONFLICT AND THE NEW DIPLOMACY

But not only are interactive technologies changing the nature of humanitarian intervention: they are also altering the nature of conflict. Marshall McLuhan said in *War and Peace in the Global Village* that "every new technology necessitates a new war."[1] This sounds like technological determinism, but when technology becomes an extension of our central nervous system, it affects the way we interact with the world, including in war. The successful use of cruise missiles, unmanned aerial vehicles (UAVs), and precision-guided weapons in Kosovo has opened the new era of unmanned combat and standoff war fighting. It is, coincidentally, the perfect panacea for the Somalia syndrome. But even standoff combat may be a transitional step towards a redefinition of weaponry. Wars, in the future, may be fought without a single bomb falling. When humanitarian intervention is required to stop the serious and widespread abuse of human rights, the deployment of militaries may be regarded as too slow and risk-prone. With the aggressive use of new technologies, a rogue state might be attacked not only by hacking into its C3 nodules, but through the electronic manipulation of its financial holdings and exchange rates; or simply by cutting off water, electricity, and telephones. The private accounts of the leaders of the regimes could be drained, their airports effectively closed, and the pressure points in the regime's infrastructure targeted. What is not yet clear is whether the use of electronic warfare in this way contravenes the Geneva Conventions, or whether any future UN Security Council would ever approve its use.

In the same way, interactive technologies are having a profound impact on the practice of diplomacy. Increasing numbers of foreign ministries, like Canada's, are now equipped with multiple global secure communications networks, both computer-and voice-based. Some of those networks can be made available literally anywhere in the world through remote access over telephone lines or cellphones. This means that a foreign service officer equipped with a lap-top and a cellphone can set up shop in a hotel room in a remote locale, and through coded access numbers, connect cost-free via telephone lines to the ministry's global communications network. With the advent of the integrated wireless communications platform, even the need for a telephone line will be obsolete. Not only can the foreign service officer become a virtual embassy in her hotel room, she will soon be able to become so in the middle of a field, if need be. Not that bricks and mortar embassies will no longer be necessary. They will. Traditional embassies will always be required in capitals to interact with other governments at a senior level, and to provide a panoply of services to the increasing numbers of our citizens travelling. But our embassies and foreign ministries will not escape the impact these technologies are having on the rest of society. Connectivity not only breaks down walls, it makes borders porous, erodes traditional hierarchies, promotes lateral thinking and unconventional networks animated by like-mindedness and shared values.

The speed and access of interactive technology is already democratizing foreign policy, not simply via real-time electronic letters to the minister, but through the creation of new partnerships. In a complex world, governments have discovered that they cannot do anything alone. In every field of foreign policy, the responsibility of governance is delivered through partnerships, – whether businesses, NGOs, artists and performers, academics and scientists, or citizens. The interactive technologies have become the lifeblood of those new partnerships, not only making them possible, but making them possible anywhere in the world. And because access to those networks is virtually cost-free, these partnerships are open and transparent; their proliferation is putting a new spin on the notion of participatory democracy.

In a connected world, the constituents of power are changing. Governments are discovering new ways to have influence and to exercise leadership, and are more sensitive to the limits of their ability to act alone. Power in today's world is not solely determined by the size of one's army, or even the strength of one's economy. Military or economic coercion still has its place, but its use in a highly interconnected world is increasingly constrained. Power in today's world is more readily constituted by one's ability to lead through the attraction of one's ideas and vision, as a way of shaping international outcomes. The campaign to ban antipersonnel landmines was a case in point. While negotiations on banning these weapons had broken down in the UN, a nontraditional coalition of the willing, including like-minded governments, NGOs, parliamentarians, and citizens (including victims), led what became a global movement. The unassailable integrity of the cause, and the broad base of the partnership, both attracted support and, through grass roots organization, put pressure on more reluctant governments to sign on. This is the new role of diplomacy in the era of human security: as a catalyst and as a network "server" – which both leads and connects, and connects through leadership.

REDEFINING LEADERSHIP

This new form of leadership is called "soft power," because its exercise is noncoercive. Governments have been in the public relations business for a long time, but this is different. Soft power is not about projecting a static image, or about "rebranding." It is about leadership through both example and exemplary actions, and through partnership. Soft power and the hard power that comes from the exercise of military muscle are not alternatives. Both are required if we are to enhance the protection of civilians in armed conflict, including through humanitarian intervention. It is rather that the changing nature of conflict, and the way in which the new technologies are affecting both the threats and the possible remedies, require a new diplomacy. And the new diplomacy simply recognizes and adapts to the changing constituents of power. Though the occupation of territory is a last-resort response to bringing humanitarian crises to an end, the soft power "occupation of minds" through peacebuilding and partnership can generate international action before intervention is necessary.

The reality of soft power, whether or not we choose to exercise it, is altering the traditional mix of diplomatic instruments. There is no substitute for leadership in international organizations and at the negotiating table. But the levers of influence are being transformed by the interactive technologies and communication at the speed of thought. Information is key to decision making in an uncertain security environment, and those representatives that are wired to it have an enormous advantage. The informal networks of the information age can make a substantial contribution to policy intelligence-gathering. Those same informal networks extend influence because of their international reach, and their ability to influence foreign governments through their own grass roots. This can magnify a negotiator's impact at the table.

Leadership based on values and reputation is conditioned by the broader background knowledge of a country. This is the perception foreign observers have of our political culture, people, and way of life. It can be shaped by high-profile domestic controversy, for better or for worse. But this perception is also fuelled by people to people contacts, particularly through the spread of cultural products that bring foreigners into the day-to-day life of Canadians. This is not a question of public relations, image-making, or the "broadcast mode." Novels, films, art, etc., are bridges between individuals, explorations of *lived-life*. What seeps through is not only the physical beauty of our country: there is a humane political and social culture from out of which our international humanitarian instincts grow. With Canada's diverse ethnic mix and its active cultural scene, our soft power "pull" internationally is significant. Every time we take up an initiative, especially where we seek to lead through the persuasiveness of our cause, that latent perception of what Canada is comes into play. It is a major contributing factor to our international credibility. Indeed, the changing constituents of international influence imply that cultural affairs should migrate from the margins of foreign policy to its core.

CONNECTING CANADIAN YOUTH TO THE WORLD

Canada launched the Youth International Internship Program in 1997 as part of a broader government youth strategy. The goal was to provide opportunities for young people to develop new skill sets and to contribute to the advancement of Canadian foreign policy through participation in some 1,850 overseas placements with nongovernmental organizations (NGOs), international organizations, and the private sector. Internships focus on the three main pillars of Canada's foreign policy: the promotion of economic prosperity, the promotion of international security, and the projection of Canadian values and culture abroad. The program connects Canadian youth to the world by sending them to over 100 countries.

Approximately one-third of the internships focus on human security issues. The interns do research; write reports; give speeches; work on advocacy issues like the global ban on landmines; do field monitoring; assist with the reintegration of refugees and the settlement of internally displaced persons; examine human rights cases; assist war-affected children; facilitate international health initiatives; promote free media; contribute to legal affairs, indigenous matters, peacebuilding initiatives, conflict resolution, and more. They bring their energy, their skills, their ideals, their creativity, and cross-cultural values to bear upon these issues. The Acadia University YIIP project, for instance, created a democratic development network using information technology for the United Nations Educational, Scientific, and Cultural Organization (UNESCO's) Culture of Peace program. In another case, Project Ploughshares, a Canadian NGO, placed a young Canadian in the early warning unit at the Institute for Security Studies in Johannesburg where he focused on small arms, peacekeeping issues, and the utility of United Nation (UN) observer missions in the African context.

Janet Boyer

"It is our hope that many of the international relationships that our youth make today will form the foundation for tomorrow's understanding and tolerance. These experiences are intended to encourage them to have the *will* to seek the resolution of future conflicts, or avoid them in the first place. After all, their generation is the first in the modern-day knowledge-based global world, whose collective intelligence will form the core of civil society. Some will become the standard bearers for our future human security agenda. Their beliefs, their advocacy for the environment and sustainable development, their knowledge of high technology, and their understanding of the principal human security issues will contribute to Canada's future role and the sustainability of the human security agenda."

Lloyd Axworthy

(For more information, please consult the website: www.dfait-maeci.gc.ca/interns/)

"– ONLY, CONNECT"

In the digital age, a country's culture and way of life connect people to people in a way that broadcast media do not. Interactive technologies are facilitating these connections as never before, which are helping to generate a global civil society rich in diversity and suffused with the tolerance inherent in a multicultural electronic environment. This is a *global* civil society, slowly taking its place in the new international order, revealing a propensity to rise above national interests to take a truly international view. Not a monolithic whole, not Hollywood's progeny, but a variegated network of networks, simultaneously grass roots and virtual, discovering the cross-cultural values that animate its increasing calls for humanitarian action. Interestingly, this emerging global civil society is not so much energized by ideology or even old-style politics, as by the very concrete, practical, and human-based concerns of the human security agenda. The manner in which individuals from a vast array of countries from both North and South have engaged in many of the initiatives that fall under the human security agenda is ample testimony that something important is going on. When this global civil society becomes self-conscious, and conscious of its common values, it will change the political landscape: voluntaristic, active, and highly democratic, a world where it will never be said of a people about to be abandoned to their fate, that it was (pace Chamberlain) "a far away country, about which we know nothing." Connectivity is becoming the central nervous system of a civil society that will be knowledge-rich and self-aware in ways that governments and traditional publics can never be. When this civil society acts in concert, it will change forever our understanding of the word "superpower."

The immediate challenge, however, is *to connect*. If the digital divide grows wider, the emerging global consensus on the humanitarian issues discussed in this book will falter. The dark side of globalization will predominate in a world where new technologies facilitate the new conflicts, and where the ghettos in globalization condemn the future inhabitants of those ghettos to poverty, insecurity, and ignorance. The digital divide risks making us all less secure, while eroding the benefits and opportunities of globalization upon which a more equitable and sustainable prosperity in both the developing and developed world depends.

Interestingly, early experience with the new technologies in the developing world is highly promising. Even a few Internet connections can make a huge difference, for example, where they link such institutions as academies of science, libraries, or agricultural schools. The institutional links are multipliers, providing access to potentially hundreds if not thousands of users. Where schools have been connected, the interactive nature of the new technology has improved literacy. International organizations like the UN Development Program (UNDP) and the Organization of American States (OAS) are using the Internet to convey "best practices" to member states and directly to a vastly expanded array of clients. The Internet leaps over bureaucratic bottlenecks to those who need, and want, to know. But it also breaks down North/South barriers altogether by bringing together activists from around the globe sharing a common interest in sustainable development. Here, local knowledge, expertise, and resources can be pooled, with or without governmental support, to tackle a particular problem, whether that be biodiversity loss or gender-related human rights abuse.

The arrival of wireless Internet platforms will revolutionize this process by connecting villages and communities that otherwise would have taken decades to connect by telephone line. Today, even the appearance of a single cellphone in a remote village brings the benefits of modern communication: medical advice; weather and crop information; even political participation. But the real pay-off of the new technologies will ultimately be in their ability to link the developing world into the knowledge economy, despite the traditional constraints of geography and income. This process will be inherently political: where there is access to information, the Internet empowers the user both politically and economically, and thereby is inherently *democratizing*. Some governments have already shown a propensity to limit access to the new technologies in order to control democratization. They have been more successful than many would have wished. The conclusion is that, while the spread of the new technologies is probably ineluctable, it will not necessarily be rapid and universal, without international pressure and assistance, even where those technologies are relatively cheap. Probably the best way forward here is through a cooperative effort involving governments, the private sector, and NGOs.

With regard to the dark side of globalization, more than a few of the papers in this book describe the ways in which the new technologies will help facilitate intrastate conflicts, whether through arms deals, international criminal activity, the harvesting of the diaspora, or money laundering. But there is a positive story too. In some postconflict societies, NGOs are helping to establish free media by connecting fledgeling newspapers to news providers over the Internet. When the activity of independent television stations in Serbia was restricted by the regime, other NGOs connected these television stations so that they could obtain direct feeds of international news through the Internet. These are imaginative combinations of old and new technology, where thinking outside the box can have a huge impact on peacebuilding in postconflict situations. But it can also be as simple as putting all of human rights law on the Web, or sharing best-practices in treating traumatized children. There is enough anecdotal evidence now to move to the next stage, which is to take a concerted view of how the new technologies can further humanitarian assistance in concrete ways. A coalition of the willing devoted to this task would move the human security agenda decisively into the digital age.

NOTES

1 Marshall McLuhan and Quentin Fiore, *War and Peace in the Global Village* (New York: McGraw Hill, 1968).

REFERENCES

Held, David, et al. *Global Transformations: Politics, Economics and Culture.* Stanford, California: Stanford University Press, 1999.

McLuhan, Marshall. *Understanding Media: The Extensions of Man.* New York: New American Library, 1964.

–. *The Global Village: Transformations in World Life and Media in the 21ˢᵗ Century.* New York: Oxford University Press, 1989.

CONCLUSION

International Relations and the New Diplomacy

ROB MCRAE

This book has sought to describe many of the foreign policy gains which have resulted by adopting human security as the lens through which to view the plight of civilians in conflict and postconflict situations. Our concern has been with the most vulnerable and often those most cruelly victimized by today's conflicts. In this respect, the human security agenda is yet a further reflection of the humanitarian instincts which have animated Canadian foreign policy for generations. It is a new and fruitful approach to a better understanding of the changes in our world, and it offers fresh insights into how best to respond.

But it is worth bearing in mind that this agenda is part of a larger foreign policy framework that governs the day-to-day work of Canada's Department of Foreign Affairs and International Trade (DFAIT). There are many other multilateral, regional, and bilateral issues, not least management of our bilateral relationship with the US, that are not reflected in this book, but which, in fact, take up a large part of the foreign minister's and the department's time and energy. The human security agenda is not, and never was intended to be, an alternative to these traditional foreign policy concerns. It is rather a complementary, new instrument with which to respond to the new conflicts and the complex crises which they engender.

Of course, our human security initiative has faced significant challenges along the way. Many of the chapters in this book draw attention to the hurdles that had to be overcome, and to the lessons that have been learned – some of them difficult, even frustrating. In addition to the many concrete lessons learned scattered throughout the chapters above, two broad conclusions can be drawn. First, the idea of human security, and the agenda of issues that emanated from it, evolved significantly over time. What started out as a United Nation's (UN)-inspired concept, with a rather amorphous connotation, was developed under Lloyd Axworthy's leadership into a diplomatic initiative and an impressive set of achievements. Of course, not all of the issues have ripened as quickly as we would have hoped. But even these, such as the uncontrolled flow of small arms, have been set on a path that both maximizes the lessons learned elsewhere and holds out the prospect of real progress.

Therefore, the second broad conclusion, related to the first, is that we have really only brought to an end the first phase of the agenda. The brush has been cleared away, the issues have been identified, and we have even had some early, in some cases unexpected, successes. This book consolidates what we have learned in this first phase, and points the way forward to the next one and the many challenges that remain. Those challenges include both relatively short-term follow-up work on specific issues, and some broader considerations of a policy nature that would expand the conceptual horizons of the human security paradigm.

THE NEXT PHASE OF THE HUMAN SECURITY AGENDA

By reviewing the proposals for follow-up from the chapters above, the next phase of work, at least in the near term, is relatively clear. Of course, it is impossible to predict now into what human security crisis the international community may be plunged in the future. But it is a relatively safe bet that many of the issues below will be relevant to our understanding of future crises and to our response. Here is a list of some of the key issues ready for fairly rapid follow-up:

- small arms and light weapons – Canada intends to play a major role before and during the 2001 UN Conference on this issue, including a Canadian contribution to the formulation of an International Plan of Action;
- humanitarian intervention – Foreign Minister Axworthy led the call for an international commission to develop a policy framework and operational template for the future, and offered Canadian support for its establishment;
- expert civilian deployments – a major problem for current peace support operations; the international community must seek to improve its capacity to train and deploy experts; Canada will enhance its domestic program;

- international civilian police – UN member-states must work to strengthen the UN's capacity for the planning and deployment of civilian police; Canada intends to contribute actively to this process;
- UN sanctions – UN Security Council members must see through the fundamental review of international sanctions initiated by Canada in order to ensure they punish transgressors, not civilians; Canada will continue to pursue the sanctions review as part of the broader economic agenda;
- the International Criminal Court (ICC) – international cooperation including in the area of developing domestic legislation is required to reach the sixty ratifications necessary for the ICC statute to enter into force;
- war-affected children – the Action Plan produced by the 2000 International Conference on War-Affected Children, hosted by Canada, will be considered by the UN Special Session on the Convention on the Rights of the Child in 2001;
- human rights field operations – the international community must promote the deployment of such teams in order to find out more about the situation of human rights in conflict-prone and postconflict countries, both as a preventative measure against future conflict and to better assist peace support operations; Canada intends to actively pursue this issue.

There are, however, other issues which are not less urgent, but which will require considerably more time for debate and reflection. These are large, complex issues, for which no single organization provides a comprehensive forum:

- the economic agendas of conflicts – we need a better appreciation internationally of the economic dimensions of conflict, as well as corporate responsibility, in order to develop levers to take the profit out of war;
- the establishment of a culture of prevention – one of the lessons of this book is that early action to prevent conflict is potentially the most effective form of humanitarian intervention, but the "ounce of prevention" approach needs better public understanding if it is to obtain broader political support;
- postconflict peacebuilding – the international community needs to formalize the full range of actions that fall under this rubric, rather than reinvent the wheel each time, in order to speed civilian deployments.

Moreover, the transition from a culture of impunity to a culture of accountability, which should result from the establishment of the ICC, will have a huge impact on the practice of diplomacy over the medium term. The indictment of Milosevic by the International Criminal Tribunal for the Former Yugoslavia (ICTY) has already given us a foretaste of the dilemmas that will face many governments in the West with links to unsavoury regimes. Not a few leaders in the world have come to power after having led rebel forces against existing, sometimes democratically-elected, governments. Without welcoming such insurrections, most Western governments argue that they recognize states, not this or that government. If a new rebel government Factually controls most of the territory within its state borders, then the international community almost always recognizes that government de facto and de jure.

However, some leaders who come to power leading rebel forces may find that they have been or soon will be indicted by the ICC, if their forces have committed crimes covered by its jurisdiction. A number of current leaders could find themselves in the same situation. In other words, we might soon face the prospect of multiple Milosevic's: sitting heads of state who are indicted for war crimes. In such circumstances, the question of how, and to what extent, we should deal with dictators and war criminals when seeking regional peace agreements will be stark. This will put a damper on the narrow pursuit of national interest by the international community's practitioners of realpolitik. It will be a period of growing pains for the international community, but should eventually deter potential rebel leaders and sitting heads of state from committing crimes that will guarantee their international isolation.

GOVERNANCE AND THE NEW DIPLOMACY

The fact that some of the most relevant questions on the human security agenda find no obvious locus in existing institutional machinery raises the issue of governance. The paradigm-shift that places human security at the heart of our concerns brings with it the need to find new ways of reaching our objectives. The reason for this is simple: most existing international arrangements and organizations reflect processes that are largely intergovernmental and consensus-based. The human security agenda seeks to create a new international norm, particularly for the treatment of civilians in armed conflict. The norms embedded in the human security agenda, as with the norms encapsulated by human rights, implicitly limit state sovereignty by asserting that no state has the right to shield itself from international obligations to protect civilians in times of war. This is not a principle that is universally accepted by all states, and it makes progress in such broadly-based intergovernmental forums as the UN difficult. The experience of multilateral gridlock in traditional forums only encourages states interested in advancing the human security agenda to seek out alternative forums, at least until sufficient momentum has been achieved. While clearly not ideal, this ad hoc approach may be temporary, as symptomatic of a period of transition, and disappear altogether once the normative shift is more pervasive, and the Copernican Revolution in international relations complete.

Because the human security agenda is normatively based, it often depends for success on a small number of leading actors, both governmental and nongovernmental, and ultimately on the sway of public opinion. In this respect, the agenda is particularly susceptible to the exercise of soft power, to the extent that it appeals for support and attracts adherents, rather than coercing allegiance. What is revealing, as this book demonstrates, is that public opinion has been surprisingly supportive of the norms which have been invoked. This lends credence to the hypothesis that the human security agenda reflects a broader normative shift under way among significant segments of the population in the West and in many developing countries.

This growing public concern for the concrete circumstances of civilians in conflict has led to increasing calls on our governments to "do something." Those calls were once exclusively directed at crises, where civilians were the victims of war or famine. Today, the demand for action is broadening to include many of the issues on the human security agenda, from landmines to war crimes. Canada has responded by pursuing this agenda by means of "the new diplomacy." Starting within or outside traditional forums, the new diplomacy creates coalitions of the willing to move difficult issues forward more quickly, while building international support. It often involves a new style of leadership, and an inclusive approach to nongovernmental organizations (NGOs) and engaged citizens; new forums, including nationally-sponsored conferences and negotiating sessions; and specific deadlines for the completion of an agreement. In terms of substance, the new diplomacy frequently shifts the terms of the previous debate onto new grounds by placing the plight of the individual at the heart of the negotiation. The landmines campaign transformed what had been an arms control issue into a humanitarian cause. Again, the normative aspect was decisive in generating international public pressure to take action now.

This inclusive and highly-participatory diplomacy has led to a new role for governments more generally. Domestically, human security depends on strong public support for an agenda that has more to do with values than national interests. (Of course many would argue that those values, including the imperatives of justice, serve our interests in a stable and secure international order.) This is why the democratization of foreign policy has been so important from the first days of the initiative. National Forums and issue specific round tables, out-reach to citizens, academics, NGOs, and companies have all been helpful in terms of better informing policymakers in government about developments on the ground, while at the same time enabling the government to network and build support for a specific course of action.

Internationally, the out-reach and inclusiveness typical of the new diplomacy has been reflected in a variety of ways. Canada has succeeded in opening up the Security Council to ground-breaking debates on the protection of civilians, and to the more routine participation of experts and NGOs. By generating a new spirit of transparency in international organizations, decisions in those organizations will be better informed and more credible to our publics. In situ, a policy of inclusiveness leads us to recognize that peacebuilding must progress from donor-driven to locally-driven strategies and programs to be successful. If they are to be truly free from fear, the citizens of postconflict societies must participate directly in rebuilding their security. Finally, the new diplomacy is all about networking. It is not enough to send instructions to Canada's representative in a given forum to ensure our views are heard. All of our embassies, and official visits, need to be harnessed in order to engage other governments, and to bring the issues to the attention of foreign publics. Key to this international effort is cooperation with like-minded countries, international NGOs, the private sector, and other international organizations. This cooperation frequently takes the shape of broad-based coalitions, which coalesce around shared objectives. To be successful, they must find the right balance between commitment to an ideal and a sufficient degree of openness and flexibility to attract new adherents.

Of course, this is not to say that every coalition of the willing is sweetness and light. It is not. The new coalitions can be fraught with differences of views as to ultimate goals and to tactics. Each participant has a different set of considerations at stake. An NGO may be hesitant to abandon the moral high-ground for a compromise with parties it has long viewed with suspicion as its adversaries, adversaries who have proved in the past to have been singularly reluctant "to do the right thing." Any government, elected to office for a specific period of time, must make a judgment about what is achievable both in terms of timeframe and substance. A government may conclude that it can sell to its more broadly-based constituency a solution that, while not perfect, moves the goal posts in the right direction. On perhaps more rare occasions, a government may choose to hold out for the best possible solution and run the risk of high-profile failure, though any government would have to consider very carefully the political risks involved. Hence, future coalitions will continue to be subject to such judgment calls and, potentially, internal divisions despite accumulated experience with their use. At the end of the day, it is wise political leadership that will be key to a coalition's success.

To the extent that coalitions of the willing are pulled in competing directions by such day-to-day judgment calls, specific near-term deadlines help manage and contain the differences. Without such fixed timeframes, it is a challenge to sustain coalitions of the willing over the longer term. The Human Security Network is a first attempt to bridge the gap between this short-term task force approach and the lowest common denominator approach of more traditional international organizations. The network significantly pushes the boundaries of the new diplomacy as never before, and has been successful to date in facilitating cross-fertilization between issues and in concerting diplomatic efforts to follow through on some of the issues noted above. The question is whether the network's very success might not lead to its institutionalization, and thus lead it to lose its flexibility and sense of shared commitment. Only time will tell. But this would have one undeniable advantage: the network would survive changes of government, and thus give the human security agenda more predictability and international staying power.

The human security agenda, and the new diplomacy with which it is pursued, elicits one further reflection on governance. Human security crises result from a complex set of circumstances and actions, and require complex and highly-integrated solutions. We see this with the new peace support operations, where the military and civilian aspects must work hand in glove to be successful. In putting together these new operations, we need to take into account such things as the need for civilian police, tailor-made disarmament, demobilization, and reintegration (DDR) programs, gender-specific peacebuilding strategies, and war crimes investigations. Indeed, the list of required elements for real-time peace support operations (PSOs) is much longer. The general point, however, is that the solutions to many of the new human security crises must involve a plethora of elements linked together horizontally. Solutions have to be holistic: if certain key elements are missing, the operation will fail, at least in the medium-term. The implication is that we need a UN that is capable of designing such horizontal strategies and implementing them, something that the UN should be uniquely positioned to do.

This same requirement for complex peace support operations has implications for domestic governance. Today, governments are called upon to supply peace support operations with a wide range of resources, from military force to police, technical and development assistance, and civilian expertise in such things as elections or human rights monitoring. A variety of government departments or agencies can be involved, creating much greater demands for coordination, especially when responding to crises. Moreover, some of the demands, such as those required in peacebuilding, can fall between the mandated scope and financial means of existing ministries. Such things as DDR may not be eligible for support because it is not strictly development assistance; and because it may not be intended for a developing country, it may not obtain funding from a given development agency. Conversely, foreign ministries and interior ministries may find that they do not have either the mandate or funding to support program delivery abroad when it comes to deploying police or civilian experts; and our defence ministries and militaries may well hesitate when soldiers in peace support operations are asked to monitor human rights.

The demands of the human security agenda require that we both re-examine and update existing departmental mandates, and establish mechanisms that maximize horizontal coordination across government. Networks will be key no less to domestic governance than to international governance, but will also raise new questions about accountability and line responsibility. We may find that the Westminister model of discrete stove-piped ministries itself needs a second look if we are to adapt our governments to the new international context.

BROADENING THE HUMAN SECURITY PARADIGM

The concept of human security is, of course, inherently broader than the notion that informs this book. There has been an advantage in pursuing and developing the concept within the area of international security and crisis response, since it has led to rapid results on a range of specific issues. But one could also apply a human security matrix to the vaster social context made up of culture, the environment, the economy, and digitalization. These, in addition to security, are the strands that form the web of globalization. It seems entirely appropriate to ask, with regard to a particular individual in a given society, how globalization has affected not only that individual's security, but his or her environmental or economic condition as well. Taking these strands together, it is the impact on human security broadly conceived – on the lived life – that should be the true measure of globalization's "benefits."

Some of those new foreign policy instruments described in this book target the relationship between conflict and globalization, as evidenced by the small arms trade, money laundering, and crime, that often fuels local disputes. Western societies cannot escape the impact of these conflicts, as the chapter on public safety makes clear. But there is also the more complex issue as to whether and how globalization is linked to "localization," i.e., reactionary instincts that find their expression in ethnic or religious extremism. If globalization is a generator of local insecurity, at least to the extent that it seems to act from a distance, then localization is the search for security in the guise of the tribe. Globalization, when it threatens local economies (no matter how inefficient), local cultures, and local traditions, almost guarantees a backlash. This is because it undermines long-standing identities and power relationships. Tribal allegiance, including ethnically-based violence and aggression, is identity-affirming in the face of insecurity and fear, i.e., when traditional social structures break down. Yet there is no reason why globalization should be immune from the demands of democratization, since it is the lack of control over globalization's effects that generates concern. By democratizing globalization, by finding local solutions to the challenges posed by globalization, we will take the heat out of localized extremism.

The human security agenda has found a particular resonance with the young. The agenda's humanitarian appeal, its focus on the individual, including the plight of children, understandably attracts youthful idealism. It may also be due to the fact that the human security initiative broke through a certain complacency in the international community that had come to accept many things, such as the mindless destruction wrought by landmines, as immune to change. The initiative has demonstrated that radical departures in foreign policy can lead to dramatic improvements in the lives of those most vulnerable. Young people seem to grasp immediately the paradigm shift that has led to this breakthrough. It all comes down to changing our mind-set, to seeing the world and its problems from a different standpoint. Perhaps this is what Vaclav Havel has in mind in calling for a "revolution of the spirit" – a heightened sense of responsibility for the planet and for each other.

It is this sense of shared responsibility, and shared values, that is most distinctive of the global civil society that has actively supported the human security agenda. Interestingly, this emergent global civil society is not monocultural, but multicultural, and its values are cross-cultural. Diversity has been key to underscoring the need for respect and tolerance in rebuilding societies that are free from fear. Indeed, it is promising for the future that the human security agenda is not viewed as strictly a Western agenda, but as an agenda that musters support in virtually every corner of the world.

Connectivity and the internet will foster, unlike anything before, a growing number of individuals who see themselves not only as the citizens of a particular country or region, but as global citizens with global concerns and responsibilities. This global civil society will by its very nature take the individual (here and now) as the starting point for any issue, because the web of personal relations that characterizes the newly-emerging global civil society is inherent in the connective technology that is its lifeblood. The human security agenda, as the product of both real and virtual networks, of governmental and nongovernmental actors in pursuit of the common good, may yet be regarded as the first step toward a truly postmodern internationalism that puts our shared humanity at its core.

Reflections on the Ghana Conference and the Freetown Visit

LLOYD AXWORTHY

Late one Saturday evening last April, on the veranda of a restaurant in Freetown, Sierra Leone, Olara Otunnu, the UN Under-Secretary-General and Special Representative for Children and Armed Conflict and I, along with Eric Hoskins – of my staff – shared a meal and postmortem of the three days we had spent together pursuing the cause of war-affected children.

The sojourn had begun in Accra, Ghana where a major conference of West African states, cohosted by Ghana and Canada, had concluded with a strong declaration and accompanying plan of action to protect children in times of war. It had been followed by a visit to Sierra Leone where, in a hectic day of visiting camps, talking with excombatant children, exchanging views with political leaders, and listening to the experiences of nongovernmental organizations (NGOs) and United Nation's (UN) personnel, we attempted to follow through on implementing key parts of the Accra agenda.

The conversation over dinner was not on the immediate, however. It centred on what the experience meant for the broader approach to human security and where the concept would go from here. In effect, it was a discussion that I hope many will have who have read this book.

Let me share some of the revelations of that evening's discussion.

First, in Accra, two governments from vastly different backgrounds, but with a common concern and interest in war-affected children, put together an active diplomatic effort, culminating in a major meeting of foreign ministers, NGOs, and military and international organizations to focus on the issue. From the meeting emerged a significant advancement of commitment and action to do something about the plight of war-affected children. Once again a coalition-building exercise centred on the prevention and protection of the most vulnerable of global citizens.

As a direct product of the meeting, President Rawlings of Ghana undertook to present the conclusions to an Economic Community of West African States (ECOWAS) Heads of State Summit – particularly those elements calling for ratification of several important international humanitarian conventions, particularly those on the International Criminal Court (ICC), and the Optional Protocol on Child Soldiers.

For those who claim that human security is only an issue for Northern developed nations, this initiative refutes such assertions. Here were the countries of one of the regions most beset by conflict taking a leadership role and advancing the cause. To me, it clearly shows that human security is a vital universal concern, with special relevance to the needs of Southern, poorer regions. As my cohost of the conference pointed out continuously, while poverty is a root cause of suffering for many people of the South, there can never be a solution until there is "freedom from fear."

Another lesson to draw from this experience is the vital importance of international humanitarian law and the capacity to make such laws work. Without the standard setting that occurs through the implementation of protocols, conventions, and treaties that prescribe an international rule of law for the individual, there is no way to hold powerful transgressors to account. Accountability and impunity were the watchwords in Accra. There was an acknowledgement that the international community had to hold accountable those responsible for crimes against humanity and make sure they are prosecuted and punished.

There is a great deal more work that must be done in this area. Scholars have been lax in not addressing this crucial issue more directly and creatively. And policy makers often cannot break out of the box. Fortunately, there has been leadership by various international NGO's, as witness the work on landmines and the ICC.

Yet, a host of emerging issues need addressing, especially those surrounding the matter of humanitarian intervention versus the classic notions of national sovereignty. The debate among West African foreign ministers in hammering out the declaration often centred on how far the reach of the international community in protecting civilians can go as opposed to the rightful responsibilities of state governments. There is still not yet the same degree of acceptance of suborning domestic decisions on humanitarian issues as there are on matters of trade, technology etc.(Even here there is a backlash.) And, of course the reasons are obvious – human rights are the most sensitive of political issues.

There needs to be a way of broadening the debate and seeking out the elements of consensus. This is why we have made a concerted effort to introduce the subject of intervention in a variety of international fora, and why we have presented speeches and papers outlining this from a Canadian perspective. It is why we have been broaching the idea of an international Commission on Humanitarian Intervention that would involve eminent persons, scholars, and the public from diverse views and regions as a vehicle to foster research, analysis, and debate.

But no one should underestimate the need for or the immediacy of this concept. As we sat on the Freetown veranda, we were sitting in a living laboratory of humanitarian intervention. From the early interventions of ECOMOG forces, to the vast array of UN personnel and equipment that were taking over to support the Lomé Agreement; to the many international humanitarian workers manning the camps, rehabilitating the victims, supplying needed technical assistance, to the outside interveners like myself and Olara Otunnu trying to advance the release of abducted children (along with direct financial assistance to make it happen) – the reality of humanitarian intervention was everywhere to be seen.

And, alas, two days after this conversation took place, the danger and complexity of such acts of intervention were all too dramatically revealed. In the north of Sierra Leone, the Revolutionary United Front (RUF) rebels attacked a demobilization and rehabilitation camp; several peacekeepers were killed, and many others were taken hostage. The fragile truce in Sierra Leone was put in jeopardy once again.

There has been a great deal of discussion in various circles on the notion of conflict prevention. Prestigious bodies such as the Carnegie Endowment have sponsored major studies. Yet, the reality, as shown in Sierra Leone, is that we are a long way from developing the means and the will to make it work.

Attempts have been made in Sierra Leone to do so. Some neighbouring countries have invested a lot of diplomatic and military effort to keep the peace. The UN has mandated a peacekeeping force, one with the precedent-setting mandate to protect civilians. And donor countries have been supplying humanitarian assistance and resources for disarmament demobilization, and reintegration (DDR).

Yet, there remains a paucity of support for the government, which itself has limited capacity. There is also a lack of coordination and integration of efforts. UN work on the civilian side is fragmented and slow.

Some neighbouring states are allowed to continue their meddling with impunity. And, world attention has drifted away – only sporadically rekindled if there is a major incident.

In other words, the ability to prevent, to rebuild, to offset the causes of conflict are still very limited and the engagement spotty. Preventing conflict, rebuilding societies still does not command the full attention of political leaders and the public alike. Until it does, Sierra Leone, East Timor, and Kosovo – and many other similar situations yet to come will continue to fester and boil.

This raises important issues: what are the tools, where are the resources, what is the commitment to make human security work? In Canada, the search for answers is underway. As pointed out earlier, as human security has evolved as a Canadian policy tenet, there has been a shift in the hows and whys of the delivery and approach. The Department of Foreign Affairs and International Trade (DFAIT) has shifted from its traditional role as analyst and advocate, to a more activist stance, putting in the field international interns, launching peacebuilding activities, and budgeting for human security measures. Similar shifts are taking place in the Canadian International Development Agency (CIDA), the solicitor general's office, Justice, and other departments as there is an increasing awareness that the security of Canadians can better be served by addressing international threats.

This has led us into a much more active partnership with like-minded countries, through the Human Security Network, and to close relationships with NGOs and private citizens. One of the initiatives under our Human Security Program is the development of a roster of Canadian experts in a variety of callings, whose knowledge and experience is needed to help resolve conflicts and preserve the peace. It is, in effect, a form of deployable "white helmets."

And, as I sat across the table from Olara Otunnu, a Ugandan of great wisdom and commitment who has long put his talents to work for international causes, I thought how crucial was the new international diplomat to human security: Olara and Carol Bellamy of the United Nations Children's Fund (UNICEF) for children; Francis Deng for displaced persons; Mary Robinson and her rapporteurs on human rights; Sadako Ogata for refugees; and, of course, Kofi Annan himself, who speaks out on these issues as no secretary-general ever has. It is crucial that the capacity of the UN – and similar capacities in regional organizations – be enhanced and broadened. This is why our human security resources are often devoted to their support.

Some of the new international players do not have a positive impact, however. In Sierra Leone, every conversation revealed the pervasive influence of the diamond trader, the arms merchant, the corrupt and the criminal who feed off the mineral riches of that country. Throughout the world, conflict and the misery it brings, is fed by the greed of the war lords, the shady entrepreneurs, and too often by legitimate enterprise!

The Angolan sanctions report[1] highlights the nexus between commerce, conflict, and corruption. It also reveals how limited or nonexistent international laws and institutions are, to say nothing of domestic laws, to deal with this global war economy. Globalization has brought with it a new lust that fuels internal conflicts and provides oxygen to the fires of violence and repression.

The international community has been working diligently and with some success to come to grips with money laundering, drug trafficking, and other transnational crimes. It is necessary that similar serious efforts be made with respect to the merchants of conflict. One only had to look at the faces of those in the rehabilitation camps of Sierra Leone to understand how heinous their crimes are and how this represents a real challenge to human security.

Finally, let me say something on how the cause of human security can be advanced by the power of the information revolution. Shortly after becoming foreign minister, I convened a group to talk about establishing an international information strategy to put Canadian skills in the field of information technology to work in advancing our international objectives. There were lots of new and innovative ideas introduced, but I could find few takers and more crucially no resources.

Nevertheless, we have continued to pursue the idea, if in small bites, as money allowed. For example, at the Santiago Summit of the Hemisphere, the prime minister announced a special program under our International Internship program for helping countries in the Caribbean and the Americas to become connected. That is why we have established specific programs to connect street rehabilitation projects and a drug information strategy network as part of our Hemispheric Dialogue on Drugs. And, we initiated a Youth Links program connecting high schools in the UK, Germany, and France with counterparts in Canada.

At Accra we moved the marker forward by supporting a project of the NGO War Child that brought together an assembly of war-affected children from West Africa with students from sixteen high schools in Canada live on the Internet. Foreign Minister Gbeho of Ghana and I participated and found it to be one of the most rewarding moments of the conference. As the young people from Canada and West Africa began to share questions, views, and experiences along the Internet, you could sense the rise of excitement and engagement in the room among the young Africans. The questions posed to the foreign minister and I were serious and pointed, and they quickly led to expressions of various ideas and concerns from the youth on both sides of the Atlantic. It truly demonstrated the power of the new information network to bind people together, to open up participation, to generate the political will of the young.

Reflecting on this over dinner, Olara Otunnu and I, with our advisers felt strongly that in the cause of mobilizing attention and support for war-affected children we needed to further expand the capacity of information systems as a means of changing the politics of human security. We discussed how the international meeting on war-affected children in Winnipeg could be made truly virtual, involving young people from the Americas, Africa, Asia, and Europe. We saw the potential for the technology to be mobilized in Sierra Leone too, helping to give young people there a real voice. We examined how the movement behind the ratification of the child-related conventions could be multiplied in strength by the power of information technology.

What this shows is that we are just at the beginning of the curve in determining the potential of this new tool. As we see the explosion in dot.com enterprises, e-commerce, and integrated networks that is rising for purposes of marketing, financing, and advertising in the private sector, we need an equivalent creative burst to serve the common good – to advance the welfare and safety of individuals.

In a few short years, the idea of human security has gone from a vague concept to a driving force in international affairs. The vocabulary, definition, and application of the idea is spreading worldwide. As the articles in this book show, it is a determining factor in shaping our foreign policy, and increasingly that of other states as it is also one way of making sense of the new reality of our world and giving structure to our policy and the allocation of our resources. And, finally and most importantly, it does offer the means to make a difference in the lives of untold numbers of people the world over.

NOTES

1 United Nations, *Report of the Panel of Experts on Violations of Security Council Sanctions Against UNITA* (s/2000/203), 10 March 2000.

Timeline: Human Security in Canadian Foreign Policy

Since 1996, Canadian foreign policy became increasingly focused on advancing human security. Over the course of the last four years, the agenda has become more explicit and more comprehensive. The following timeline documents the evolution of human security in Canadian foreign policy, highlighting key initiatives, major milestones, and seminal international events.

1996

March: Release of the *International Response to Conflict and Genocide: Lessons from the Rwanda Experience* (multidonor evaluation of the international response to the Rwandan Genocide).

March: Sharm el-Sheikh Summit of the Peacemakers, focuses on terrorism.

May: United Nations (UN) Review Conference approves modest changes to the Conventional Weapons Convention dealing with use of landmines. Canada and a group of other states, plus nongovernmental organizations (NGOs), begin discussions on options to pursue a more comprehensive ban.

April: Appointment of Louise Arbour as Chief Prosecutor of the International Criminal Tribunal for former the Yugoslavia (ICTY) and Rwanda (ICTR).

April: First Organization of American States (OAS) ministerial meeting on terrorism at the Interamerican Specialized Conference on Terrorism, Peru.

July: The Lyon G-8 Summit: Canada succeeds in having "human security" figure in the G-8 chairman's statement on political issues, noting the UN's crucial responsibility in this regard.

July: The G-8 Summit also approves creation of a regular forum for G-8 action on crime, known as the Lyon Group. Also followed by the G-8 Paris Ministerial Conference on Terrorism, it establishes twenty-five points for implementation.

September: National Forum on Canadian International Relations launched. Focus on peacebuilding and a Canadian international information strategy. Supports a broader agenda of engaging civil society in foreign policy.

September: Minister Axworthy's first speech to UN General Assembly. First use of terminology of human security in Canadian foreign policy speech. Proposes creation of a roster of Canadian experts on human rights for deployment in UN human rights field operations.

October: Canada hosts conference of interested states to explore options for addressing the landmine crisis. Minister Axworthy proposes negotiation of a comprehensive treaty banning landmines to be signed by December 1997.

October: Minister Axworthy delivers seminal speech outlining the concept of peacebuilding and launching the Canadian Peacebuilding Initiative. Initial focus on critical war to peace transitions in postconflict societies. Creation of a Peacebuilding Fund in the Canadian International Development Agency (CIDA).

November: Submission of the Graça Machel report on the impact of armed conflict on children to the UN General Assembly.

November / December: Crisis in eastern Zaire. Canada offers to lead multinational force (MNF) to deliver humanitarian assistance to refugees. MNF for Eastern Zaire terminated without deploying into the field, following return of refugees to Rwanda.

December: Signing of Guatemala Peace Accords, ending more than thirty years of civil war. UN General Assembly approves establishment of verification mission (MINUGUA).

1997

January: Beginning of term of Kofi Annan, seventh secretary-general of the UN.

February: launch of Youth International Internship Program, supporting young Canadians seeking overseas experience with NGOs, international organizations, or the private sector.

February: Inauguration of the Canadian Resource Bank for Democracy and Human Rights (CANADEM), the roster of Canadian human rights experts; expanded to include experts in democracy and peacebuilding.

February: Inauguration of annual Canadian government-NGO peace-building consultations in Ottawa.

May: Release of the Organization of Economic Cooperation and Development (OECD) Development Assistance Committee Guidelines on Conflict, Peace, and Development Cooperation.

August: Establishment of Peacebuilding Program in Department of Foreign Affairs to complete CIDA's Peacebuilding Fund.

September: Appointment of Olarra Otunnu as Special Representative of the Secretary-General for Children and Armed Conflict.

September: Meeting in Oslo negotiated comprehensive treaty to ban production, stockpile, and use of landmines.

October: Nobel Peace Prize awarded to Jody Williams and the International Campaign to Ban Landmines.

November: Launch of UN civilian police mission to mentor and train Haiti National Police (MIPONUH).

3–5 December: Landmark conference in Ottawa where 122 governments sign Landmines Treaty. 3 December, Canada becomes the first country to sign Landmines Treaty, also the first country to submit ratification to UN secretary-general. 5 December, Ottawa Mine Action Forum issues an "Agenda for Mine Action" to assist in implementation of the Ottawa Convention describing $500 million in mine action programs pledged by the international community.

December: Launch of Carnegie Commission report on Preventing Deadly Conflict.

1998

January: UN Office of the Coordinator for Humanitarian Assistance (OCHA) is created as part of Secretary General Annan's UN reform package.

April: UN Crime Commission agrees to launch negotiations on a Transnational Organized Crime Convention, with specific protocols on firearms, trafficking in migrants, and trafficking in women and children.

May: Signature of Canada/Norway bilateral Plan of Action to promote human security (Lysøen Declaration).

May: The InterAmerican Drug Abuse Control Commission of the OAS agrees to launch the Multilateral Evaluation Mechanism (MEM) on drug policies; Canadian Deputy Solicitor-General Jean Fournier appointed as chair of the negotiations.

May: The Coalition to Stop the Use of Child Soldiers is launched.

July: Successful adoption in Rome of statute to create an International Criminal Court (ICC).

August: NGO meeting in Orillia, Ontario established the groundwork for International Action Network on Small Arms.

September: Canada and Norway host meeting of foreign ministers in New York to create cross-regional coalition of governments supporting human security, establishing the Human Security Network.

September: Fortieth ratification of the Landmines Treaty, resulting in its entry into force six months later, thus marking the fastest ever adoption of a disarmament treaty.

October: Canada elected for two year mandate on the Security Council. Increased transparency of the council and human security as cornerstones of the campaign.

October: Crisis in Kosovo temporarily averted by negotiations led by US Ambassador Richard Holbrooke. Organization for Security and Cooperation in Europe (OSCE)-led Kosovo Verification Mission created.

December: Canada enacts its own legislation on combatting bribery of foreign officials which allowed ratification of the OECD Bribery Convention and triggered the entry into force of the OECD Convention.

December: Canada signs the ICC Statute.

1999

January: Canada assumes two-year term on the Security Council. Canadian permanent representative to the UN, Ambassador Robert Fowler, appointed to chair Angola Sanctions Committee.

January: Rebel Armed Forces Ruling Council/Revolutionary United Front (AFRC/RUF) invasion of Freetown, Sierra Leone, triggers atrocities and humanitarian crisis.

February: Under first Canadian presidency of the Security Council, Canada convenes open debate on the theme of "protection of civilians." Presidential statement requests secretary-general to prepare a report to the council in September.

March: Kosovo Verification Mission withdrawn.

March: Start of North Atlantic Treaty Organization (NATO) air campaign against government of the former Yugoslavia in response to human rights violations in Kosovo and collapse of Rambouillet peace talks.

May: First ministerial meeting of the Human Security Network, hosted by Norway, held in Bergen.

May: Hague Appeal for Peace, the largest civil society peace conference attended by over 10,000 activists. Site of the official launch of the International Action Network Against Small Arms.

May: Conclusion of East Timor negotiations between Indonesia and Portugal.

May: First Meeting of states parties to the Landmines Treaty, in Maputo, Mozambique.

June: UN authorizes electoral mission to East Timor (UNAMET) to supervise popular consultation.

June: G-8 foreign ministers in Cologne negotiate a Security Council Resolution bringing an end to the Kosovo conflict. Government in Belgrade withdraws military forces. UN Mission approved by United Nations.

June: International Labour Organization approves new Convention on the Worst Forms of Child Labour.

July: Negotiation of Lomé Agreement between government of Sierra Leone and RUF to end civil war in Sierra Leone.

August: Fiftieth anniversary of the Geneva Conventions.

September: Widespread massacres in East Timor by militias, following victory of independence option. Indonesia withdraws military presence and agrees to establishment of Australian-led peace enforcement force (INTERFET).

September: UN secretary-general presents report to Security Council on Protection of Civilians in Armed Conflict, making fifty recommendations for action. Canada leads negotiations on Council Resolution 1265 accepting secretary-general's report.

September: UN secretary-general's speech to the UN United Nations challenges the organization to address the question of humanitarian intervention.

September: Minister Axworthy delivers keynote address to Carnegie Endowment for International Peace, at meeting organized by the International Peace Academy on Protection of Civilians.

October: Security Council authorizes new mandate for peacekeeping force to assist the signatories in implementing the Lomé Agreement in Sierra Leone (UNAMSIL).

October: The Interamerican Drug Abuse Control Commission of the OAS approves mechanisms of the Multilateral Evaluation Mechanism. First trial multilateral evaluation of all OAS member states scheduled for release at the Quebec City Hemispheric Summit in April 2001.

October: Canada's governor general delivers Speech from the Throne setting out the goal for the government of Canada to "achieve meaningful progress on a global human security agenda."

December: Minister Axworthy tables Canada's ICC legislation making Canada the first country to table comprehensive implementation legislation.

December: UN Security Council debate on findings of UN investigation into Srebrenica.

December: G-8 foreign minister's meeting in Berlin on conflict prevention.

December: Adoption of UN General Assembly resolution to convene an international conference on the "Illicit Trade in Small Arms and Light Weapons in all its Aspects" in 2001.

2000

January: Successful conclusion of final round of negotiations in Geneva on the Optional Protocol to the Convention on the Rights of the Child on the Involvement of Children in Armed Conflict.

February: Minister Axworthy delivers Hauser Lecture on International Law at New York University School of Law, furthering the discussion on humanitarian intervention.

March: Release of the Angola Sanctions Committee report, identifying specific individuals involved in breaking UN sanctions against the National Union for the Total Independence of Angola (UNITA); recommends broad measures to increase the effectiveness of UN sanctions regime.

April: Second Canadian presidency of the Security Council, leads to approval of council resolution on implementing recommendations of the secretary-general on protection of civilians (SC 1296).

April: Council issues presidential statement on increasing the effectiveness of UN sanctions regimes and reducing negative humanitarian impact economic sanctions.

April: Council accepts recommendations of the report of the Angola Sanctions Committee. Council debates findings of UN investigation into the Rwandan genocide.

April: Canada and Ghana host Conference on war-Affected Children in West Africa for fifteen Economic Community of West African States (ECOWAS) member states. Produces the Accra Declaration and Plan of Action.

May: Second ministerial meeting of the Human Security Network hosted by Switzerland in Lucerne.

May: Attack by RUF on peacekeeping forces in Sierra Leone almost leads to collapse of UN mission. British government deploys military force to evacuate foreign residents and secure the airport. Security Council subsequently approves significant increase in force size.

June: Canada hosts OAS General Assembly in Windsor, Ontario. Foreign minister's debate held on human security. General Assembly adopts Canadian-led resolution. OAS mission of Secretary-General Gavaria and Foreign Minister Axworthy authorized to address postelectoral crisis in Peru.

June: Human Security Program established for five-year period in the Department of Foreign Affairs, with new resources allocated in the 2000 federal budget.

June: Release of the Northern Dimension to Canada's foreign policy.

June: Canada first country to sign the Optional Protocol to the Convention on the Rights of the Child, on the Involvement of Children in Armed Conflict.

June: Canada first country in the world to adopt comprehensive implementing legislation for the ICC Statute.

July: Canada ratifies the ICC Statute.

July: G-8 foreign ministers meeting in Miyazaki, Japan, approves comprehensive statement on conflict prevention.

September: UN Millennium Summit held in New York. Launch of UN Special Commission on Humanitarian Intervention and Sovereignty.

September: Canada hosts International Conference on War-Affected Children in Winnipeg.

October: Minister Axworthy/Canada launches Regional Centre for Human Security in Amman, Jordan.

December: Fiftieth anniversary of the UN High Commissioner for Refugees (UNHCR).

Contributors

DAVID ANGELL is currently a member of Canada's Security Council delegation in New York. He has also worked at the Canadian Embassy in Washington and on the senior staff of the Northern Ireland peace process in Belfast and Dublin.

ALAN BONES At the time of writing, was responsible for Regional Security in the Regional Security and Peacekeeping Division. He has also had postings in Mexico and Malaysia.

MICHAEL BONSER is the 1999–2000 Cadieux-Léger Fellow in the Policy Planning Staff.

TERRY CORMIER is currently director of the International Crime Division, and is the Canadian head of delegation to the Lyon Group, the G8 crime group. He has held postings in Hong Kong, Singapore, France, Congo-Kinshasa, and in Brussels at the Mission to the European Union.

PATRICIA FORTIER is currently the director of the Regional Security and Peacekeeping Division. She has been posted in Costa Rica, India, Kenya, and Zambia. In 1988–90, she was Security Council officer for Iraq, particularly sanctions, and for missions in Haiti and Central America. She has also worked with human rights and environmental nongovernmental organizations (NGOs) abroad.

ROBERT FOWLER at the time of writing, was ambassador and permanent representative of Canada to the United Nations (UN) in New York, and had represented Canada on the Security Council since January 1999. During his career, he has also served as assistant secretary to the cabinet (Foreign and Defence Policy), and as deputy Minister of National Defence. Robert Fowler is currently the Canadian ambassador to Italy.

ELISSA GOLBERG is a policy adviser (Humanitarian Affairs) in the Human Rights, Humanitarian Affairs, International Women's Equality Division. She has been working in the Global and Human Issues Bureau since 1996.

MARK GWOZDECKY is currently director of the Nuclear and Chemical Disarmament Implementation Agency. He was one of three key Canadian strategists throughout the Ottawa Process and was later appointed coordinator of the Mine Action Team. He has also held postings in Korea, Syria, and the Philippines.

SAM HANSON is currently Canada's ambassador in Bosnia and Herzegovina, and was a member of the Kosovo Task Force in 1999. In previous assignments abroad, he has served as special representative and chargé d'affaires in Croatia, and has also served at the Permanent Mission to the UN in New York, in Namibia, Tanzania, Yugoslavia, and at the Canadian Delegation to the North Atlantic Treaty Organization (NATO) in Brussels. In Ottawa, he has held the position of deputy director in the Corporate Planning and Resource Management Division, the UN Affairs Division, and the Intelligence Services Division.

PAUL HEINBECKER, at the time of writing, was the assistant deputy minister for Global and Security Policy. Currently he is serving as ambassador and permanent representative at the Permanent Mission to the UN in New York. He has served in Sweden, Turkey, Washington, and as ambassador in Germany, as well as at the Permanent Delegation of Canada to the Organization for Economic Cooperation and Development (OECD) in Paris. Paul Heinbecker has also been assistant secretary to the cabinet in the Privy Council Office and senior policy adviser in the prime minister's office.

ERIC HOSKINS is currently senior policy Adviser to Foreign Minister Lloyd Axworthy. Trained as a physician, Hoskins has a doctorate in public health and epidemiology from Oxford University. Prior to his current position, he worked for nearly ten years in war zones in both

Africa and the Middle East, including Sudan, Ethiopia, Somalia, Burundi, and Iraq.

DON HUBERT is a senior policy adviser in the Peacebuilding and Human Security division of the Department of Foreign Affairs, currently on leave and living in Dhaka, Bangladesh. He is also a research fellow at the Centre for Foreign Policy Studies at Dalhousie University.

DAVID LEE is currently director general, as the special coordinator for Haiti and as adviser for the management of the International Security and Cooperation Business Line. He has also held the positions of director general of the International Organizations Bureau, and director general of the Bureau of Commercial and Commodity Relations. During the Uruguay Round of multilateral trade negotiations, he served as chief negotiator on trade in services and coordinated Canadian involvement in the investment and intellectual property negotiations. He has served postings in Japan, Switzerland, and Iran as well as at the Mission to the European Union (EU) in Brussels, and the Permanent Mission to the UN in New York.

DANIEL LIVERMORE was the Canadian ambassador to Guatemala from August 1996 until September 1999, and is currently the ambassador for Mine Action. During his career, he has also held the positions of director of the Regional Security and Peacekeeping Division, director of Policy Planning, director of the Human Rights and Social Affairs Division and has been seconded to the Privy Council Office. In addition to Guatemala, Daniel Livermore has been posted to Santiago (Chile), Washington, and to the Permanent Mission to the UN in New York.

JENNIFER LOTEN, an anthropologist specializing in gender analysis, is currently policy adviser (Gender, Small Arms) in the Peacebuilding and Human Security Division.

ROB MCRAE is currently the deputy permanent representative at the Canadian Joint Delegation to NATO. He has served as the director of Policy Planning Staff and as the deputy director of the Environment Division. During his career, he has also served in (then) Czechoslovakia, the United Kingdom, and Yugoslavia. His most recent book was *Resistance and Revolution. Vaclav Havel's Czechoslovakia.*

VALERIE OOSTERVELD is currently legal officer with the Human Rights and Humanitarian Law Section in the UN, Criminal and Treaty

Law Division. She is also a member of the Canadian delegation to the International Criminal Court Preparatory Commission negotiations. Valerie previously served as director of the International Human Rights Program at the Faculty of Law, University of Toronto.

VICTOR RAKMIL is currently the director of the Corporate Security Division. During his career, he has served as a member of the Southern Africa Task Force, where he managed sanctions against South Africa, and on the NATO desk. He has also held postings in India and Africa. Prior to his work with the department, he worked at the International Energy Agency during the 1979 oil crisis.

DARRYL ROBINSON currently works in the UN, Human Rights and Humanitarian Law Section of the Department of Foreign Affairs and International Trade (DFAIT). He has served on the Canadian delegation to the ICC Preparatory Committee, the Rome Diplomatic Conference, and the ICC Preparatory Commission.

JILL SINCLAIR is currently the director general of the Global and Human Issues Bureau. As director of the Arms Control and Disarmament Division she led the Ottawa Process resulting in the Ottawa Convention Banning Antipersonnel Mines, and was Canada's first ambassador for Mine Action. She has served in Cuba and (then) Czechoslovakia.

MICHAEL SMALL has been a member of the Canadian Foreign Service since 1981. He is currently the director of the Peacebuilding and Human Security Division in DFAIT. He has also served overseas in Canadian missions in Malaysia, Brazil, Costa Rica, and Mexico.

ROSS SNYDER, at the time of writing, served as deputy director of the Peacebuilding and Human Security Division. He has held the positions of deputy director of the Caribbean and Central America Relations Division as well as deputy director of the Economic Relations with Developing Countries Division. Ross Snyder has also served in Haiti, Tanzania, and Washington.

CARMEN SORGER is currently senior policy Adviser in the Peacebuilding and Human Security Division, working on the issue of war-affected children.

ROMAN WASCHUK is currently deputy director (political) of the Policy Planning Division. He has also served in Russia and Ukraine.

SIDEBAR AUTHORS

STEPHEN BOLTON is currently working as an analyst in the International Crime Division at DFAIT. He is formerly professor of history and international relations, Universidad Externado de Colombia, Bogota, Colombia.

JANET BOYER is currently a program officer working on the DFAIT, Youth International Internship Program.

MIKE ELLIOTT is currently the desk officer responsible for NATO in the North American and Euro-Atlantic Security and Defence Relations Division. He was previously desk officer for UN peace support operations and a member of the department's Zaire Task Force in 1996.

MARK GAILLARD is currently the desk officer responsible for Small Arms and Light Weapons in the Nonproliferation, Arms Control, and Disarmament Division.

DIANE HARPER, at the time of writing, was responsible for police policy in the Regional Security and Peacekeeping Division.

BARRY PARKINSON is a former foreign service officer (1992–6) who has since worked for DFAIT on a consultative basis. His focus has been on peace support operations, especially the nontraditional deployment of experts to operations in, for instance, Kosovo and East Timor.